TAMERS OF DEATH

God's foundation is my foundation and my foundation is God's foundation. Here I am on my own ground, just as God is on his own ground. Actions spring up from this ground without asking *why?*   *Meister Eckhart*

TAMERS OF DEATH

VOLUME ONE

The History of the Alexian Brothers from 1300 to 1789

CHRISTOPHER J. KAUFFMAN

A CROSSROAD BOOK

The Seabury Press   New York

1976
The Seabury Press
815 Second Avenue
New York, N.Y. 10017

Library of Congress Cataloging in Publication Data

Kauffman, Christopher J.   1936–
Tamers of death.
"A crossroad book."
Includes index.
Contents: v. l. From 1300 to 1789.
1. Alexian Brothers—History. I. Title.
BX2890.K38   271'.07   76-24469   ISBN 0-8164-0314-7
Printed in the United States of America

and life's not a paragraph
and death i think is no parenthesis

e. e. cummings

To my wife, Helen,
who made these words real for me

THE LOCATIONS OF THE ALEXIAN HOUSES
IN THE LOW COUNTRIES
AND THE RHINELAND CA. 1550.

CONTENTS

PART THREE
THE DECLINE OF THE MEDIEVAL CELLITES AND THE EMERGENCE OF THE MODERN ALEXIANS

PREFACE

Writing this book has been a taming process for me. It originated in the wilderness of vague conjecture cluttered with apprehension and ambivalence. As I made progress I was directed and encouraged by many scholars, Alexian Brothers and friends. I am very grateful to John Francis Bannon, S.J., who introduced me to the need for this book.

The Alexian Brothers were my primary aids. The two Superiors General, Brothers Felix Bettendorf, C.F.A., and Augustine Lohman, C.F.A., responded to my every need with understanding, direction, and support. The Alexian Provincials, Brother Ludger Goeller, C.F.A., in Germany, Brother Dominic Walsh, C.F.A., in England, Brother Florian Eberle, C.F.A., in the U.S. and Brother Clemens Aarts, C.F.A., in Belgium, kindly directed me through their provinces and lightened the burdens of archival work by the warm spirit of Alexian hospitality. In each of the Provinces there were Brothers who were particularly concerned with making myself and family at home: Brothers Goar Nalewaja, C.F.A., and Joachim Wetzke, C.F.A., in Germany, Brothers Edmund Kelly, C.F.A., and Peter Mannion, C.F.A., in England and Ireland. I am deeply indebted to those historians who over the years have done valuable research on the Alexian past. Martin Birken of the University of Bielefeld, who is writing a dissertation on the Brothers—origins to the Reformation—provided me with valuable bibliographical information. Brother Damien Stayaert, C.F.A., of Boechout, Belgium, is an expert on the Cellites of Germany and the Low Countries, as are Brothers Cornelius Kearney, C.F.A., and Andrew McKenzie, C.F.A., in England and Ireland, and Christopher

Lynch, O.F.M., and Gregory Isenhart in the U.S.A. So many Alexians have contributed to the business and pleasure of writing this book that to the entire Congregation I am indebted.

As this work developed from research to writing, Ms. Att McDowell, Mr. Benjamin Shearer, Father M. A. Haworth, S.J., Professor George Hickenlooper, and Professor Wolfgang Karrer kindly helped me with difficult textual materials in Flemish, German, and Latin. Once the rough draft was completed Professors George Hickenlooper, Robert E. Lerner, James Hitchcock, José M. Sanchez, Wolfgang Karrer, Charles Fleener, and Ms. Ann Galati read parts or all of the text. I am very grateful for their comments, corrections, and criticisms.

To acknowledge my wife's help is like thanking the sun and air for one's sustenance. Her typing and proofreading ability were very helpful, but it was her spirited person, her understanding of the more straining aspects of research and writing, and her genuine enthusiasm for this project that have left a permanent imprint on this book. Finally, thanks are due to our children, Jane, Christopher, and Kathryn Ann for preventing me from taking life and work too seriously.

INTRODUCTION

To write an introduction to a historical monograph entails a self-examination for the historian. He must ask himself whether he is a descendant of the Positivist school, which stresses the accumulation of statistical data, or an heir of the Romantic tradition, with its accent on the discernment of the zeitgeist of a given epoch. Though both schools in their nineteenth-century origins sought to provide alternative paths to historical certitudes, few of their twentieth-century students share that confidence. Caught in the current world of skepticism, historians are led to offer their interpretations of epochs, such as the late medieval period, in tentative terms.

When the historian is seeking to organize religious events of the past into an orderly composition and place them within the framework of cultural history, he must engage in an analysis of his own views about the relationship between religion and culture. This entails plunging into one's notion of the problem of historical causation. For the student of Franciscan, Dominican, or Jesuit history the weight of self-exploration is lightened by the written or printed communication of his main cast of characters, e.g., the documents authored by Dominic and his followers. Though the historian may still be compelled to reflect on his views regarding the distinctions between the cultural deposits in the language of the thirteenth century and his own culture-bound semantics, he may be supported in the process by allowing his characters to speak for themselves.

The original Alexian Brothers were oral-folk mendicants who participated in a broad heterogeneous religious movement. Because there is no one founder whose presence permeates the establishment of the institution and because the

I

oral-folk character of the early brothers precludes documentation of their motives, ideals, and attitudes, one must rely upon
inference to reconstruct the Alexian foundation period.

The cultural gap between the historian and the anonymous
founding brothers is, in the following pages, bridged by one
major principle of interpretation: in spite of the secularity of
twentieth-century culture, contemporary man who has experienced a religious dimension in existence may vicariously situate
himself in the thoroughly religious culture of the fourteenth
century by immersing himself in the writings of the female
counterparts of the brothers (Beguines), of those who appear
paradigmatic of their spirituality (Meister Eckhart), of those
who have studied their milieu (Huyskens), and particularly
of those other modern historians (Huizinga) who have made
similar journeys into the shadowy lanes of folk society in the
late Middle Ages.

Though this hermeneutic is not meant to strike a blow at
abstract theories of social change, it does presuppose that men
may be authentically motivated by religious ideals which, however rooted in a given culture, possess a degree of autonomy
free from what the Marxist refers to as the superstructure. It
also presupposes a critical view of the contemporary scholarly
trend to reify every portion of the human condition (e.g.,
those descendants of the Positivist school of historiography—
cliometricians—who quantify the past as if all human experience were grist for the computer). A belief in the human spirit
places one in the Romantic tradition, but the foregoing
hermeneutic is also opposed to the deterministic implications
of the zeitgeist that the Romantic historian often perceived
as the overriding causal reality in history.

The interpretive bridge that will be used in this book to
span the gap between cultures—i.e., those human experiences
of the historian that are analogous to the fourteenth-century
Alexian life—is derived from a philosophical position covering
an enormous amount of theoretical ground. The concept of
limit-situation helps to remove some of the clutter; it is a
concept that may be transferred from the philosopher and
theologian's intellectual framework to that of the historian

groping for a principle to understand the past and to find a language capable of coherently expressing that past.

David Tracy has observed of limit-situation and limit-language:

> The concept limit-situation is a familiar one in the existentialist philosophy and theology of the very recent past. Fundamentally, the concept refers to those human situations wherein a human being ineluctably finds manifest a certain ultimate limit or horizon to his or her existence. The concept itself is mediated by "showing" the implications of certain crucial positive and negative experiential limit-situations. More exactly, limit-situations refer to two basic kinds of existential situation: either those "boundary" situations of guilt, anxiety, sickness and the recognition of death as one's own destiny, or those situations called "ecstatic experiences"—intense joy, love, reassurance creation. All genuine limit-situations refer to those experiences, both positive and negative, wherein we both experience our own human limits (limits-to) as our own as well as recognize, however haltingly, some disclosure of a limit-of our experience. The negative mode of limit-situations can best be described with Karl Jaspers as "boundary situations." Such experiences (sickness, guilt, anxiety, recognition of death as one's own destiny) allow and, when intense, seem to demand reflection upon the existential boundaries of our present everyday existence. When an announcement of a serious illness—whether our own or of someone we love—is made, we begin to experience the everyday, the "real" world, as suddenly unreal: petty, strange, foreign to the now real world. That "limit" world of final closure to our lives now faces us with a starkness we cannot shirk and manages to disclose to us our basic existential faith or unfaith in life's very meaningfulness.[1]

Documents on the Alexian past such as papal bulls and city hall records can situate the historian in time and place as well as provide a glimpse of some of the attitudes toward the Brothers; they do not introduce him to the Brothers' own religious perspectives. A historian who can view aspects of his personal experiences as limit-situations disclosing the religious dimension must incorporate these activities into his perspective as he situates himself among an anonymous group of Brothers. The historian and his faceless characters do not share common cultural sensibilities or common experiences. Even though their cultures instruct them differently on certain of their shared biblical sources or statements of belief, the twentieth-century man can at least by analogy and inference give real substance to the Alexian shadows as they pass from the fourteenth to the sixteenth century.

A fivefold conclusion is derived from this principle of interpretation and its application to the Alexian past. These oral-culture mendicants lived out of the New Testament, which converted them into apostles of Jesus; their mendicant life in urban squalor was implicitly grounded in the sacred, i.e., they lived their poverty in quasi-mystical terms as embodiments of Jesus; the specific calling, their charism, was gradually discerned as being one of ministry to the "outsider," the plague victim, the insane, to whom they brought sacramental ritual and symbol at bedside and graveside; after 175 years on the borderline (somewhere between the monastery and the parish) they institutionalized themselves into a religious order to preserve their tradition and to guarantee their future.

The Brothers refracted cultural trends from their origins, and as culture passed from the medieval to the modern they were compelled to reintegrate their original charism, a process which unconsciously engaged them prior to the French Revolution but was not concluded until the mid-nineteenth century. It is this latter period with which volume 2 of this work is concerned.

The story of the Alexian Brothers is alive with limit-situations—sacrament, ministry, plague, mental illness, rejection, charism. Ironically, their house in Aachen was located on the "ditch," adjacent to the town walls "limiting the city." Plague victims whom they nursed and buried were not only placed on the limit of society but, like the lepers, were frequently situated in separate colonies beyond that limit. The mentally ill were most commonly placed in "jails" within the city-gate limit of the town. The attitudes toward death, the plague, and insanity were expressed in language symbolic of the limit-character sensibilities of the folk who dwelt in a world populated by saints and demons with phenomenal powers to intervene in the limit-drama of human existence.

When one is led to reflect upon his own limit-situation he is humbled by a glimpse of the transcendent, reluctant to presuppose a disclosure of a "limit-of" our experience and to presume that his experiences are universal and neatly applicable to Everyman. The person who is a historian must, therefore, be cautious in rendering by analogy the limit-situations so apparently abundant within and paradigmatic of the evolution of the Alexian existence. He must not presume that a real harmony exists between himself and the early Brothers. Instead, he employs that limit-situation theory as a way of organizing the Alexian past into a coherent and integral composition. Hence, the theory provides a model for expanding his understanding of the past; the limit-situation model, like analogy, should not be viewed as certifying the truth but merely as a methodological device for reconstructing some truths. Similarly, when such limit-content terms as *charism* and *sacrament* are used they are not meant to exalt the work of the Brothers. These words are intended to convey the real meaning of their lives. Hence, as we move through their past we must remove the cosmetic imagery of stereotyped portraits that sentimentalize those touched by sacrament and by charism. The oral-folk Brothers lived in urban squalor which by today's standards was "poor, nasty [and] brutish." Their bedside and graveside ministries contained sacramental and charismatic witness but it was mediated by hard, backbreaking work.

But one must be cautious and avoid romanticizing the past. As G. G. Coulton remarks, "There is a terrible temptation to deprecate this poor workaday world to which, after all, we are wedded, in comparison with the meretricious charms of the imaginary past."[2] The workaday worlds of the medieval and modern Alexians are as different as the medieval town and the modern metropolis. But in spite of the distinctive cultural milieu which forms their different religious perspectives, this and the following volume are predicated on the conviction that a strong continuum of charism stretches from the medieval Brot-Beghard to the modern Alexian Brother. Though today's Brothers have developed sophisticated health-care institutions, they still dwell, like their Beghard founders, in quiet inconspicuousness.

To compensate for the total absence of documents revealing

the thoughts of the Brothers themselves, Brother Paul, an ideal-type Alexian, will occasionally provide an imaginary monologue, adding flesh to the silent skeletal images. Also, in order to make the story manageable, it was necessary to limit our focus to three Alexian houses, Cologne, Aachen, and Antwerp, which have been significant foundations since their origins in the fourteenth century.[3]

PART ONE

✝

FROM BEGHARDS AND LOLLARDS TO ALEXIAN BROTHERS

1

The Voluntary Poor
and the *Vita Apostolica* in
Late Medieval Society

I

The late medieval ancestors of the modern Alexian Brothers evolved from a popular lay-religious movement in the Low Countries and in the Rhineland. First appearing in Cologne, Aachen, and Antwerp during the first half of the fourteenth century, the "Alexians" experienced a continuous struggle for existence until they were finally approved as a religious order in 1472. For over a century and a half they traveled what is commonly referred to as the *via media*, the middle path. As laymen who chose a life of apostolic poverty and service to the impoverished of the towns, the early Brothers dwelt midway between the monastery and the secular city. Unlike the Franciscans and Dominicans of the thirteenth century, relatively little is known about the foundation, the organization, the specific motivations, and the particular religious and social world-view of the "poor men" who later called themselves

Alexian Brothers. We know of no one founder, no early rule, no chapter meetings, and they have left us neither letters nor diaries.

Much of our knowledge is, therefore, gathered by studying the larger movement of which they were a vital part. In Cologne they were called *Lungenbrüder* and *Begarden*, in Aachen *Brot Begarden*, and in Antwerp *Matemannen* and *Lollarden*. They all shared the name *willige Armen*, i.e., voluntary poor. By the fifteenth century their most common names were *Cellebroeder*, *Celliten* and *Fratres de Celles*. These specific appellations place them under the popular generic term *Beghard*, one which has been used by their contemporary observers and by today's historians to designate the male counterpart of the earlier and more numerous female travelers along the *via media*, the *Beguines*.

The etymology of *Beguine/Beghard* has elicited much scholarly controversy. The earliest interpretation traced the origin of *Beguine* to Lambert-le-Begue (the Stammerer), a priest of mid-thirteenth-century Liège whose fame as a vitriolic spokesman against simony and as a protector of pious lay-women has been well established.[1] Henry Charles Lea views the term as simply a derivation of the German verb *beggan*, meaning to beg or pray.[2] Herbert Grundmann related it to the Catharist heretics of twelfth- and thirteenth-century southern France, the *Albigensians*.[3] A definitive etymology may never be achieved, but each of these interpretations reveals something about the early Alexian way of life.

Like Lambert, the poor men of Aachen, Cologne, and Antwerp may be associated with a reform reaction against the abuses of the church, particularly the secularism of the clergy. The Brot-Beghards of the Rhineland did combine the two meanings of *beggan*, as they begged—"Brot durch Gott" (Bread for the sake of God)—and considered that cry a part of their general prayer witness. Because they were also harassed by local bishops and papal inquisitors, the charge of heresy played a major role in their early history. The modern Alexians are, therefore, an extraordinary remnant of the late medieval reform movement which, because it was so varied, harks back both to the heterodoxy of Waldensians and to the orthodoxy of the Franciscans and Dominicans. The common strand woven throughout the movement was their dedication to the ideals of the *vita apostolica*.

Reform movements in the church have traditionally followed one of three paths. Gregory VII and Innocent III, who represent reform from above, directed juridical and structural changes infused with papal idealism. The monastic reformers of Cluny and Citeaux illustrate a revival of the austere detachment found in the scriptural origins of Western monasticism; they stressed communalism and a rigid interpretation of the three vows as the means to personal perfection and the sanctification of society. The *vita apostolica*, which sought a regeneration of society from below, was a direct-action movement accenting the evangelical witness to the gospel of Jesus. The latter was by far the most revolutionary path because its missionary zeal inspired many groups to devise their own particular route to the original apostolic community.

The *vita apostolica* was ultimately derived from the Acts of the Apostles. St. Luke's account of the early church in Jerusalem was the first elaboration of Christian communalism. Both in his Gospel and in Acts, Luke stressed Jesus' love of sinners, his forgiveness, and his loving concern for the impoverished lower classes in contrast to his severe attitude toward the self-righteous aristocrats who abuse their power and wealth.[4] "The one thing necessary is repentance, abdication of self, and on this the gentle, tolerant Luke takes a firm stand insisting on unflinching and complete detachment, . . . especially from riches."[5] This theme is clearly expressed in Acts 2:42–47 where Luke describes the early Christian community in Jerusalem.

> These remained faithful to the teaching of the Apostles, to the brotherhood, to the breaking of bread and to the prayers. The many miracles and signs worked through the apostles made a deep impression on everyone.
> The faithful all lived together in common and owned everything in common; they sold their goods and possessions and shared out the proceeds among themselves according to what each one needed.[6]

Luke's narrative of the fraud of Ananias and Sapphira also illustrates the theme of selflessness and sacrifice. Ananias and Sapphira were a married couple who sold their property but secretly kept a portion of the proceeds rather than turn it all over to the apostles. Both were struck dead for their crime, i.e., love of money.[7] Luke refers to the way the apostles shared their food; and because service to the poor became so time-consuming, seven deacons were appointed to carry out these tasks.[8]

Western monasticism also derived its inspiration from Luke's account of the Jerusalem church. Augustine and Benedict identified the communal life as the path to Christian perfection. Ironically the *vita apostolica* of the late Middle Ages was directly influenced by the reforms of Pope Gregory VII, a former monk from the monastery at Cluny. Gregory urged a return to the apostolic virtues of the gospel. The irony appears when one notes that Gregory's reforms ultimately led to a drastic departure from his view of the apostolic life, as the followers of the late medieval *vita apostolica* struck out on a divergent path, away from the monastery toward a Christian witness within the secular world. Thus, the evangelism so characteristic of the *vita apostolica* originated with the Hildebrandine reforms, but the apostolic mission was reinterpreted. The monastic *vita apostolica* of the eleventh century was expressed in the monks' personal holiness, communal life, liturgy, and stability. Service to the secular order was expressed in the monastery as the mode for Christianizing and civilizing secular society. The fresh manifestation of the *vita apostolica* stressed the evangelism of the early church. "Preaching, itinerant preaching—as opposed to monastic stability and as distinguished from episcopal preaching—was central to this new *Vita Apostolica*."[9]

The new way expressed itself in a variety of groups ranging from the Canons Regular (who revived the Augustinian communalism of the secular clergy) to disparate lay movements such as the Humiliate in Northern Italy and the Beguines and Beghards in the Low Countries and the Rhineland. Common evangelical and gospel themes bound them all together to the new *vita apostolica*—preaching, poverty, brotherly love, and the directives from the Sermon on the Mount.[10] Twelfth-century lay piety, influenced by the revival of Scripture as well as the widespread Crusade idealism, manifested a devotion not to the Glorified Christ but to the earthly Jesus of Nazareth who sanctified humanity by his passion and death. Because the laity had no institutional ties they could adopt the *vita* with greater ease and spontaneity than the clerical or monastic communities: "Layfolk wanted not less religion but more of the right kind."[11] A common negative strand is also apparent: they rejected the monastic ideal, particularly as it was embroidered into the feudal fabric.[12] Even the austere Cistercians possessed large abbeys. When the followers of the new *vita* committed themselves to giving witness, this was not limited to the traditional world of feudal society but was primarily directed to the people of the towns and cities, which were greatly altering the medieval landscape. As Ernst McDonnell comments: "Socially, intense devotion to the apostolic life coincided with the communes and the louder articulation of townsmen on matters of faith and politics. Urban centers, and more especially the cloth industry, were in ferment. As an ascesis for urban society, the *Vita Apostolica* befitted a climate in which the silence and prayer envisaged by St. Jerome for monastic precincts was no longer at home."[13]

The late-eleventh- and early-twelfth-century chronicler Bernold of Constance was one of the first to testify to new lay piety in Germany: "In these times (around 1091) there flourished in many places in the German Kingdom the common life, not only among priests and monks committed to religious stability, but indeed among laymen, who offered themselves and their belongings very devotedly to this common life. . . ."[14] In the twelfth century, towns, guilds, and professions frequently organized themselves into religious fraternities. However, those who lived a common life, referring to themselves as *pauperes Christi*, dedicated themselves to the *vita caritatis*.

Pauperes Christi groups were representative of either literate or oral culture. In contrast to the monasteries, these groups infused with the dynamic lay piety of the day would tend to represent folk or oral culture. Though an enormous amount of study has been concerned with the perspective formed by the spoken rather than the written word, such study has not been applied to the evangelism of the *pauperes Christi* groups, including the original Alexians. If we are to compensate for the total lack of documentation illustrative of the Alexian-Beghard view of the *vita apostolica*, we must attempt to apply the general knowledge of oral culture to this folk-mendicant way of life.

Walter J. Ong, S.J., who has traced the evolution of both the spoken and the written word, provides us with a general frame of reference from which we can make certain inferences about the ways in which the Beghard-Alexian experienced the word of God.[15] These inferences suggest the following fictional reconstruction. An itinerant preacher appears in a town square near the market place; infused with the idealism of the *vita apostolica*, he recounts Gospel narratives, stressing the Sermon on the Mount, the parable of the rich man (which illustrates the theme—give everything to the poor and follow me), as well as a dramatic account of the passion and death of Christ. Though the preacher may be literate and have a historical perspective, which allows him to distinguish past from present events, the thoroughly oral character of his folk listeners urges the people to absorb the spoken word as a living real event. One man (let us call him Paul) absorbs the word of God into the recesses of his interiority. This experience compels him to continue to nourish the living realities of Jesus within by explicitly adopting the *pauperes Christi* way of life.

The world of the monasteries allowed the literate monk to develop a historical perspective where time formed a link between the gospel days and his own life of dedication to the gospel ideals. He, therefore, would have to strain himself in order to absorb the word of God as deeply as Paul, whose oral-folk condition formed an unconscious bridge between past and present. Time's historical space was meaningless to Paul as he received the word of God as a present event. Professor Ong elaborates on the conditions of an oral culture in which the word is "a happening." He views the sound-dominated oral culture as situating "man in the middle of actuality and in simultaneity," in contrast to the literate culture in which "vision situates man in front of things and in sequentiality."[16] Thus as a member of a sacral folk community Paul listens and utters religious words which to him convey simultaneously the past and the present. The Jesus-happening within Paul was persistently expressed in his *pauperes Christi* existence. By adopting the principles of the Sermon on the Mount, the life of poverty, and the sacrificial life for others, he was performing ritual and symbol which were in an oral-culture sense sacramental Jesus-happenings. The Beghard Alexian ritual was at bedside and graveside—"limit situations," which to the oral Christian were rich in symbol. The Beghard Alexian must have viewed his *vita apostolica* not as a revival of the early apostolic church in Jerusalem but as a real presence within the Acts of the Apostles.

Originally monks and canons attended to the poor and sick. The rise of the towns and the return of many Crusade veterans who were homeless, sick, lame, and poor necessitated new responses to the drastically new urban scene. One of the early nonmilitary confraternities dedicated to nursing was the Hospital Order of St. Anthony. Originating in France in the late eleventh century, in 1247 they adopted the rule of St. Augustine and the organizational structure of the Canons Regular. The Hospital Order of the Holy Spirit (which also originated in France) was officially recognized as an order by Innocent III in 1198. Both these orders spread into Germany in the thirteenth century, but by the end of that century, when the original Alexians made their first appearance, the continuous population increase exacerbated the desperate need for nursing. Indeed, it was the thirteenth-century growth of the cities that prompted the proliferation of *pauperes Christi* groups who wished to identify with and serve the ever increasing numbers of poor city folk.[17]

During this period as capitalist enterprise developed, bringing social and political changes, town life gradually drove a wedge into feudal agrarian society. Sophisticated banking and commercial processes, combined with the rise in town population, eventuated the need for trained bureaucrats, lawyers, and judges to attend to the increasing complexities of governing city, state, and church. The emergence of the great modern universities fulfilled the need for trained officials and promoted a more sophisticated, intellectual world-view suitable to the needs of the burgeoning city classes.

Richard W. Southern traces the development of medieval Humanism to its climax in the university towns. In contrast to Renaissance Humanism which was to stress a total immersion into ancient Greek and Roman lifestyles, medieval Humanism was concerned with the relationships between man's dignity and nature, between the natural and the supernatural worlds: "... nature is seen as an orderly system, and man—in understanding the laws of nature—understands himself as the main part, the key stone of nature."[18] Beginning in the late eleventh century this "scientific" Humanism (vis-à-vis the literary Humanism of the Renaissance) reached its fullest intellectual expression in the Scholasticism of St. Thomas.[19] Just as man rationalized the ultimate relationships between the sacred and the profane, he also sought to humanize politics, economics, and social relationships. Medieval Humanism and urban life simultaneously reflected the departure from the simple village existence of the feudal manor; the new cultural currents of the twelfth and thirteenth centuries stressed man's independence in thought and life in contrast to his secular dependence upon the feudal lord and his intellectual dependence upon a religious tradition in which divine causation was responsible for every event in his life.

The pontificate of Innocent III (1198–1216) has frequently been referred to as the zenith of the medieval papacy. Because Innocent was a superb jurist who introduced many reforms reflecting a rationalization of church governance, one may also view his pontificate as representative of the development of medieval Humanism. The Fourth Lateran Council (1215) clearly illustrates the papacy's preeminent position: "over 70 patriarchs, nearly 400 bishops, over 800 abbots and priors and representatives from the various secular courts responded to Innocent's convocation."[20] As a student of Roman law,

Innocent skillfully drafted seventy decrees touching upon almost every aspect of church and moral discipline, including judicial procedures for heresy trials, the new religious duties for laymen, annual confession and communion, regulations concerning preaching, clerical education, tithes, the relationships with Jews. One decree prohibited the institution of new religious orders without papal consent, a law that was to haunt the Beghards.

Perhaps the prestige of the papacy was never greater than during the era of Innocent III but, as Walter Ullman points out, his pontificate contained both "the strengths and weaknesses of the papacy as an institution of government."[21]

> Its strength lay in the formulation, fixation, and application of medieval Christian doctrine, in its axiomatic belief in its ability to shape society by the Christian idea embodied in Law—a grandiose conception and an equally grandiose aim, but whose weakness was that it was hardly capable of being translated into reality. Reality and the natural frailty of mankind could not be mastered by ideas alone. In no other phase in the history of the medieval Papacy was there so stark a contrast between actuality and the ideal Christian theme of a rebirth, of a veritable renaissance of mankind.[22]

"Francis, go and repair my church which, as you see, is falling down."[23] In 1206 St. Francis took as his "bride" Poverty and made his first step on the mendicant path of regeneration, an omen of a "veritable renaissance of mankind." When Innocent III met with St. Francis there was, like Southern's description of medieval thought, "a dialogue between Aristotle and the Bible," the rational world of Innocent encountering a thirteenth-century embodiment of the scriptural Jesus. The laws of the Fourth Lateran Council and the evangelism of the mendicants shared an identical goal, repair of the church which was "falling down."

The Franciscans, and later the Dominicans, dedicated themselves to rebuilding the walls, which were undermined from within by the ignorance and laxity of the clergy, by the worldliness of the traditional monasteries, and by the power politics and affluence of the hierarchy. The Albigensians were battering the walls from without with the ramrods of anticlericalism.

Innocent responded with the law (Lateran Council), and with the sword (the Albigensian crusade); the Friars Minor and the Friars Preachers responded with the power of the word through preaching, and by the power of example through the worldlessness of the *vita apostolica*.

From the vantage point of the Beghard house on the *via media*, the church walls must have appeared, as they did to St. Francis, to be in great disrepair. Implicit in the foundation of the Alexians was that strain of orthodox anticlericalism which may or may not have expressed itself explicitly among individual brothers who traveled through the lanes of urban poverty, nursing the sick, burying the dead, and preaching the scriptural Jesus in word and deed. The apostolic poverty which bound these laymen together was a scriptural witness against the worldliness of the church. Indeed, the *via media* was paved with the words of the gospel, and lay people who followed this path represent the success of the itinerant gospel preachers of the day. The simple scriptural idealism infused into the Alexian foundations was a form of lay piety which, like the legal idealism of Innocent III, the scholastic idealism of Aquinas, and the mendicant idealism of Francis and Dominic, demanded standards of Christian life so high that the ever present cracks in the medieval church walls, the marks of human frailty, appeared as scandalous deviations from the Christian ideal.

As the scriptural character of the early Alexians developed they were, no doubt, stimulated by the mysticism of Meister Eckhart (ca. 1260–1327), a German Dominican who frequently preached in Cologne. Eckhart's mysticism symbolizes the change in religious attitudes from thirteenth-century Scholasticism to a more personalized view of the way man relates to God. By the fourteenth century, Scholasticism had developed into a richly sophisticated style of logic that could engage only a tiny intellectual elite. Though sermons to the laity in the vernacular were not uncommon, they were generally "colorless affairs, a distillation of academic recollections seasoned with lurid stories."[24] On the other hand, Meister Eckhart appears as the "first academic voice which delivered arresting and original truths to an audience far beyond the lecture room."[25] Southern sees Eckhart as the first great spiritual light to respond to the needs of the burgeoning towns of the north. Both Aquinas and his mentor Aristotle decried the decline of virtue marked by the rise of towns. By the fourteenth century, urban life had developed to such a degree that it was able to contribute its own unique cultural forms, modes of life, and climates of opinion. Eckhart's new religious message garbed in fresh symbol and metaphor was to fourteenth-century fluid town society what Scholasticism was to the more hierarchically structured thirteenth century.

> God's foundation is my foundation and my foundation is God's foundation. Here I am on my own ground, just as God is on his own ground. Actions spring up from this ground without asking *why*?[26]

Man and God shared identical foundations; the stress was on the individual's ability to reach God, omitting but not necessarily excluding the clergy, the sacraments, the saints, and the hierarchical church structure. Eckhart's way to holiness must have been very appealing to the early Alexian, a layman dedicated to a life of poverty and service and searching for spiritual direction distinctive from that offered by the monastery and the parish church. Meister Eckhart's mysticism was appropriately expressed in the spoken word and therefore dwelt comfortably within the oral culture. There were no spacial or temporal distinctions between "God's foundation and my foundation." There is a radical identity between the believer and God, the same sort of identity as existed between the *pauperes Christi*, Beghards, and the Christ of the Gospels.

II

In discussing thirteenth- to fifteenth-century urban life there is a historical hazard of focusing only on those aspects which form a continuum with the present, i.e., capitalism, bureaucracy, statecraft, bourgeois lifestyle, individualism, and humanism—as if the old medieval village man had been totally eclipsed by what were actually nascent forms of modern culture. But, as Huizinga long ago emphasized, these forms were mere saplings in a forest dominated by tradition.[27]

It is difficult for twentieth-century man, who has his origins in the scientific explanation of life found in medieval Humanism, to appreciate the feelings, sensibilities, and "world-view" of traditional medieval man. Because contemporary man is anxiety-ridden in his complex, pluralistic, and technological society, he mistakenly cloaks the medieval peasant and town artisan in the garb of "simplicity." This view is buttressed by another popular notion which romanticizes man's security in the "Age of Faith." The truth is that medieval society was bound together in one church, but varieties of belief circulated within that institution. Popular cults of saints and relics were often abused. Although the church frequently struggled against this popular tendency she was unable to prevent the spread of superficial and superstitious practices. Huizinga states:

> Even the profound faith in the Eucharist expands into childish beliefs—for instance, that one can not go blind or have a stroke of apoplexy on a day on which was heard Mass, or that one does not grow older during the time spent in attending Mass.[28]

Such simplemindedness sharply contrasts with the complex intellectual sophistication of Scholasticism, but the anxieties from which these fantasies spring reveal complex feelings of fear and confusion. Traditional medieval man, particularly the town-dweller, was also subjected to itinerant preachers, ranging from doomsday dances of the flagellants to semi-mystical orations by the Brothers of the Free Spirit. The Age of Faith contained a continuous dialectic between mystery and superstition and between orthodoxy and heterodoxy, a dialectic that testified to the fundamental insecurity of traditional man.

We have noted two medieval cultures—the literate culture of Humanism and the oral culture of the folk. Though each had a distinctive perspective on Christian reality there were obvious bridges between the two. In terms of ideal types the contemplative monk and the preacher or scholar friar did share with the Beghard-Alexian nursing and burial minister common religious traditions, rituals, and symbols which placed such profound events as birth and death into a cosmic plan. However, the literate monk or friar may view it more as a mystery-plan capable of rational elucidation, while the Beghard-Alexian would tend to see himself and his ministries within a divine mystery-drama. The anxieties of the traditional man, whether he belonged to the literate or the oral culture, were every bit as intense as those of modern man. The meaning of existence may have been clearly prescribed by religious custom, but the ever persistent reality of appeasing a vengeful God must have been at least as awesome as modern man's quest for money, status, power, and an occasional glimpse of the meaning of existence.

During the fourteenth century, one which Robert E. Lerner labels "The Age of Adversity," the cultural insecurity of the Middle Ages exploded with a gloomy array of tragic events, many of which were frequently interpreted as heralding humanity's end.[29] Lynn White, Jr., describes the period from 1300 to 1650 as "the most psychically disturbed era in European history."[30] It was characterized by "abnormal anxiety," which "arose from an ever increasing velocity of cultural change compounded by a series of fearful disasters."[31] It gradually came to a close in the mid-seventeenth century when "ordinary people" began to have "an absolutely novel and relaxed attitude toward change."[32] The Hundred Years' War, which began in 1338, initiated a new epoch in military history that terminated with the last religious war—The Thirty Years' War (1618–1648). Continuous waves of pestilence inundated Europe from 1347 until the end of the seventeenth century while famine continuously haunted the continent. As symptoms of the anxiety, White lists, among other things, the witch mania, the persecution of Jews, and the macabre centrality of death portrayed in the arts. To cope with profound change, Europeans frantically searched for scapegoats and took a perverse pleasure in witchburning, torture, and the cult of death.[33]

Though historians may disagree with the sweep of White's theses, few would take issue with his stress upon the profound significance of the Black Death (1348–1350), which decimated the population of Europe by almost 30 percent. The economic and social expansion of the thirteenth century was followed by population decline and economic contraction. Historians stress the following causal factors in explaining the crisis of the fourteenth century: the previous century placed too great a burden on the marginal lands thereby creating food shortages; the climatic changes were characterized by longer and colder winters and shorter and damper summers; the development of regional agricultural specialization, which with a crop failure could spell tragedy. Although there was a constant threat of famine throughout the Middle Ages the famines of the fourteenth century were particularly frequent and severe.[34] The dependent towns were hard hit by crop failure and the steady economic decline brought low wages, unemployment, and social conflict. Prophets of the "endtime," particularly during and after the plague (e.g., flagellants) appeared credible and experienced spurts of vast popularity. The Alexian "founding Brothers" were, therefore, responding to the call of the *vita apostolica*, which in turn was a response to the never ceasing cries of the urban beggar, leper, moron, lunatic, and those wretchedly impoverished by the economic conditions of the era. The evangelism of the *vita apostolica* must have been deeply incorporated into the lives of these men as they confronted the harshness of an age of continuous adversity.

III

In a history of the church, the chapters on the fourteenth and fifteenth centuries could also be labeled "age of adversity." In the early thirteenth century Innocent III, Francis, and Dominic attempted to rebuild the walls of the church with the papal ideas of law and order, and the mendicant zeal of poverty and preaching. A hundred years later the papacy had lost an enormous amount of its prestige: in its renewed struggle with the Hohenstaufen emperor its supranational basis diminished as it veered toward its French ally; its secular concerns became embroiled in petty political struggles; thirteenth-century Humanism influenced many to regard the papacy not in terms of its theoretical primacy but on its moral content, depending on the current occupant of the papal throne. For the first time the term "bad Pope" was uttered.[35] During the early fourteenth-century church-state struggle between Boniface VIII and Philip IV of France, the Pope was taken prisoner by French troops. Even after Boniface's death Philip demanded a posthumous trial of the Pope on the grounds that he was a fornicator and a heretic. Clement V, a Frenchman elevated to the papacy in 1305, thought it more convenient to remain in France until the Council of Vienne (1311) had terminated. He died in Avignon. His five successors also intended to return to Rome but the journey was never convenient. This Avignese papacy (1305–1378) obviously symbolized the decline in papal prestige since the days of Innocent III. Many contemporary critics, particularly in the German states, considered the papacy an appendage of the French state; Petrarch considered the Avignese papacy as the whore of Babylon and the Pope as the Antichrist. In spite of such a decline the papal bureaucracy was functioning smoothly, and present-day historians disagree with the contemporary critics by stressing the relative competence, statesmanship, and independent leadership of the Avignese popes. Nonetheless, the adverse contemporary opinion leads one to conclude that there was a distinctive crisis of papal authority.[36]

Mendicant zeal had also departed from the spirit of Francis and Dominic. During the early fourteenth century the Franciscans were divided as to the proper interpretation of poverty and had shifted from the edge of medieval society to become a vital part of the church "establishment." This of course was crucial for their survival, but as ensconced insiders they tended to view the Alexian mendicants on the *via media* as hypocritical lay competitors for donations. The Dominicans experienced a similar evolution, as their chapter meetings reveal a deep concern with the oversecularized and propertied character that accompanied success.[37] As official representatives of the papal

Inquisition, both mendicant orders came into direct contact with the early Alexians. Fourteenth-century church and society were riddled with crises from below and above. Since we have no documents to inform us of the early Alexian view of this age of adversity we can only infer from the profound depth of the religious and secular challenges of the era that these pious laymen were probably too involved in the daily rigors of the *vita apostolica* to theorize on the course proper to four-teenth-century church and society. However, as they wandered through the slums of Cologne, Aachen, and Antwerp they were actively pursuing the ideals of the gospel, unconsciously repairing the walls that were so visibly undermined by all sorts of adversities.

The evolution of the Alexian habit, 15–17th centuries.

The evolution of the Alexian habit, 15–17th centuries.

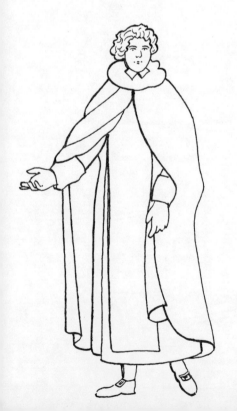

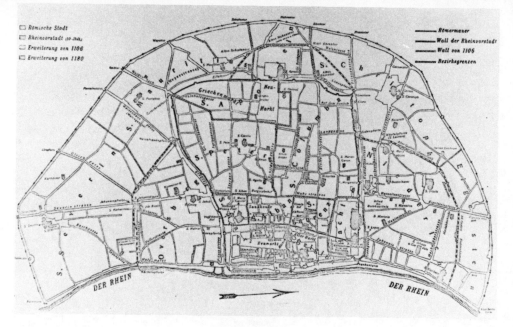

Medieval Cologne.

The location of the Cologne Lungenbrüder house.

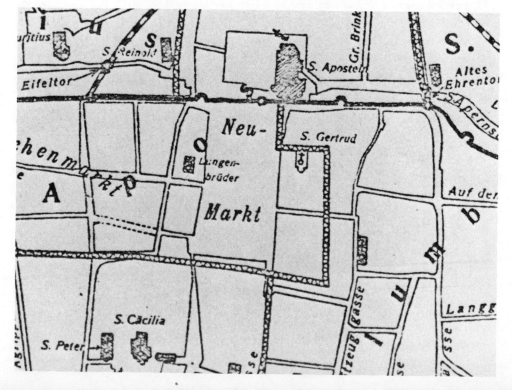

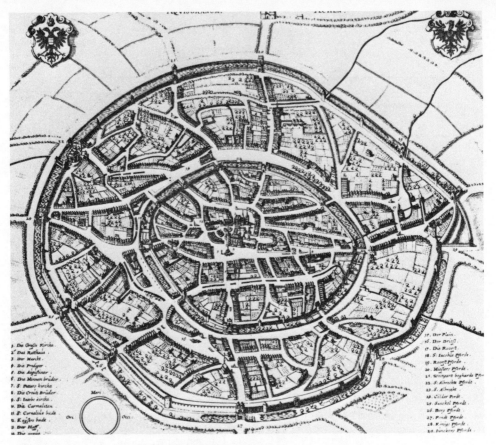

Medieval Aachen. The Alexians have been dwelling on what is today's Alexianergraben, the street immediately above the cathedral, since at least 1334.

Medieval Antwerp. The Alexian house was located on Cellebroedersstraat near the top left gate.

2

Cologne Beghards
and Charges of Heresy

Economic and social historians have linked dissident movements such as those of the Beguines and Beghards to the rise
of towns and capitalism, as if these groups represented poor
women and men economically unable to adjust to the burgeoning money economy—i.e., the urban proletariat.[1] No doubt
social causation played a role in the proliferation of Beguine
houses, since life in a Beguinage could offer women liberation
from a mandatory marriage or provide a condition of economic security in widowhood. Perhaps some Beghards were
refugees from the ranks of the urban proletariat. On the other
hand, documents reveal that the presence of wealthy aristo-
cratic ladies in many Beguinages, the rigid religious practices
of the Beguine-Beghard houses, and the varieties of apostolic
works—in leprosaria, hospitals, pesthouses—characterized
many of the groups on the *via media*. Such tasks could be
performed only by persons motivated by religious rather than
simply social or economic considerations. Herbert Grundmann, who extensively researched the broad contours of the
twelfth- and thirteenth-century religious movement, has permanently put to rest those theses which stress only economic
and social factors. Grundmann traced the movement as a
European phenomenon, which included such heretical sects as

the Albigensians and the Waldensians, such orthodox orders as the Humiliates, the Franciscans, and the Dominicans, and such suspect groups as the Beguines and the Beghards—each a diverse manifestation of the same zeal to adopt the *vita apostolica*.[2] Because the Beguine-Beghard houses developed spontaneously without a founder or a rule, the movement was by its very nature heterogeneous and defies rigid categorization. We may infer that each house had a distinctive character, yet fell into a rough type according to whether the stress was upon the contemplative or the active life, and whether it was attached to a specific trade or begged for its livelihood. The Low-Country Beghards were more settled and engaged in craft works, while the Rhineland Beghards were more mendicant and itinerant. The former were referred to as Webbeghards (Weaving Brothers)—the latter as Brot-Beghards. The Alexian Brothers of Cologne and Aachen were originally Brot-Beghards.

Around 1300 there were two Beghard houses in Cologne, zum Olvunde in the Streitzeuggasse and zum Lungen in the Lungengasse, so called because it was dominated by a wealthy butcher's shop that proudly displayed its trademark containing two lungs.[3] In 1290 Olvunde housed only two Beghards but by 1310 they were recognized as an orthodox community with permission to have their own chapel. We may infer, therefore, that the Olvunde Brothers had prospered. Shortly after this they became Margaretbrüder, then in 1328 they became tertiaries of the Franciscans. Because laymen on the *via media* were subject to criticism and harassment many Beghards and Lollards, particularly in the Low Countries, adopted the rule of the Third Order of St. Francis as a means of self-defense as well as of achieving official status within the church. Two centuries later Olvunde evolved into a regular Franciscan house.[4]

Toward the end of the thirteenth century a group of Beghards settled in the cemetery of St. Mauritius. Then after living in a house on the Fleischmengergasse, in 1300 they relocated in the house of Gerhard von Kluppel on the Lungengasse, which was referred to as Erklenz or Zome Kluppel.

Because the Beghards on the Lungengasse gained prominence throughout that section of the city close to newmarket and in the parish of Holy Apostles they were called *Lungenbrüder*, a nickname that has followed them into modern times. From the start the Lungenbrüder were engaged in nursing the impoverished sick and poor of the community. Their first habit included a gray mantle and hood and a black scapular. Though medieval nursing would be considered merely custodial by modern standards—i.e., attending to the sick and providing physical and spiritual comforts—it fulfilled a vital need in the urban squalor of the day. If the patient was terminal, nursing included preparing the body for burial. It seems therefore a natural consequence of their ministry to the poor that these early Alexians involved themselves in what came to be one of their hallmarks, the burying of the dead.

On August 3, 1306 Father John of Krefeld bought Erklenz from von Kluppel and donated it to the Beghards, who were then under the leadership of Brother Nicholas.[5] No sooner had these early Alexians gained their first house than they experienced the first of many waves of persecution. Henry of Virneburg,[6] who became archbishop of Cologne in 1306, was determined to rid his diocese of all Beguines and Beghards. Not only was he, like many bishops, suspicious of those on the *via media* who lived a religious life outside the officially recognized religious orders, but he was the first prelate to associate the Beghards with heresy.

The *vita apostolica* harked back to the primitive church when there was no standardized diocesan and parish structure. The principle of apostolic poverty had been incorporated into the *vita canonica* with the establishment of the Augustinian Canons Regular but, as noted earlier, the *vita apostolica* had widespread appeal among those laity who formed *pauperes Christi* groups. Some Beghards and Beguines, as in the diocese of Liège, came under the tutelage of members of the hierarchy or of official religious orders and were easily recognized as orthodox. Others, who stressed the need for general clerical reform before they could subject themselves to episcopal direction, were frequently considered dangerously heterodox, particularly because they proclaimed the literal message of the gospel in their teaching and preaching.[7] Even the early Franciscans suffered episcopal censure as they wandered into dioceses preaching and teaching the principles of penitence, humility, and simplicity. *Pauperes Christi* communities that also assumed the mendicant roles were obviously suspect. The cosmopolitan observer in today's world may not be disturbed by streetcorner preachers dressed in religious attire, but it is quite common for noncosmopolitan people to be upset by such nonconformity. The practice of poverty also offends the sensibilities of today's "man on the street" who would tend to criticize the voluntary poor as hypocrites with "holier-than-thou" pretenses. Because religious nonconformists suffer abuse and misunderstanding in the modern secular world, it is readily understandable why the early Alexian Beghards were subject to abuse. Not only were they considered hypocritical, but because they begged they were frequently called slothful as well as unjust, for they were accused of taking alms that rightfully belonged to the involuntary poor.

Nearly a century before Archbishop Henry's anti-Beghard assault, Innocent III had proscribed the establishment of new religious orders without prior papal approval. Ad hoc religious communities spawn popular confusion, said Innocent—but the more compelling reasons were the proliferation of heretical sects and the inability of the local bishops to contain the spread of lay institutes.[8] Though the thirteenth century witnessed the official establishment of Franciscans, Dominicans, Carmelites, and Hermits of St. Augustine, the unofficial (extra-regular) Beghards were not absorbed into these new religious orders but, rather, remained lay mendicants. Perhaps many illiterate Beghards would have been attracted to either the Franciscans or the Dominicans were it not that by the mid-thirteenth century these communities had high educational qualifications for their aspirants.[9] Though the extra-regular Alexian-Beghards and the Franciscans had adopted a mendicant way of life, the Alexians were responding to specific health-care needs of the urban poor. Thus, we can safely say that the early Alexian was hardly a frustrated Franciscan; he appears as a self-conscious layman who was adapting the mendicant life to a fresh need. Unlike the Franciscan whose papal privileges protected him from local church authorities the Beghard dwelt in permanent insecurity.

The first direct anti-Beghard decree was issued at the second Synod of Fritzlar (1259), which was chaired by the archbishop of Mainz. Although the decree did not include a charge of heresy there was a strong implication that Beghards were potential heretics. Archbishop Gerhard of Mainz decreed that those Beghards who publically begged "Brot durch Gott" "should be warned on three successive Sundays or feast days by their priests to abandon their peculiarities, to conform to the accepted Christian way of life and recognized habit, to refrain from preaching 'underground or in other secret places,' and not to consort with Beguines or to imitate them."[10] The secular clergy at the Synod of Trier in 1277 made a similar complaint against Beghard preachers as disseminators of heresy. Robert Lerner sees the anti-Beghard reaction in the context of the altered views toward the friars. "By the late 13th century the latter were losing much of their pristine zeal though enjoying many ecclesiastical privileges and their enemies began to take advantage of public disenchantment by pressing for restrictive legislation. The total effect of this was a far less favorable climate for apostolic living and Beguines and Beghards began to suffer accordingly."[11] In self-defense the friars frequently lashed out at the Beghards as pseudo-religious. Thus Archbishop Henry of Cologne appears to have been partially influenced by this attitude when in 1307 he condemned those "Beggardos" and "Beggardas" who refer to themselves as *apostolici*. He charged them with violating church law, custom, and orthodoxy on four counts: (1) by establishing an independent religious institute with a distinctive religious habit unattached to an officially recognized religious order, the Beghards violated the decree of the Fourth Lateran Council that prohibited the initiation of religious orders without papal approval; (2) as Brot-Beghards they unjustly solicited alms instead of working for their living and injuriously competed with the legitimized beggars of the mendicant orders; (3) without official recognition they publicly preached and often interrupted the friars during their preaching with the intention of engaging them in a public dispute; (4) they preached a heresy as "they said that whoever did not follow in their path could not be saved and that all those moved by the Spirit of God were not under law (Gal. 5:18) because the law was not made for the just (I Tim 1:9)."[12] Henry accused them of considering themselves without sin and of believing that "simple fornication is not a sin." Under the threat of excommunication the Beghards were to resume the dress, deportment, and respectable work of ordinary laymen.[13]

The Beghard-Alexians on the Lungengasse were apparently considered uncontrite *apostolici*; their pastor at Holy Apostles Parish excommunicated them and denied them the sacraments.[14] However, these early Alexians had made a favorable impression upon some influential citizens of the city who successfully appealed to Henry to rescind the bans of excommunication. On September 3, 1308 the Cologne Brothers were declared non-*apostolici* and allowed to resume their former way of life of serving the sick and burying the dead dressed in habits suitable to such work.[15] Had these men been self-styled streetcorner preachers proclaiming to be moved by the spirit to be above the law, the city patricians would never have advocated their case to Henry. On the contrary, they probably would have opposed them. Since there are no records of any arrests or trials resulting from the decrees of 1307 we can presume that if such *apostolici* were common in Cologne they were not easily identifiable or were itinerant preachers who could flee to distant places of protection.

As mentioned, Archbishop Henry of Virneburg was the first to charge the Beghards with a specific heresy. Until that time, they were considered suspect "outsiders" on the fringe of orthodoxy. From 1307 to well into the fifteenth century the Beghards were consistently identified as *apostolici* who soon became known as the Brethren of the Free Spirit. Because the early Alexians in Cologne and Aachen were Brot-Beghards, they too were frequently investigated for heresy. But as in

1307–1308, whenever the official church sought heretics among these communities, local city notables intervened on the Brothers' behalf. Occasionally, the Brothers may have housed few *apostolici*-Beghard, but it is highly improbable that they stressed public preaching as a major expression of their apostolate. From the consistently favorable response among prominent laymen, it appears that the hallmark of the early Alexians (one that time has strongly etched into their tradition) was their keen sense of public service. They preached their dedication to the *vita apostolica* more through action than word: they identified their belief in poverty by serving the impoverished. As early as 1308 when the Cologne patricians came to their aid, they were recognized as fulfilling a vital need. As a lay organization they theoretically led a precarious existence in a society that cherished official positions with official garb for the various ranks of ecclesiastical and secular authority. In actuality, however, this early recognition among the insiders of the city council illustrates that, regardless of how they fitted into the church, they were indeed accepted as providing a necessary service for the benefit of society.

Because these Alexians in Cologne and later in Aachen set up permanent cloister-type houses and were strongly endorsed by the city fathers, it seems unfortunate that they adopted the name Beghard. Unlike the Brot-Beghards condemned by various diocesan councils, they were not primarily itinerant preachers. Though they begged for their bread, they did not avoid manual labor but worked voluntarily in the homes of the poor and in the cemeteries of the city. They did not live by a trade, so it would be wrong to refer to them as Webbeghards, i.e., Weaver Brothers. In spite of its fuzziness, we are therefore compelled to accept the fourteenth-century name Brot-Beghard, the one that both they and the townspeople used. (When one considers the inappropriateness of the term, there is some consolation in the fact that for years scholars have warned us against generalizing on the multifarious Beguine-Beghard movement.) Ironically, as Henry of Virneburg was attempting to rid his dioceses of Beghards, the bishop of Liège was granting the Beghards of Maastricht the right to possess their own chapel and cemetery.

Perhaps the early Alexians were mistakenly associated with the heretical doctrines of the Brethren of the Free Spirit because of either the implicit or explicit mystical characteristics expressed in their way of life. The followers of the *vita apostolica*, like enthusiasts in all religions, tend to identify a life of sanctity with a return to the foundations. The *via media* departed from the contemporary corruption of the parish and of the cloister in search of the Divine Source of belief. Apostolic poverty was not an end in itself but the means whereby one discovered the radical continuity between Jesus and his living apostles. Poverty was, in this sense, a way of gathering together the fundamentals of self as a first step toward a selfless loving of God and his creatures. Through the witness of poverty, the early Alexian thus displayed a general tendency toward mysticism. In contrast to that of the preacher-prophet Brot-Beghard, the Alexian form of mysticism was probably expressed more in terms of social-action witness and within the cloister than in direct public evangelization.

The German word for an authentic groping for mystical bonds of unity between man and God is *Mystik*, in contrast to the vulgarization of the cult of mysticism characterized by hysterics, which is *Mysticismus*.[16] The fourteenth-century attacks upon the Brot-Beghards as Free Spirit heretics probably resulted from their *mysticismus* interpretation of authentic mysticism. One could easily absorb the mystical metaphors of Meister Eckhart literally and thereby distort their meaning. For example:

> The soul has something in itself, a spark of knowledge beyond reason, that never goes out. This is the spark which is so near God that it is a single same one with him and carries in itself the image of all creatures. He who remains in God has five things. The first, that between him and God there is no difference but they are one. . . .[17]

The language of love is metaphor and if Eckhart's language is taken in nonmetaphorical sense then the foregoing would mean that human nature is divine. The cardinal belief in the heresy of the Brethren of the Free Spirit is the identity of God and man, which places man above the law. Such anti-nomianism ("the true Christian is above the law") was scrip-turally rationalized by quoting St. Paul that the follower of Christ is free from all laws. The illiterate mendicant Brot-Beghards who stressed preaching could easily adulterate mystical metaphors by literal interpretation. If the early Alexians did infuse mysticism into their way of life, the following remark by Eckhart seems to comprehend their priorities: "As I have often said, if someone were in ecstasy like St. Paul's and knew of an ill person who needed from him a small broth, I consider it far wiser that you willingly leave your ecstasy and serve in greater love of the needy one."[18]

In 1307 the Cologne Brothers were considered members of that curious sect, the Brethren of the Free Spirit. Because the decrees of the Council of Vienne identified this sect with Beg-hards, the Alexians, as well as other groups on the *via media*, were frequently associated with heretical mystical-antinomian-ism.

A major historical problem has developed regarding the origins, nature, and popularity of the Free Spirit heresy. Some have traced it to Amoury of Bene's pantheistic beliefs, which were condemned at Paris in 1210. The followers of Ortlieb of Strasbourg, "Ortlibians," who preached the founder's apocalyptic mysticism, have also been considered founding fathers of the heresy.[19] Norman Cohn views Tanchlem, the eleventh-century heresiarch at Antwerp, as probably the first Free Spirit adept.[20] Gordon Leff and Robert Lerner, who have done the most recent research on the heresy, see it originating as a strain of mysticism from a peculiar religious climate rather than from any one specific heresiarch. They thus agree that the heresy was "a state of mind" that was not in-fused into a particular sect. Lerner departs from Leff, how-ever, when the latter states that "its incidence was inseparable from the Beguines and Beghards."[21] As we shall see, Lerner contends that the heresy was not only a "state of mind" but also one that was elaborately fabricated by the minds of its opponents.[22]

The famous bishop of Regensburg, Albert the Great (d. 1280), was the first to condemn the heresy comprehensively. In his *Compilatio de Novo Spiritu* Albert listed the various Free Spirit doctrinal errors as ranging from the identification of God and man to man's liberty from all moral obligations.[23] In 1310 Marguerite Porete, a mendicant mystic from Hainault, was executed in Paris as a heretic. Author of *The Mirror of Simple Souls*, Marguerite had embraced mystical beliefs that the Inquisition considered antinomian. Henry Lea therefore considers her "the first apostle in France of the German sect of Brethren of the Free Spirit."[24] A few years prior to her execution, the Inquisitor of Lorraine accused her of spreading her doctrines among "the simple folk called Begghards."[25]

The most dramatic link between Beghards and the Free Spirit Brethren was forged at the Council of Vienne (1311). Presided over by the first Avignese pope, Clement V, the council was called primarily to promulgate the liquidation of the Knights Templars. There is evidence to support Clement's own fear of the Free Spirit heresy in Italy, but since his bull *Ad Nostrum* was directed to the errors of "an abominable sect of malignant men known as Beghards and faithless women known as Beguines in the Kingdom of Germany,"[26] it appears as if Henry of Virneburg greatly influenced Clement. The eight errors condemned by *Ad Nostrum* were:

1. That a man in this life can attain to such perfection that he is incapable of sinning or surpassing his present degree of grace, since to do so would make him more perfect than Christ.
2. That he no longer needs to fast or pray for he has gained such control over the senses that he can allow them complete freedom.
3. That he is free from all obedience to the church.
4. That the free in spirit can obtain full blessedness in this life.
5. That every man so blessed does not need the divine light of glory to love God.
6. That the need for virtuous actions belongs to the imperfect man only.
7. That sexual intercourse is not a sin when desired.

8. That there is no obligation to rise before Christ's body in the elevation of the host, or to show him any other signs of respect, since this would entail descending from their heights of contemplation and so mean imperfection.[27]

To be mistakenly associated with the Brethren of the Free Spirit must have been profoundly disturbing to the Cologne Brothers. We have no evidence of their reactions to those who would place them in the category of amoral anarchists; we may assume that one reaction may have been to further restrict the behavior of the Lungenbrüder community to the practical services of nursing the sick and burying the dead; in short, to shun any sort of activity that might be construed as Free Spirit evangelization.

Another Clementine decree of the Council of Vienne was specifically aimed at the extra-regular Beguine movement. *Cum de Quibusdeim Mulieribus* identified Beguines as pseudo-religious who wore religious garb, abided by no prescribed rule, and did not take the canonical vows for the religious life. The decree also stated that Beguines were preaching "as if possessed by madness . . . opinions which are contrary to the Catholic faith."[28] Just as Henry of Virneburg excommunicated all recalcitrant Beghards and Beguines in Cologne, Clement V forbade women to pursue the life of a Beguine upon pain of excommunication. The two Clementine decrees were not published until 1317; Clement presented them to the theologians for refinement but their publication was further delayed by Clement's death (1314) and the long interval between that time and John XXII's pre-publication work on the decrees. Though *Cum de Quibusdeim* contained a qualifying remark granting protection to "good Beguines" the immediate effect of the decrees was apparently a widespread persecution of both Beguines and Beghards in northern Europe. As Leff points out:

> Clement V's Bulls marked the beginning of a new era in medieval heresy, which lasted until the Council of Constance. Henceforth the Beguines, Beghards, and the heresy of the Free Spirit became one of the preoccupations of the Church and one which exercised it perhaps more consistently than any other heresy until Huss. . . . [Unlike the

Waldensians and the Hussites who posed a direct challenge to the Church, the Free Spirit heretics] were less an alternative from without than rivals from within, postulating ... not so much a new religious form as the pursuits of the existing one on their own terms.[29]

Henry of Virneburg (1306–1322) and his successor, Walram Von Julich (1332–1349), continued to issue anti-Beghard decrees throughout the first half of the fourteenth century. In 1310 the provincial synods of Trier and Mainz followed Henry's lead by passing anti-Beghard legislation. Though there was no specific reference to Free Spirit antinomianism, the Trier decrees included a condemnation of those who "received or gave alms to beghards who called themselves 'Apostles.' "[30] It also repeated Henry's condemnation of the practice of begging "Brot durch Gott."

In 1317–1318 John of Dürbheim, bishop of Strasbourg and a member of the Council of Vienne, waged war against the Free Spirit Beghards and Beguines. Historians note the widespread mysticism in Strasbourg; perhaps not coincidentally, Meister Eckhart was preaching there during the persecution.[31] Like Archbishop Henry of Cologne who found "good Beghards" at Zum Lungen, John's diocesan inquisition confronted the problem of distinguishing between orthodox and heretical extra-regulars. The situation became more muddled when John XXII issued the bull *Sancta Romana* (1317), which appeared to proscribe the Third Order of St. Francis. After many appeals, presumably on behalf of good Beghards and Beguines, John XXII was compelled to issue another bull, *Racio Pecta* (1318), which urged protection for orthodox Beguines particularly in Germany and the Low Countries.[32]

The Strasbourg inquisition charged many Beghards and Beguines with being Free Spirit heretics. Those who recanted were compelled to wear the cross of the penitent, while the recalcitrant were transferred to the secular authorities for punishment. Though we know of no executions in Strasbourg, there is evidence of the stringency of the persecution in that many "heretics" fled the city.[33]

Numerous sources reveal widespread Free Spirit heresy in Cologne during the 1320s. In 1322 Walter of Holland (Walter the Lollard), an itinerant priest-preacher, willingly accepted burning at the stake rather than abjure his ways and inform the authorities of his disciples. Wild stories of midnight orgies have been related about this "priest of the devil."[34] Walter's followers were supposedly rounded up after one of these orgies and, according to one chronicler, over fifty were burned. Through such chronicles Cologne has frequently been considered a mecca for Free Spirit orgiastic gatherings. Recent historians are reluctant to accept such stories uncritically but even a scholar like Leff views them as proof of the penetration of the Free Spirit heresy among the Beghards of Cologne.[35] Only one historian completely rejects them. Lerner concludes:

> It does not require any great amount of scientific criticism to recognize that the recurrence of such stories is no proof of their veracity. Just as fearful children imagine the most lurid shapes in the dark, so can grown men believe in potent fables concerning movements that they fear and do not understand. Further comments along these lines may be left to the psychologist, but the historian may recall the charges of ritual murder, sexual promiscuity, and adoration of obscene divinities launched against the early Christians as well as against other minority groups throughout the ages.[36]

The single document which links the Brethren of the Free Spirit and the early Alexians is a confession by a supposedly former Free Spirit adept, John of Brünn. The confession is not from an original document but is taken from a fifteenth-century manuscript. Though undated, the confession was probably made in the early 1340s, when John was entering the Dominicans.[37] He prefaced his remarks by stating that he was confessing to Brother Gallo (Gallus of Novo Castro), an inquisitor from Bohemia, regarding the sect of the Beghards-Beguines and the Free Spirit heresy. Though there is some textual confusion with his statement that he had been a Beghard for twenty years and an adept of the Free Spirit for eight years, it seems that, since in the context of the confession these two categories are not mutually exclusive, he was actually twenty years a Beghard, during eight of which he was an adept. According to his testimony, John was apparently a man of

status and means who sought the perfect Christian life. He
was instructed by his spiritual mentor, Master Nicholas, to
leave his wife and go to Cologne in order to enter a Beghard
house dedicated to a life of poverty. John settled matters with
his wife, to whom he gave half his wealth, and entered the
Beghard house near the chapel of St. Stephen. Because his mentor, Nicholas, was also master of that house and Nicholas de
Mysene was master of the Lungenbrüder house, and because
the location fits that of the Lungengasse, historians have concluded that John entered the house of the early Alexians.[38]
After giving the Beghards all his money as a sign of his sub-
mission to them, John was introduced to the ascetic practices
of the house. ". . . The true follower of poverty has nothing
for his own but, like Christ on the cross, should be devoid of
all things temporal."[39] He then stood before them stripped
of all his clothing, whereupon they clothed him in a tunic made
of one hundred pieces of cloth as a symbol of the many abuses
which he would suffer. He was warned that he would be called
a heretic but instructed to be humbly patient as he went about
the city with a fellow Beghard begging for alms. The first
phase of his spiritual development was characterized by the
respect he owed only to the authority of his community and by
self-denial and mysticism. Because the official church did not
understand Christ's poor, he must not confess to a priest but
to one of the Brethren. He was told to deny the prompting
of his nature and through meditation submit to the will of God.
If he were genuinely moved by God he could violate the rule
to beg only with a companion and pursue alms on his own.
John was also instructed that as one of Christ's poor he did
not have to abide by church regulations on fasting and could,
if he were hungry, secretly eat behind the shield of his tunic.[40]

The confession went on to state: "I am of the Free Spirit,
and all that I desire I satisfy and gratify. Should I seek a
woman in the still of the night I satisfy my cravings without
any feelings of conscience or sin; for the spirit is free, and I
am also a natural man. Therefore I must freely satisfy my
nature by deeds."[41] He listed various other situations in which
his freedom would justify his actions. For example, if fornica-

tion led to the birth of a child, the offspring could legitimately be killed by drowning or could be labeled as the child of a clergyman who could better afford to raise the child than the poor Brethren of the Free Spirit. This anticlericalism extended to an attack upon the entire sacramental system, which was so often defiled by the prevalent corruption of the clergy. Men and women should not, therefore, fear excommunication, for once they had achieved freedom they were no longer bound by laws, including those of the Pope and archbishops.[42]

Leff points out that even after John had achieved his freedom from the law he held apostolic poverty to be sacred, and he persisted in the mendicant life at the same house. Leff explicitly accuses the Lungenbrüder house of being engulfed in heresy.

> We are thus forced to conclude from John's testimony that the Free Spirit was practiced not only by individuals and possibly clandestine conventicles [Walter of Holland and his disciples] but by entire Beguine [sic] houses in which there was a *Cursus honorum* from the austerities of initiation to final acceptance as an adept.[43]

Leff is also of the opinion that the Free Spirit heresy must have been extensive, since it would be difficult otherwise to explain the persistent anti-Beghard-Beguine attitudes of popes, local synods, inquisitions, and "self-proclaimed adherents" such as John of Brünn.[44] Though he admits that not all Beghards were heretical adepts, Leff obviously accepts John's witness, which implied that the early Alexian house was a school for the most outrageous heretical behavior of the late Middle Ages.

In contrast to Leff, Rufus Jones dismisses John's confession as bearing "all the marks of being the work of a degenerate. It is no more reliable than the testimony of a condemned witch to the existence of witchcraft in the community."[45] Jones accepts the credibility of those who gave witness to orgies of immorality, but John's confession "is wholly worthless as evidence of the moral character of the Beghards," because he knew "that his own standing with the Dominicans would be improved by his ability to make out a damaging case against their enemies."[46]

Lerner, the most recent commentator on John of Brünn's testimony, also appears as a defender of the moral character of the Lungengasse Beghards. Rather than completely dismissing John's confession, Lerner accepts it as containing "kernels of fact." There is evidence to support John when he remarks on the apostolic life and the Free Spirit beliefs regarding the annihilation of man's exterior nature as the means to union with God. Lerner sees a contradiction when John describes his freedom to sneak food within an otherwise stringently ascetic life. Such a description too easily fits the "hostile stereotype of Beghards as hypocrites."[47] Lerner agrees with the explanation of why the Lungenbrüder were cleared of heresy in 1308; he cites the fact that notable citizens of Cologne would never have supported them if they were in any way associated with the libertine way of life narrated by John of Brünn.[48] He also concurs with Rufus Jones's conclusion that John "went out of his way to cooperate with Gallus of Novo Castro [the inquisitor of Bohemia determined to weed out the Free Spirit heresy] in order to be accepted as a Dominican."[49] Lerner concludes that the interpretation of John's confession is ultimately subjective, "but modern experience has instructed us to be wary of lurid confessions of paid state witnesses or political converts and common sense might indicate that if heretical beghards did believe in the possibility of supernatural perfection they did not seriously advocate drowning children like worms."[50]

Those documents in the Cologne city archive cited by Brother Bernhard Giergen and Johannes Asen add some credibility to John's witness. Nicholas de Mysene, John's mentor, was procurator of the Lungenbrüder house from 1321–1326. Apparently, he was removed from office after the house experienced difficulties, which Asen considers the result of conflicts between the church authorities and the Brothers but which Eva Gertrud von Neumann contends were primarily financial.[51]

Regardless of the exact nature of these difficulties the Brothers once again turned to prominent citizens for support, Rutger and Sophia Overstoltz. Though the Overstoltzes seem to have responded favorably, they refused to be replacements for Nicholas as lay procurators for the house. Brothers Gottfried von Wireburg and Heinrick von Bachem became procurators on December 26, 1328. Brother Bernhard reports further unspecified difficulties over the next twenty years. The situation was ultimately resolved when two noblemen, Johann von Horn and Gerhard von Weinsberg, joined Brother Johann von Molenhiem to act as procurators in June 1349.[52]

It appears to be more than coincidental that the trouble of 1326 occurred simultaneously with the Cologne Synod of 1326 that condemned the works of Meister Eckhart as heretical. If such a famous preacher could be accused of heterodoxy perhaps the Brothers, under the direction of Nicholas, were accused of being guilty by association. Of course Nicholas could have been an antinomian heresiarch of the amoral type described by John of Brünn, but since there is no evidence of a trial and since he seems to have vanished from the scene, one is left with mere conjecture. What appears certain, however, is that the noblemen of the city would never have lent support to the Lungenbrüder if the Free Spirit heresy was running rampant throughout the house; nor would the Brothers have successfully approached them had they not been confident of the general orthodoxy of their house. Lerner's conclusion seems to come closest to the mark when he invokes common sense as the guide to understanding John's confession. Perhaps John did indeed, like the entire community, come under the tutelage of Nicholas who, we may infer, was a self-styled mystic. John's commentary on the ascetic lifestyle of the Lungenbrüder may also be accepted as true. He may have witnessed Nicholas's mystic utterances which, like those of Marguerite of Porete, could have contained remarks on the freedom of a spirit dwelling in God. Unlike Marguerite, Nicholas may not have concluded that God would implicitly direct the free spirit to follow only the promptings of nature. Yet it is unlikely that after twelve or even twenty years John was raised to the status of Free Spirit adept. Even if Nicholas was an adept, the troubles of 1326 and the plea for outside support among the Cologne nobility must have diminished his influence. John stated that he entered the Beghards when Nicholas was "master." Since we may date his entrance at the earliest as 1321, his eight-year experience as an adept could not have begun before 1329, long after Nicholas had presumably suffered disgrace. It seems inconceivable that after the Cologne house had been closed for over a year, and must have been under the close scrutiny of Archbishop Henry of Virneburg and his successor, it would embark on such a dangerous heretical course. John could have fabricated the entire story or may have along with one or two others experienced a periodic flight of free spirit which he rationalized on an adulterated mystical basis. If the latter is true then that could explain "the troubles" of the 1320s and '40s when the Brothers themselves apparently purged such deviants from the community. Perhaps John himself was purged and in his confession sought revenge. John did not mention the charitable work of the Brothers. If the Lungenbrüder were not primarily engaged in nursing the sick and burying the dead, then it is highly unlikely that as a mere Brot-Beghard community constantly under suspicion of heresy they could have been so consistently successful in appealing to the local nobility. We need go no further in exploring either the contradictions or the various explanatory inferences ramifying from the confession of John of Brünn. Regardless of its credibility, the testimony does signify the extent of the anti-Beghard climate which not only permeated the fourteenth and fifteenth centuries but is even contained in those contemporary histories that accept the reports of John and others.

Zum Lungen is the first well-established German cloister which later housed a community referred to as Cellites. This name, along with the term "poor ones," was used by popes in their protective bulls which granted privileges to the Brothers. Brot-Beghard became so associated with heterodoxy that both the Brothers and the papacy either consciously or unconsciously avoided using the term. However, because the townspeople continued to refer to them as Brot-Beghards or Beghards, it appears as if they recognized the orthodox meaning of the term.

This Cologne house, as well as other Beghard and Lollard houses, continued to experience public and official church harassment. The dark cloud of the Free Spirit heresy, so closely related to the ethereal climate of fourteenth-century Rhenish and Lowland mysticism, hovered over the early Alexians. Though it must have been a continual source of anxiety, their persistence in the face of adversity ultimately strengthened these founding Brothers.

3

The Brot-Beghards
and Lollards in
Aachen and Antwerp

I

The Beguine-Beghard movement flourished in the Low Countries, particularly in the city of Liège. Located on both banks of the Meuse, the city has a rich religious history. Indeed, the foundation of Liège as a city stems from the decision of Bishop Hubert to move his see from Maastricht to the site of Liège (717–718). His predecessor, Lambert, had constructed an oratory there and was later murdered on that spot; Hubert, impressed with the number of miracles occurring at the venerable site, decided to establish his diocesan seat at Liège. Around the year 980, it became an ecclesiastical principality under the Holy Roman emperor, with the prince bishop of Liège as a suffragan of the archbishop of Cologne.

Once considered the "Athens of Europe" because of its fine Cathedral School, Liège later earned the title "the city of priests." Because the diocese harbored so many women extra-regulars, Liège could have been appropriately dubbed the city of Beguines. When Pope Urban IV (1261–1264) was

an archdeacon in Liège he wrote a booklet on the proper
guidance and direction of the Beguine way of life. Bishop
Robert of Liège (1229–1246) gave the booklet the authority
of a rule demanding that all Beguine convents observe its
prescriptions. The so-called Beguine Court (i.e., Beguinage),
therefore, originated in Liège and when Urban IV became
pope he assumed the role of patron over the Beguines of
Liège.[1] So extensive was the movement in this diocese that in
1267 Bishop Henry conferred privileges upon seventeen of
their communities. According to a document of 1266, some
Beguines and Beghards were associated with work in pesthouses and hospitals; however, in 1288 the bishop decreed that
if Beguines wished to receive diocesan privileges, they must
reside in a Beguinage and if they lived outside a court they
must not wear special garb. The decree also stipulated that if
they were engaged in a trade which provided them with more
than ten marks income they were exempt from paying taxes.[2]

The ancient imperial city, Aachen, was located in the Liège
diocese. As early as 1262 Aachen was known as a center for
Beguines, many of whom lived in their own homes rather than
in courts. According to the pattern adopted in Liège, Henry
encouraged them to move into a Beguinage outside the city
where they could enjoy all the privileges of a Beguine court
including their own chapel and spiritual director; apparently,
most of the Aachen courts were dependent upon manual labor
for their livelihood.[3]

The Liège Beghards followed the general pattern of Beguine development. For example, as cited earlier, in 1308 the
Beghards of Maastricht received permission from the bishop
of Liège to have their own chapel and rector. They, too,
earned their living through manual labor, particularly weaving,
which earned them the status of Webbeghards. Just as there
were Web- and Brot-Beghards in Cologne, so also Aachen
housed both groups. Webbeghards once lived on what is today's Kapuzïnergraben.[4] Clement V, the same pope who lashed
out at the Beghards as Free Spirit heretics, sanctioned the life
of these "weaving brothers" by granting them permission to
have their own chapel. Characteristic of the Webbeghards,

this house followed the rule of the Third Order of St. Francis. Because their chapel was dedicated to St. Servatius of Maastricht and because their way of life and the timing of their official recognition corresponded to the patterns established in the western portion of the diocese, the Aachen Webbeghards presumably owed their origins to the general movement in the Low Countries.[5]

Situated in the northwestern edge of the Rhineland, Aachen was not only influenced by developments in the Low Countries but by the currents of the Rhine valley as well. We have already noted (Council of Mainz, 1259) the appearance of Brot-Beghards, mendicants who live entirely on charity, in the Rhine valley. It is not surprising therefore that in Aachen and Cologne both types of Beghard communities developed their distinctive ways of life.

The earliest document evidencing the presence of the Brot-Beghards in Aachen is a 1334 city hall notice of a gift of alms to the "poor" Beguines and Beghards.[6] The document refers to the Brot-Beghards located on the *Scharportzgrave*, which is today's *Alexianergraben*.[7] Hence for over six hundred years the Alexian presence has persisted on that street, which during the fourteenth century was a ditch along the town walls, symbolic of the outsider situation of these self-styled mendicants. Though we have no real evidence of their pre-1334 existence, one historian has traced Alexianergraben to 1172 when it was referred to as *Begarden-graben*.[8] Perhaps lay mendicants did dwell on that graben in the twelfth century, but if we are designating the Alexian Founding Brothers by the characteristic ministries that persisted to modern times, then we must focus on the fourteenth century for the clear identification of the Alexian "species" from the generic Beghard.

Without documentation it is impossible to localize the origins of the Aachen Brothers. Because their lifestyle seems to have closely resembled the Brot-Beghards of the Rhineland it is probable that their founders originated to the east, perhaps even Cologne. Yet, since we know that lay mendicant groups characterized by the cry "Brot durch Gott" spontaneously sprang up throughout the Rhineland, it is equally possible that these poor Beghards were natives of Aachen.

The prehistory (before 1334) condition of the Aachen Brothers also leaves us with conjecture about the possible adversities they may have suffered as a result of Archbishop Henry's anti-Beghard persecutions and the Council of Vienne decrees. Perhaps because of Liège's absorption of Beguines and Beghards into the official church milieu, the Aachen Brothers did not represent a threat to orthodoxy as did the Lungenbrüder to the Cologne archdiocese.

Just as the Cologne city council continuously supported the early Alexians, the Aachen city council recorded gifts to the poor Beghards in 1334, 1338, 1344, and 1346.[9] Again, it is very unlikely that prominent men of the city would extend such charity to these Beghards had they been at all suspicious of heterodox beliefs. On the contrary, the Aachen city council must have been rewarding them for their charitable service rendered for the common good. Unlike the more cloistered Webbeghards, the Brot-Beghards identified the *vita apostolica* with voluntary poverty and service to the poor. They thus begged for alms to support themselves in their apostolate.

The graben on which they dwelt ran along the ramparts of the old city, and so the "graben-life" may thus symbolize the existence of these early Alexians. As travelers on the *via media* they lived on the edge of church society in contrast to the established religious orders who dwelt at the center of *religio*. Though their way of life contained an implicit protest against the secularism of both parish and monastery, their service to the community was recognized as an orthodox Christian response, at least by the city council. Perhaps they were harassed by the mendicant friars and abused by those who would heckle any nonconformists, but it was not until the papal Inquisition was introduced in Germany in 1369 that the Aachen Brot-Beghards experienced their first battle for survival. However, before witnessing this dramatic series of events, it is necessary to shift the focus to Antwerp, where in 1345 a group of Lollards established a house that later became a major Alexian cloister.

II

Antwerp's strategic location along the river Schelde as it flows to the North Sea (sixty miles from the city) was crucial to its development as a great commercial city. The etymology of the name *Antwerp* illustrates its strategic importance—*anda werpum*, in front of the accretion.[10] Though it was not until the fourteenth century that Antwerp became a bustling commercial city, its ships accompanied Godfrey de Bouillon on the First Crusade (1096). The merchant path from Cologne passed through Aachen and veered to Antwerp.

The first extra-regulars of Antwerp founded a Beguinage in 1240. Though they experienced a period of prosperity and respect, symbolized by the privileges of having their own chaplain and cemetery, later they suffered persecution.[11] The first Antwerp Brothers were called *Matemannen* and *Lollarden*. *Matemannen* has been translated as "poor men who live a humble existence." The following medieval lines illustrate its meaning:

> I see no one noble on the earth who is not mighty and rich. How do they alone have nobility and the mate volk [small people] have none?[12]

The etymology of the term *Lollard* is Middle Dutch, meaning "mumbler." The Oxford English Dictionary (OED) contains a specific reference to the Alexians in its etymology of the term *Lollard*.

> The name was originally applied c. 1300 to the members of a branch of the Cellite or Alexian fraternity (also called lollerbroeders) who devoted themselves especially to the care of the sick and the providing of funeral rites for the poor. In the course of the 14 c. it was often used of other semi-monastic orders, and sometimes, by opponents, of the Franciscans. Usually it was taken to connote great pretensions to piety and humility, combined with views more or less heretical. Hence early mod. G[erman] lollhart chiefly applied to Beghards.[13]

Dietrich von Kurze is the most recent scholar of the continental Lollards, as distinguished from the disciples of Wyclif in England. After tracing the various interpretations of the term he concludes that *Lollard* is derived from *lollen, lullen,* i.e., to mumble or stammer.[14] Unlike the OED, von Kurze does not associate the Lollards primarily with the Alexian family. He refers to the Cellites as "municipal Lollards" who, by their ministries, were able to survive as voluntary poverty groups in spite of adverse public opinion and attacks upon them by the clergy.[15]

The Chronicler Jan van Hoesen (ca. 1334), a schoolmaster from Liège, described the Lollards as members of the poor classes who united in order to take care of the sick of the poor and bury the dead.[16] Though von Kurze may be accurate when he states that the origin of *Lollard* cannot be traced to one specific group, it does appear that one of its most common usages was in reference to Cellite communities. Because of their illiteracy, the early Cellites were probably noticed mumbling the funeral chant as they performed their public burial rites. Father Floris Prims tied the origins of the Low Country Lollards to the Brot-Beghards of Cologne ca. 1300.[17] There is no evidence of Brot-Beghards as such appearing in the Netherlands; Beghards there were exclusively Webbeghards, i.e., semireligious communities characterized by stability and a common trade, particularly weaving. However, like the Brot-Beghards, many Lollards were itinerant mendicants who shared the same apostolate as the Lungenbrüder of Cologne. Thus it is likely that the Cellite Lollards of the Low Countries and the Brot-Beghards of the Rhineland represent independent spontaneous expressions of the *vita apostolica*; yet without accurate documentation it is impossible to trace either independent or common Alexian sources. Perhaps in the late thirteenth century there was a charismatic leader responsible for the birth of the community and because he was illiterate there is no written evidence of his role. If they did originate in Germany, then the trade routes from the Rhineland to Antwerp may have been their path. When they first came to Antwerp they lived a scattered existence throughout the city. "In 1342," remarked one chronicler, "there started to gather in the city of Antwerp many devoted men, who served the sick and buried the dead, and exercised many works of love toward their neighbors. Those were the Cellbrothers."[18] On October 1, 1345 Henrik Suderman, a prominent merchant from Dortmund, Germany, declared before the Antwerp aldermen that he had given, "to the praise and glory of God and to the salvation of his soul, his house along the Corte Mere"[19] as the living quarters for the *Matemannen*, who were called *Lollarden*. He noted the itinerant life of the Lollards as he opened the house to them regardless of from "whichever country they come"[20] assuming that they were "leading a good life."[21] Suderman stipulated that the house was to be governed by three persons chosen by him: Arnold van Horonst the elder, Hostin van Eversbeke, and the former owner of the house, Jacob van Brussel.[22] Though the Lollards were not the legal owners, the foregoing "board of governors" was directed to handle their authority with the Council of the Brothers.

Five years before this, Suderman established a charitable residence for elderly homeless men. Perhaps there he first noticed that the Lollards, who probably nursed the old people, were in need of their own house. The house that Suderman provided for them was situated near the Cattle Market, directly behind Suderman's residence, which he later gave to the Beghards (Webbeghards).[23] Apparently there was some conflict between the Lollards and the Beghards, as the aldermen intervened concerning the use of the wall that separated the two pieces of property.[24] Obviously Suderman's prominent position strengthened the Lollards' status in the city. As long as he and the original board of governors were presiding over their house the Antwerp Brothers dwelt in security.

The Lungenbrüder of Cologne, the Brot-Beghards of Aachen, and the Lollards of Antwerp were intimately related through their common *pauperes Christi* ministries and their oral-folk absorption of the Scriptures. Perhaps each of these three communities was aware of the others but documentation revealing direct lines of communication among them does not appear until the early fifteenth century. The founderless Beghard and Lollard-Alexians represent a spontaneous submovement within the broad *vita apostolica* movement. It is likely that, like the Cologne Brothers, the Aachen and Antwerp communities experienced some misunderstanding, public or church harassment, and even some form of discrimination and persecution.

Each community was dedicated to the poverty expressed in administering to the sick. Unlike other nursing orders, these Brothers did not construct hospitals but, rather, attended to the sick in their homes. This common characteristic appears to reveal their emphasis upon a personal approach to the patient. This facet of their existence will be thoroughly explored elsewhere, but it is appropriate to note here the character that each of these three communities spontaneously expressed. Our fictional "Brother Paul" was, then, primarily a *pauperes Christi* mendicant who brought Jesus to the sick. He was called to the bedside of the dying where his evangelical fervor was uttered in prayer and service. Though we have no documents to verify the Brothers' pre-plague burial ministry, their ministry to the dying must have included at least preparation for burial. As the Black Death spread through the Rhineland and the Low Countries these Brothers became thoroughly immersed in burial rites. Before the plague they administered to persons on the limits of existence; during the plague their ministry to entire towns struck by catastrophe was heroically evidenced. Their original ministry, a general ministry to the dying and the dead, was to become particularized when they encountered one of the most tragic events in the history of European civilization—the Black Death.

4

The Black Death, Expansion
and the Inquisition

I

The fourteenth century is characterized by the adversities of war, famine, and economic depression, but the most devastating series of events is associated with the Black Death. Originating around the Black Sea, the plague was imported to Europe through its commercial towns. Prior economic and social adversities had made European society particularly vulnerable to the deadly disease. Boccaccio witnessed its destructive force:

> ... In men and women alike it first betrayed itself by the emergence of certain tumors in the groin or armpits, some of which grew as large as an apple, others as an egg, some more some less, which the common people called gavocciolo. From the two said parts of the body this deadly gavocciolo soon began to propagate and spread itself in all directions indifferently; after which the form of the malady began to change, black spots or livid making their appearance in many cases on the arm or the thigh or elsewhere, now few and large, now minute and numerous. And as the gavocciolo had been and still was the infallible token of approaching death, such also were these spots on whomsoever they showed themselves.[1]

The epidemic reached Cologne in December 1349. Contemporary accounts of the German death toll range from one-third to two-thirds of the population; recent studies, from one-fifth to one-third. The most conservative figures for Cologne, Aachen, and Antwerp would be 10,000, 3,500, and 2,500 victims, respectively. Within three years—1347 to 1350 —twenty million Europeans died, twice the number of those who perished in World War II.[2] To medieval man, thoroughly lacking medical knowledge necessary to evaluate the cause of the plague, the Black Death heralded civilization's doom. Referred to as the *Jungfrau* in Germany, the plague was everywhere personified in various forms as the Angel of Death. The church in Germany was particularly hard hit. The *Jungfrau* who "flew through the air in the form of a blue flame, and in this guise was often seen emerging from the mouths of the dead,"[3] struck down over one-third of the higher clergy in Germany. Though many religious apparently deserted their cloisters, chronicles reveal their work among the plague victims. Such work elicited heroism from those committed to the nursing apostolate. One witness remarked that physicians and priests "were seized by the plague whilst administering spiritual aid; and, often by a single touch, or a single breath of the plague—stricken, perished even before the sick person they had come to assist."[4]

As communities dedicated to nursing, the Brot-Beghards of Cologne and Aachen and the Lollards of Antwerp were so crucially affected by the Black Death that the plague marks a turning point in the history of the Alexian Brothers. Indeed, a popular historical view placed their origins during the time of the Black Death. For example, in the 1907 edition of *The Catholic Encyclopedia* John J. A'Becket claims that the Alexian Congregation "had its origin at Mechlin, in Brabant, in the fifteenth [sic] century during the terrible ravages of a pest called the 'black death.' "[5] He even refers to a specific founder, Brother Tobias, who supposedly united a group of laymen dedicated to nursing and burying the plague victims. A'Becket probably relied upon the work of Etienne Binet, a seventeenth-century Jesuit who wrote a book on the founders of religious orders.[6] Johanne Nohle, author of a classic work on the plague, noted the work of the early Alexians: "Fearless and indefatigable were also the Poor Friars [a common fourteenth-century term applied to the Brothers] whose order was founded by a certain Tobias on the middle course of the Rhine in the middle of the fourteenth century."[7] Perhaps Nohle was influenced by Binet, but there is also a sixteenth-century chronicle containing references to Tobias.[8] Though as a founder Tobias lacks all credibility, the legend illustrates the plague's impact upon the history of the Brothers.

Even the author of the Alexian piece in the 1967 *Catholic Encyclopedia* views the Congregation as evolving "from the needs of the victims of the Black Death of 14th century Europe."[9] Though there is an abundance of documents to verify the pre-plague existence of the "Poor Brothers," the plague seems to have acted as a catalyst in bringing this thoroughly amorphous lay ministry movement into some primitive form of organization. Only after 1350 are there records of various communities of Brothers acting in concord. Ernst McDonnell and Walter Marx, who are primarily concerned with church history in the Low Countries, share the opinion that until the Black Death the Alexians were pious laymen indistinguishable from Beghards and Lollards. McDonnell speculates that, after the plague, scattered brothers "began to come together in cloisters, living in cells like those used by monks, but not adopting a monastic rule."[10] Since the word *Brot-Beghard* did not exist in the Low Countries, the term *Beghard* applied to that area could mean *Lollarden*, *Matemannen* or *Webbegharden*. It would seem that Webbeghards did not evolve into Alexians. On the other hand, *Matemannen* and *Lollarden* were names applied to the founding Brothers in Antwerp. Other *Matemannen* and *Lollarden* were very poor brothers who frequently lived in humble quarters near local hospitals where, along with Beguines, they nursed the sick.[11] It is very probable that during the plague these "hospital Lollards" gained status in the community, received gifts from the city fathers, and developed a specific identity. Because they were doing the same work as those Brothers in Aachen, Cologne, and Antwerp, they seem to have gradually become conscious of their common ministries.

54

Though nursing included preparation for burial and frequently participation in the burial of the dead, the latter ministry gained great momentum during the plague years. The funeral chant of the Brothers must have been both a haunting refrain and a source of consolation, as the survivors knew that their deceased friends and relatives, in spite of the dangerous conditions, would receive a sacred burial. The ministry of a new religious order is normally in response to a need neglected by society. The Alexians did not originate in response to the needs of the plague but they gained their distinguishing hallmarks by responding to those struck by the plague, a task that few had the courage to perform. This is indeed a measure of their asceticism and their uncomplicated dedication to the *vita apostolica.*

There are no records of the Brothers' attitudes toward the plague nor to their burial ministry during this period. Had the Brothers been motivated merely by a desire to serve the general welfare by removing the pest-stricken bodies from the city, then one doubts whether they would have persisted. Nor is it enough to say that they possessed an enormous amount of charity for their fellow human beings. It appears that to appreciate the historical nature of their heroic plague efforts one must again attempt to penetrate their oral-folk perspective. Let us return to "Brother Paul" who, after he absorbed the word of God as "a real happening," assumed the life of poverty and the nursing and burial ministries as the means whereby he believed Christ was continuously made present.

His witness to the sick and the dead was not a nice act committed by a charitable person, nor was it the fulfillment of a social need. Instead, it was a religious response to a religious need. The dying person is approaching the *limit* of his earthly existence. In the limit-situation the dying religiously gropes for the traditional rites and symbols appropriate to the limit-character of his existence. Paul's ministry included, besides the physical care, the chanting of *Pater Nosters* and *Aves* and probably the *Miserere* and the *De Profundis*, psalms that formed the core of the funeral chant. We may also infer that Paul inconspicuously preached at bedside.

Though we would now refer to this as counseling, that is far too contemporary a term for what he performed. The deathbedside words he uttered were ritual invocations for the redemptive Christ to be present in this profound situation. As will be discussed later, since the Sacrament of Extreme Unction was not a frequent privilege for the poor, one may infer that the Brothers anointed the sick and dead bodies with sacred oil as well. Transpose these rituals to the plague condition and one may conclude that the entire culture was passing through a limit-situation. The Alexians responded to the plague victims because that was their unique calling, or charism. The plague victim was an obvious outsider struck by the Angel of Death.

The "hospital Lollards" of the mid-fourteenth century were called *Cellbrüder*, or Cellites, in the fifteenth century. The name could come from one of two derivations of the Latin word *cella*: either the monastic "small room" or cell, or the underground storage room—*cella*—which many historians have loosely applied to also mean grave. *Cellbrüder* could therefore mean either brothers of the monastic cells or gravebrothers. Because their burial apostolate evolving from the plague became their unique feature, "gravebrothers" is a popular interpretation for *Cellbrüder*. However, Marx and McDonnell, who view the organizational development as evolving from the plague, prefer the monastic meaning; they conclude that after the Black Death the loosely structured hospital Lollards came together in a cloister of monastic cells.[12] Regardless of which is the proper etymology, both interpretations depend upon the profound impact of the plague for the development of the early Alexians.

The Black Death, therefore, probably had the following effects upon the Brothers: it strengthened the towns' appreciation of their vital works; it provided stability to those groups of hospital Lollards who without recognition could have gradually disappeared; it occasioned in many towns a common contractual arrangement between the Brothers and the city hall, which certified the early Alexians as a burial guild with exclusive rights for the preparation and burial of the dead. Stabilization and status meant not only local expansion into suitable cloisters but general expansion throughout the Rhineland and the Netherlands. Of the fifty-four Cellite houses that existed on the eve of the Reformation, the vast majority were founded after the plague. Before 1350 houses existed in Cologne, Aachen, Antwerp, Louvain, Mechlin, and Thienen; in the latter half of the fourteenth century they settled in Ghent, Bruges, Brussels, Hasselt, Diest and St. Troiden.[18] However, it was not until after 1400 that the Brothers entered the cities of the northern Netherlands (the Dutch Netherlands of today). The effects of the plague upon the evolution of the Alexian Brothers were compounded when one notes that there were recurrences of the deadly epidemic in 1357–1362, 1370–1376, and 1380–1383. With each new wave the services of the Brothers became more highly regarded.

Not until the next century did the various houses establish regular channels for communication and organization, but the results of the plague provided them with a common identity from which they could gain a common consciousness, such consciousness becoming the necessary basis for further development as a nascent religious order.

Black Death culture contained explosive extremes. Chroniclers reported the heroic but more frequently stressed the decline of morality, the cult of public penance (flagellants), and varieties of macabre behavior such as grave-robbing. Since biblical narratives possessed an abundance of instances when God's wrath imposed plagues upon a degenerate unfaithful people, this tradition provided the common explanation for the appearance of the *Jungfrau*. Colossal catastrophes frequently bring out the worst as well as the best in human nature. Traditional biases, prejudices, and frustrations shifted from implicit to explicit expression. Depending on local leadership, a community could publicly traffic in the most amoral acts, could become consumed with passionate rage toward outsider groups, and toward economic, social, and religious elites. The outsider group most commonly attacked was the Jewish community. Beginning in southern France, the pogroms spread throughout Germany. A plague-confused public could easily be led to believe the stories of how the Jews had set about poisoning the wells, butchering Christian youths, and other equally horrid tales. Because Jews were excluded from all forms of property ownership and from the guilds, many became money-lenders. In an era of economic contraction and depression, money-lenders were viewed as parasites on the poor and unfortunate. Thus traditional prejudices combined with economic conditions smoldering below the surface before the plague set off a volcanic explosion of gross anti-Semitism in which tens of thousands of Jews were publicly executed, usually with the approval of both secular and religious leaders.

Strasbourg and Cologne were exceptions. In the former, it was the bishop who, in conflict with the secular arm, whipped up the anti-Semitic rage of the people. Cologne, avoiding such a pogrom, actually expressed concern for the Jews in the form of a letter from the city council.[14] The Avignese Pope Clement VI issued a bull condemning the persecution, but it apparently had little effect. Even in the twentieth century, which witnessed the Holocaust, the anti-Semitic violence of the catastrophic mid-fourteenth century is viewed as one of the bloodiest chapters in the history of Western civilization.

The flagellant movement did not originate with the Black Death. There is evidence of it among Italian monks as far back as the eleventh century. During the thirteenth and early fourteenth centuries, flagellant movements appeared in eastern Europe. The plague-flagellants claimed to have heavenly sanction through a letter written by God specifying the plague as divine punishment and the penance of flagellation as a worthy sign of man's plea for forgiveness.[15]

The movement was particularly strong in Germany. Although chroniclers tell of how the "Brotherhood of the Flagellants" or "Brothers of the Cross" would daily scourge themselves and each other, historians question how widespread the movement was. Yet few deny the general popularity with which it began. Pope, bishops, and secular notables encouraged the cult until the flagellants began to demand a commitment of thirty-three years instead of thirty-three days. The church establishment was also critical of their prophecies of the "end time," and their claims to heal the sick, raise the dead, and exorcise devils. What began as a popular movement led by "respectable" classes of society became a fringe movement with an appeal to the rootless and desperate groups in society. Until mid-1349, the flagellants enjoyed widespread support in Germany and the Low Countries. Frightened by what had devolved into a heterodox group that frequently attacked the simoniacal abuses in the church, Clement VI, advised by the Flemish monk Jean de Fayt, issued a bull on October 20, 1349 condemning the movement and demanding its immediate suppression.[16]

Ultimately the flagellants evolved into an extremist sectarian group with strong anticlerical and anti-Semitic views. Nohl quotes Clement VI:

> Already flagellants under pretence of piety have spilt the blood of Jews, which Christian charity preserves and protects, and frequently also the blood of Christians, and, when opportunity offered, they have stolen the property of the clergy and laity and have arrogated to themselves the legal authority of their superiors on which account it is to be feared that their boldness and impudence will produce no small degree of perversion if strong steps are not immediately taken to suppress it.[17]

Zeigler reports that "cases were heard of Flagellants interrupting religious services, driving priests from their churches and looting ecclesiastical property."[18] Perhaps Zeigler is paraphrasing Clement's letter, but since he does not document his statement there is no supportive evidence for these cases. Be that as it may, the following statement, also undocumented, is unworthy of an author who has otherwise done an admirable work on the Black Death: "other heretics—Lollards, Beghards, and Cellites—made common cause with them [the flagellants] in contesting the authority of the Catholic Church."[19]

Apparently Zeigler's reference to the Cellites is dependent upon his reading of Lea's work on the Inquisition, which contains an almost identical indictment of the Lollards, Beghards, and Cellites. To verify his statement Lea cites two chronicles which, because they were written in the fifteenth century, are not primary source material for an accurate Cellite-flagellant association; instead they reflect the traditional biases against extra-regulars.[20] Prims notes that during the plague the early Alexians in Antwerp were harassed because they were associated with the Brothers of the Cross. Though Prims defines the latter not as flagellants but as members of a community founded in Liège (1211) by Theodore de Celles (the modern Crosiers), they could have actually been the flagellant Brothers of the Cross.[21] If so, this is the only possible "Cellite-flagellant" relationship because these Brothers were thoroughly engaged by their burial apostolate and apparently shunned overt anticlerical protest.

II

During the Black Death the only evidence of anti-Beghard harassment toward the early Alexians occurred at Antwerp. In Germany, however, the excesses of the flagellant movement, the declining danger of the plague, and a spirit of peaceful coexistence between pope and emperor encouraged the renewal of anti-Beghard activity. As heretics in the guise of pious laymen, the flagellants hurt the cause of the Beghards and Beguines who, though they may have been thoroughly orthodox, were frequently confused with heterodox groups.

Because of the bitter conflict between Emperor Ludwig and the Avignese papacy, the papal Inquisition never penetrated Germany. When Charles IV became emperor in 1347 a spirit of mutual respect developed between emperor and pope. In 1348 Clement appointed the first inquisitor for the empire. The plague intervened but Charles IV and Clement VI were vigorous antiflagellant leaders, and after the epidemic had spent its course Pope Innocent VI (1352–1362), following the lead of his predecessor Clement, reintroduced the papal Inquisition in Germany. He was particularly concerned with the "pestiferious madness" of the Beghards.[22] Though Charles IV did not obstruct the work of Innocent's inquisitor, John Schadeland, neither did he provide the political support necessary for a successful antiheresy pursuit. The Inquisition was, therefore, not a serious threat until 1369 when the emperor became its champion. The story of Charles's shift to a pro-Inquisition position is not entirely clear. Urban V (1362–1370), who was an energetic reformer, was very concerned with the Beghard-Beguine challenge to orthodoxy, with the then apparent decline in Christian morality, and with the need for a restoration of papal prestige by returning the papacy from Avignon to Rome. Upon his succession he immediately commissioned four Dominicans as inquisitors for Germany. Shortly after his return to Rome, Urban had a historic meeting with Charles IV, the first such pope-emperor encounter in the Holy City since 1220. The following June (1369) Charles issued his four Lucca edicts through which he clearly placed the prestige and power of his office at the service of the papal Inquisition in his empire.

The first of the four edicts (June 9, 1369) is most significant. Charles directed all spiritual and temporal authorities to cooperate with the papal Inquisition in its pursuits of the heretical Beghards and Beguines, the "willige Armen" (voluntary poor) who beg "Brot durch Gott"; all those persons who participated in or were in any way supportive of their way of life were automatically executed. The other three decrees were concerned with specific instructions on the ways in which bishops and princes were to aid the papal inquisitors, with the censorship of all Beghard-Beguine literature, and with the procedures for disposing of the heretics' property.[23]

Charles's pro-Inquisition edicts may have been motivated by his loyalty to Urban, which was strengthened by their historic meeting; by his need to consolidate his power over the prince-bishops of the empire; or, what is more likely, a combination of both political and ecclesiastical concerns. By brandishing the imperial sword in defense of the papal Inquisition, he certainly earned the nickname *Pfaffenkönig* (papal emperor).[24]

The two major inquisitors commissioned to prosecute the

Beghards were Walter Kerlinger and Louis de Caliga. Though they were first appointed in 1364 their activity did not gain momentum until after the Lucca edicts were issued. Kerlinger was chief inquisitor and gained great notoriety from his "successful" trials of Free Spirit heretics.[25] Louis de Caliga was responsible for the dioceses of Cologne and Trier, but since documents reveal his presence in Aachen, it is probable that he was assigned to Liège as well. Armed with a personal letter from the emperor and well versed in the anti-Beghard-Beguine Clementine decrees, he examined the Aachen extra-regulars for heresy. A single document signed by Friar Louis was a directive (dated February 22, 1370) to the Aachen city council assigning to it responsibility for retaining the houses of the Beguines and Beghards until the pope or the emperor had decided what was to be done with them. Two months later Charles assigned the property to the city council which, with its alms, had built the Beghard-Beguine houses.[26]

From these two documents we are unable to discover the particulars of Caliga's prosecutions in Aachen. Obviously some Beghards and Beguines were considered heterodox and had their houses confiscated. Since there is no evidence of inquisitional trials nor any follow-up investigation resulting from Louis's visitation, the residents in the closed houses must have been declared nonconformists rather than heretics.

Because the early Alexians were the only Brot-Beghards in Aachen, we may infer that Friar Louis did examine their customs and beliefs. They were either cleared of all suspicion of heresy or temporarily closed on the grounds that as extra-regulars on the *via media* they were in violation of church law and leaned toward heterodox beliefs. It is highly unlikely that they were closed, as city council records would have noted that fact, particularly in light of the council's consistently favorable view of the Aachen Brot-Beghards.

Gregory XI, the last of the Avignese popes, who succeeded Urban VI in March 1371 was also a firm anti-Beghard pope. In January 1372 or 1373 Gregory wrote to Charles IV as well as all the spiritual and temporal authorities in Germany urging cooperation with the Inquisition's persecution of Beghards and Beguines and the flagellants, who had experienced a recent revival.[27] The subsequent persecution must have been particularly severe on all extra-regulars. For example, in 1374 three Beghard houses in the dioceses of Liège, Trier, and Strasbourg registered a complaint with the Avignese papacy. In early 1374 four notables representing these three extra-regular communities had traveled to Avignon where they voiced opposition to the unjust persecution of Christians in the Rhineland and Brabant.[28] Albert Huyskens also reports that representatives of houses in Cologne, Trier, and Mainz pursued papal approval for extra-regulars in their dioceses.[29] He tells how they explained to the Pope that the Beghards and Beguines throughout Germany, Brabant, and Flanders dwelt in poverty and chastity, were loyal subjects of their bishops, regularly attended services in their parish churches, and served their neighbors in humility and charity.[30] Gregory's response to this latter request took the form of a rescript dated April 6, 1374. The Pope instructed the archbishops and bishops of these dioceses to investigate the way of life, customs, constitutions, and orthodoxy of those that had registered complaints and, according to their findings, punish the guilty and protect the innocent. Gregory did not specify the houses by name, nor did the rescript contain references to Beguines or Beghards. Instead he referred to these pious laypersons as "poor ones."[31]

The papal mandate was effective; armed with the rescript, "poor ones" in the dioceses of Worms and Liège appealed to their bishops for an investigation to clear them once and for all of all suspicion of heresy. On May 13, 1375 John, bishop of Liège, ordered all priests and pastors of his diocese to admit the extra-regulars into their churches for all services and to assist them in their way of life.[32] Since Aachen was in the Liège diocese, the early Alexians were probably encouraged by Gregory's rescript and the decree of their bishop. Indeed, the efforts of the "poor ones" to gain papal approval signaled a new phase in the evolution of the Beghards in the Rhineland, Flanders, and Brabant. Though Gregory did not explicitly approve of their way of life, he did order the bishops to protect those orthodox extra-regular communities. Yet such legal protection depended upon the bishops' discretion. And because bishops were also ordered to cooperate with the Inquisition, the anti-Beghard-Beguine persecution continued.

In January, 1375 the Cologne city council wrote to Gregory XI protesting the methods used by the Dominican inquisitors to examine "poor men and women" who beg in accordance with Scripture.[33] The magistrates told the Pope that they had organized their own investigation of these groups by inquiring of their pastors regarding their orthodoxy and the integrity of their mendicant way of life. Satisfied that they were good Christians, the city fathers informed the Pope of the unjust tactics employed by the Dominican inquisitors: "Forsooth, most holy Father, this inquisitor propounds to these poor and unlettered laymen such difficult and unanswerable questions that a great theologian can scarcely offer a solution to them without much deliberation and consulting of books. Over these questions mere laymen ought not to be examined; it seems sufficient that they know the articles of faith as befits laymen."[34] Though we know of no immediate papal response to this complaint, eventually such complaints did bring satisfaction.

Lambert Bern, bishop of Strasbourg, was a bitter enemy of the Beguines and Beghards. A close confidant of Charles IV and one who witnessed the promulgation of the 1369 Lucca edicts, he followed in the footsteps of another anti-Beghard prelate of Strasbourg, John of Dürbheim.[35] Though his attack included quotes from the earlier papal bull *Ad Nostrum*, Lambert did not stress the doctrinal deviation of the extra-regulars but lashed out at their unorthodox way of life. According to his decree, the lay mendicants on the *via media* who begged, wore religious garb, elected their own superiors, and confessed to one another and performed prayer or flagellant-like penances represented a threat to church stability.[36] He appears to reflect the then typical anti-Beghard-Beguine prejudice, i.e., that lay voluntary-poverty communities were pseudo-religious orders in violation of the Fourth Lateran Council's decree against new religious orders.

Lambert's attack was launched on August 19, 1374, four

months after Gregory XI issued his mandate urging the hierarchy to be careful that they did not punish innocent "poor ones." Because shortly after his August 19 letter Lambert became bishop of Bamberg, and because the Dominican and Franciscan friars who had been spiritual directors of the Beguines used Gregory's April rescript to protect the extra-regular houses, Lambert's battle never materialized into a full-scale war.[37] But this Strasbourg situation may serve as an example of the continued harassment of lay institutes even after Gregory's 1374 rescript. The fact that Lambert's actions were not atypical is revealed by the need Gregory felt to issue another bull in December, 1377, one which became a milestone in the evolution of the early Alexians. Written to all the bishops of Germany, Brabant, and Flanders, this bull, *Ad Audientiam Nostram*, appears to be a direct response to anti-Beghard prejudices. However, Gregory once again avoided Beghard-Beguine terminology as he referred to some "poor persons of both sexes living humbly and honestly in purity of faith, in decent clothing and habits, as well as in poverty and chastity. . . ."[38] He seems to have purposely opened his letter with an approbation of the various extra-regular lifestyles. He said that many of these poor persons had been unjustly and unduly disturbed "by both bishops and inquisitors as guilty of 'heretical depravity' . . . because of their attire."[39] The Pope also alluded to the way in which the poor ones had even been denied the sacraments because of their officially unrecognized habits. He therefore ordered the bishops "not in any way to molest these poor persons . . . because of their habit . . . and do not permit them to be molested by others as much as you are able to prevent it. . . ."[40] If after an investigation the bishops found that some poor persons had been excommunicated because of their habits, Gregory ordered the bishops to absolve them and restore them to the sacraments.[41]

The one papal inquisitor most frequently cited as responsible for the unjust prosecution of the poor persons noted in Gregory's 1377 bull is John of Boland, who was, mistakenly, believed to have been appointed in 1373.[42] However, as Lerner's research reveals, John of Boland was not appointed until sometime shortly before February 17, 1378, when Charles IV ordered authorities throughout the empire to co-operate with John and the Inquisition.[43] Thus, it could not have been John who so unjustly exploited the ignorance of the poor laymen as described in the complaint written by the Cologne magistrates. Indeed, by the time he was appointed to pursue heresy in the dioceses of Cologne, Trier, and Liège, the early Alexians were protected by Gregory's bull. Perhaps during his visit to Aachen in the spring of 1378 John examined the Brot-Beghards. Though he stated that he had found some heterodox extra-regulars whom he had dismissed from their houses, it is very likely that any Brot-Beghards, now considered in that vague "poor person" group, were found innocent.[44] Since John was appointed in 1378 it can no longer be held that the bull of 1377 terminated the second wave of anti-Beghard-Beguine persecution. No doubt it did play a role, but the death of Charles IV in 1378 and the ramifications of the Great Schism, which began in the same year, also helped to diminish the Inquisition's pursuit of heretics among the extra-regular followers of the *vita apostolica*.[45]

In *Ad Audientiam Nostram* Gregory did not grant papal approval to all extra-regulars but merely protected them from flagrant abuses by bishops and inquisitors. Responsibility for protecting the innocent and punishing the guilty now rested with the local bishop. Since John, bishop of Liège, had already initiated his investigation in May 1375, he probably considered his duty fulfilled. On February 3, 1375 Archbishop Frederick of Cologne appointed John de Cervo, a doctor of laws, and Henry Suderland, a scholastic at St. Geron, to initiate an investigation according to the mandate of *Ad Audientiam Nostram*. If any "poor persons" had been unjustly excommunicated because of their religious garb, de Cervo and Suderland were to summon them to court where they were to be granted absolution. In 1382 the Lungenbrüder of Holy Apostles parish applied to de Cervo requesting him to investigate their way of life and grant them an official declaration of approval. These early Alexians were not harassed by their bishop or inquisitor but by "jealous persons . . . instigated by the devil and by those who envied them their place, slandering them with accusations and persecuting them outrageously."[46] It is possible their accusers were mendicant friars who were jealous of their success in begging alms from the notable citizens of the towns.

John de Cervo's report (December 10, 1382) reads like a copy of Gregory's bull. He stated that these poor persons were "good Christians and staunch followers of the Catholic faith, living in poverty and chastity, clothed in honest and becoming vestments, visiting the churches piously, were obedient to the precepts of Holy Mother Church, honoring the shepherds of their souls, the prelates and the Apostolic See, and beside that they were in good standing and enjoyed the best reputation. They were not involved in heresies of any kind ... [and] served each other for the love of God and performed works of charity as far as possible."[47] The Lungenbrüder, therefore, took full advantage of *Ad Audientiam Nostram*'s implementation in Cologne.

From John's testimony it seems as if the Cologne Lungenbrüder had finally achieved permanent status within the diocese. Though without a rule and direct papal approval, they were still on the *via media*. The Aachen Brot-Beghards may also have demanded an investigation to clear them of suspicion either after the 1375 decree of their bishop or after Gregory's bull *Ad Audientiam Nostram*. The Antwerp Lollards did obtain a copy of the bull but apparently did not feel the need to use it until the 1390s. It is interesting to note that about this time these Lollards were first experiencing a shift in their name from *Lollard* to *Cellebroeder*: "Lollardis in cellis commorantibus" (May 13, 1376).[48] Since from their origins these Lollards of both sexes seem to have developed out of the pre-plague hospital brothers and sisters who, after the pestilence, gathered together in separate cloisters (double cloisters) the argument that the term *Cellebroeder*, or *Cellite*, derives from this "gathering into cells" is supported by these documents. It seems very likely that the generic *Lollard* was ultimately dropped in favor of this specific *Cellebroeder* in order to avoid the derogatory connotations associated with the terms *Beghard* and *Lollard*. All the terms had by the 1370s entered slang to designate lay religious extremists, nonconformists, hypocrites, and heretics. These early Alexians of Antwerp, Aachen, and Cologne successfully struggled against the attacks by the papal Inquisition, the hierarchy, and Charles IV. They succeeded in achieveing a papal response and in the struggle gained important friends in the local communities. Perhaps most important, the successful fight for survival strengthened their confidence in the integrity of their way of life and encouraged common consciousness among the various houses, the essential first step in organizing a viable religious order.

Eleven months before he issued *Ad Audientiam Nostram* (January 11, 1377) Gregory brought the papacy back to Rome. The crisis referred to as "the Babylonian Captivity" had been terminated; but when Gregory died on January 27, 1378, a new crisis followed, the Great Schism. Gregory's successor Urban VI immediately alienated the College of Cardinals by his stress upon the monarchical as opposed to the oligarchical style of rule. Five months after they had elected Urban, the College of Cardinals declared Urban's election invalid. They said they had acted under duress because the Roman mobs demanded an Italian pope. After unsuccessfully pleading for Urban's resignation they elected a new "pope," Clement VII. After each had excommunicated the other and an Urbanist military campaign threatened his life, Clement moved his papacy to Avignon. For forty years Christendom was ruled by two and sometimes three popes. Europe eventually divided into two papal camps. France, Scotland, Aragon, Castile, and Navarre supported Clement; most of Italy, Germany, Hungary, England, Poland, and Scandinavia adhered to Urban, while the Low Countries were split between Clementine and Urbanite camps.[49]

The effectiveness of the papal Inquisition suffered during the early years of the Great Schism. The German emperor was apathetic to the threat of heresy and therefore contributed to the relative calm during the 1380s. The storm was renewed, however, when in 1390 Waldensians were discovered in

Mainz. Three papal inquisitors, Martin of Prague, Peter Zwicker, and Eyland Schoenveld, vigorously pursued the Waldensians and revived the war against the Beghards and Beguines.[50] The "poor persons" were once again subject to inquisitional and diocesan suspicions and, as in the 1390s, appealed to the Pope for protection. As John de Cervo's testimony indicates, some groups of "poor persons" such as the Lungenbrüder had by the 1390s gained friends in diocesan chanceries. Hence, when the anti-Beghard-Beguine spirit was revived they could rely upon these influential friends to lodge complaints at Rome protesting against the assaults upon innocent extra-regular communities. Such complaints reached the ears of Urban VI's successor, Boniface IX (1389–1404), in the fall of 1393. On January 7, 1394 Boniface responded to these protests by issuing a mandate addressed particularly to the archbishops of Cologne, Trier, and Mainz and their suffragans (including that of Liège) and in general to the hierarchy of Germany, Brabant, and Flanders.[51]

Unlike Gregory XI, Boniface was not responding to injustices against these "poor persons" because of their attire but, rather, he wrote in response to reports of inquisitors and bishops who molested the innocent people because of "their way of life and the pious works which they do...."[52] Like Gregory, he urged them to investigate such groups, punish the guilty, and protect the innocent. The "poor persons" whom Gregory defended may have been exclusively early Alexians or they may have been a variety of extra-regular groups. Boniface's "poor persons" were specifically Alexians; he described their works of charity as "visiting the sick, and, if there is a need, even staying with them, guarding them and nourishing them, and also whenever they are asked to do so they give ecclesiastical burial to the bodies of the deceased faithful...."[53] No lay community of the times, other than the early Alexian Brothers and the Black Sisters (Celletinen, in Germany) was known for both nursing the sick and burying the dead. Boniface also referred to the "poor persons" of both sexes who lived in double cloisters. Though the German Beghards worked closely with Beguines in Cologne and

Aachen, the double-cloister arrangement was nonexistent. However, that was the common characteristic of the Cellites and Black Sisters of the Low Countries. They frequently situated their houses next to each other, apparently for mutual sustenance in their spiritual and charitable exercises. Considering the prejudices of the day, one could presume that such an arrangement could have led to scandal. For this reason, it is probable that the complaints to the Pope originated in the Low Countries where double cloisters were common.

According to custom bulls were not sent to the addressed ecclesiastic officials but to the representation of those who had requested a letter of protection. In Cologne two priests (referred to as *pauperes Christi*) on behalf of the "poor ones in Christ" submitted the bull to the judge of archepiscopal court, the aforementioned John de Cervo, who provided it with the necessary legal confirmations.[54] A copy of the bull is located in the Aachen archives of the Alexian Brothers (the oldest document in the collection), which indicates that the Brot-Beghards of that ancient city must have secured it for their protection. Though the bull is of great historical significance for its recognition of the specific Alexian ministry, Boniface had a noticeable change of heart almost immediately after he had issued his 1394 bull.

Apparently some Beghards and Beguines had offended inquisitors and bishops by using the 1394 bull in their defense. In 1396 Boniface issued *Sedis Apostolicis* in which he ordered fresh investigation of all "Beghards, Lollards, or sisters." He also included the "*pauperes Pueruli*" on the list of possible heretics.[55] He stated that for a hundred years these groups had slandered church law and had formed institutes with their own habit, rule, and superiors, not approved by the church. Noting that some of these religious had invoked papal privileges, Boniface therefore officially repealed those concessions.[56] We may presume that John de Cervo, who was prosecuting heresy in Cologne during the 1390s, maintained his respect for the Lungenbrüder during the waves of anti-Beghard persecution in the late 1390s and the early 1400s. The Brot-Beghards of Aachen were also probably protected by the bull as well as by

the city council; the latter had made a gift to the house in
1390. The Brothers in Antwerp, who dwelt in a diocese that
had declared its neutrality in the Great Schism, were probably
not affected by either the favorable '94 bull or the negative
'96 one.

Father Prims discovered a very significant document in the
archive of Our Lady's Chapel (Antwerp) which sheds new
light upon the papal relations with the Cellites in the Low
Countries. In this papal bull addressed to the bishop of Utrecht
(dated July 15, 1396), Boniface IX urged the same protections
to the Brothers as he did in the 1394 bull.[57] Apparently friends
of the Brothers had registered a complaint regarding the
implications of the January 31, 1396 bull, which lashed out at
all lay institutes as houses of heresy. Though Prims states that
this bull was probably used to defend the Antwerp Brothers
against their enemies, it is curious to note that when they did
appeal for city council protection they did not refer to the
favorable 1396 bull but to Gregory XI's 1377 one.[58] Perhaps
since the 1377 bull specified papal protection for those poor
persons who were molested because of their religious garb, the
situation in Antwerp may have demanded not the protective
1396 bull but, rather, Gregory XI's specific references to the
orthodoxy of garb. Regardless, the Antwerp Brothers successfully appealed to the city council for protection, and the
following reveals how the council became a sort of board of
trustees with police rights for these early Alexians.

> We, the bailiffs and aldermen take under our care and protec-
> tion, the house and estate with her possessions and all land that may
> be added, situated on the Cattle Market (Egg market) with the
> poor brothers, who now possess this estate, or those who will possess
> it hereafter and who want to live in obedience to God, to the holy
> Church and her prelates, according to the letters of Pope Gregorius.
> And should someone do these brothers any harm and we should hear
> about it, then we would let the guilty person be whipped and cor-
> rected. Might, on the other hand, one of the brothers, not lead a
> honorable and peaceful life, as their statutes prescribe and we should
> hear about it, then we would, after seeking the advice of one of
> their regents, make them leave their house and institute. And is there
> such a person in Antwerp, who practices the same charity as the

brothers, that he then should go into their house, as that their estate is founded thereto, so as to conduct oneself honorably in it and to handle the affairs as the other brothers, such are the decrees.[59]

When Henry Suderman founded the Antwerp house he relieved the Brothers of legal matters regarding ownership and management of their property by establishing an administrative board. It is likely that after the original administrators died, promient citizens, perhaps aldermen, replaced them. This resolution of the city council was, therefore, based upon the traditional arrangement that the aldermen noted after reading Suderman's 1345 letter establishing the house. However, to shift from a private to a public board of control must have significantly altered the role of the Brothers in the civic life in Antwerp. The appeal and the decision reveal that a mutuality of self-interest existed between the Brothers and the city council. Without full documentation this particular contractual relationship appears as the first legal document setting forth the civic status of the Brothers, a condition that strongly affects their permanence as a service group for the community.

Due to the jealously guarded autonomy of the hierarchy in the Low Countries, the papal Inquisition was not active there. However, Jacob of Soest, one of the major inquisitors of the 1390s, did appear in Utrecht (ca. 1393) where he investigated the Sisters of the Common Life, a contemplative community on the *via media*.[60] Florens Radewijns, the "superior" of the Brethren of the Common Life, succeeded in exonerating the sisters of such charges as forming a religious order without papal approval and praying in the vernacular. Perhaps the Antwerp Brothers faced similar charges. Regardless, interesting parallels may be drawn between the Brethren of the Common Life and the early Alexians.

III

The paucity of documentation revealing what it was like for the Brothers to dwell continuously in the shadow of suspicion may receive some compensation by examining the early history of the Brethren of the Common Life; by analogy one may gather a deeper appreciation of the life of the early Alexians. Because the Brethren drew vocations from the literate classes, the historian can gather from their recorded sayings and writings a vivid picture of their development. But for that very reason, the historian of the Alexians who is concerned with nonliterate men of a primary oral culture must cautiously develop parallels in the subjunctive mood.

The Brethren originated in Deventer where Gerard Groote (1340–1384) formed a community of priests and laymen who lived a life of voluntary poverty and asceticism. Though they had a definite intellectual character, they stressed contemplation and mysticism. In their early years they took no vows and followed no recognized rule; they were, like the early Alexians, lay pilgrims on the *via media*. Groote, who never went beyond the office of deacon, was well known for preaching the need for penance as the leaven of Christian society. Groote and his followers were ridiculed for their pretentions to be members of a religious order in violation of the decree at the Fourth Lateran Council. Groote's defense reads as a fourteenth-century apologia for the Alexians as well.

> No one may found a new religious order without the Pope's permission, but it is not wrong, I believe, for two or more persons to live together in observance of certain rules, or the rule of rules, namely, the Blessed Gospel. . . . The mere name religio signifies but little; it is not the name which determines the nature of a thing. . . . There are many who are not protected by the mere name religio, and yet may be more religious than those whom the Church calls religious.[61]

Professor Hyma reports that the Brethren, like many extra-regulars of the day, were frequently molested on the streets and called "Beghards and Lollards . . . and commended to burn in hell or some other suitable place of torture."[62] The slanderous insults aimed at the Brethren were frequently instigated by jealous friars. When Gerard Groote was dying, one of his followers (R. R. Post speculates that it was Thomas à Kempis) supposedly remarked, "The opponents will rejoice and the worldly will mock us: they have no leader now, thus they will soon perish. If they had dared to laugh at us and curse us while you lived, what will they do when you are dead."[63] No doubt the Brot-Beghards in Aachen and the Lungenbrüder in Cologne, particularly since they lacked a founder and the education of the more intellectually oriented Brethren, were subjected to such ridicule. However, since the Alexian ministries brought them into daily contact with those in need, perhaps they were not harassed as much as the Brethren, lay preachers who urged penance and righteousness.

The Brethren did experience an encounter with the papal Inquisition when, around 1400, the ruthless prosecutor Eyland Schoenveld accused them of being a dangerous sect. By this time the Brethren had, like the Alexians, won some powerful friends. One of them, the bishop of Utrecht, intervened and protected the Brethren from a heresy trial.[64] In spite of their progress toward recognition as orthodox followers of the *vita apostolica*, both the Brethren and the early Alexians sent representatives to the Council of Constance (1414–1418) to seek papal confirmation of their respective ways of life.

At the turn of their first century, the Cellites could look back with pride to their phenomenal expansion. Perhaps the primary cause of their growth was the four waves of plague, which expanded the need for their nursing and burial ministries. Yet the path of progress was strewn with obstacles, particularly harassment by inquisitors and the hostility of many other mendicants. At the turn of the century the church was fractured; Christendom was still divided by the Great Schism. This infected rupture added credibility to those groups that criticized the church's pursuit of wealth and power. The followers of British theologian John Wyclif, who were called Lollards (a pejorative term imported from the Netherlands), advocated a propertyless church modeled on the ancient Jerusalem Community. Wyclif appears as a precursor of Luther; his doctrines included belief that salvation is attained solely by faith, that Baptism and the Eucharist were the only valid sacraments, and that Christ is found not in traditional church practices but only in direct revelation in Scripture.

Scandalized by the secularism of the church in its monastic, papal, episcopal, and pastoral forms, Wyclif doubted the validity of the sacraments administered by corrupt clergymen. Imported into Bohemia where anti-Romanism, anticlericalism, and heterodoxy were already flourishing, Wyclif's doctrines intensified a volatile situation. The Bohemian reform movement turned into a revolution under the leadership of John Hus. The Bohemian revolt was a multifaceted movement caused by complex political, economic, and social, as well as religious factors. Gradually during the first decade of the fifteenth century the Great Schism was healed and an ecumenical council was convoked at Constance to resolve the problems of church unity, the legitimate authority of the papacy, church reform, and the threats from England and Bohemia. Though far down on the agenda of the council fathers, the Cellites also submitted an appeal to the council seeking once and for all an end to harassment and persecution. Eyland Schoenveld, the infamous Dominican inquisitor with numerous executions to his credit, had apparently harassed the Beghards in the diocese of Augsburg. Records of the Council of Constance reveal that a poor layman from that diocese, Jacob Sutzman, appealed to the Pope for redress of grievances on behalf of these Beghards who were unjustly persecuted by Heinrick Schoenveld (probably Eyland).[65] As supportive evidence for his case, Sutzman included testimonials from various places where extra-regular communities resided. These sixteen testimonials were not merely concerned with demonstrating the orthodoxy of the generic Beghard or Lollard but specifically of the early Alexians. The Council of Constance commissioned the papal vice chancellor, the cardinal bishop of Ostia, to take charge of the case. The bishop delegated his authority to a Cardinal Angelus. On January 24, 1416 the sixteen testimonials were confirmed, notarized, and given the official seal of the Cardinal.[66] These documents contain rich reflections on the work of the early Alexians.

The various cities in which the testimonials were taken illustrate the mode of life of Alexian-type communities throughout what is today Belgium, the Netherlands, and northwest

Germany. The list includes the following cities in chronological order: Mechlin (November 12, 1405), Lier (November 12, 1405), Haarlem (November 17, 1405), Antwerp (November 21, 1405), Brussels (November 22, 1405), Herzogenbusch (November 22, 1405), Delft (December 10, 1405), Maastricht (December 16, 1405), Louvain (November 5, 1413), Korssendong (November 22, 1414), Mechlin (September 23, 1415), Brussels (September 23, 1415), and Cologne (October 9, 1415).[67]

It is impossible to discover why 1405 and 1415 were such significant years. Perhaps the houses existing in the year 1405 were all responding to a common need—to have their orthodoxy certified. Some testimonials indicate that the Brothers begged, others mention manual labor as the means of subsistence. The Mechlin, Antwerp, and Cologne testimonials specify the nursing and burial ministries of the Brothers; the others refer to their charitable works in general. They were called "pious laymen" in Mechlin, "pious poor men . . . living in the house of the cell" (*domus de cella*) in Lier, "brodertgens" in Haarlem, "certain laymen" in Antwerp, "brothers of the Cell" (*fratres de cella*) in Brussels, and the same (*fratres dicti celli*) in Herzogenbusch, "die Broertgens" in Delft, "brothers" in Maastricht, "Cell Brothers" (*fratrum cellarum*) in Louvain. By 1415 their name had evolved to "Cell Brothers" in Mechlin, and "honest laymen" in Cologne. Thus *Cellite* was obviously developing as the most common name, while *Lollard*, a pejorative conveying a heretic of any stripe, was nearly extinct. The testimonials stress their marks of orthodoxy: reception of the Eucharist, confession to priests, and obedience to pastors and prelates. Since a few mention "fervent meditation" it seems that these early Alexians possessed a strong contemplative strain to buttress their active apostolate.[68]

Of the three houses which concern us, only the Aachen Brot-Beghard community did not have a testimonial. The Antwerp documents indicate the fifteenth-century derivation of the *fratres de cella*:

> Jacobus dictus de Parijis, pastor and Canon of St. Mary's Church in Antwerp, diocese of Cambrai, attested November 21, 1405 that in

his parish for a long time certain laymen were living, walking in simple and decent dress, living in common in poverty, mutually serving each other piously and in charity, and begging their necessary livelihood modestly. They were, he stated, visiting his church by day and night, assisting there at the divine service and the sermons with prayers and fervent meditation, giving themselves to the works of charity especially in such a manner that they carried the dead bodies of rich and poor of the whole city, after being requested, to the churches, practicing also other virtues and like good and faithful Christians as everyone may see, living faithfully and obeying the precepts of the superiors announced by him and his confreres, not being charged with excommunication as far as he knew.[69]

And for Cologne:

The priest Johannes de Gynet alias de Novimago, pastor of Holy Apostles church in Cologne, made known to all regardless of rank and order of position in a document verified by his parish seal, October 9, 1415, that for a long time, honest laymen were living in his parish in the house called "tzo dim Klueppel" by the people also called "tzo der Longen," dressed in simple, honest, and decent garments, living together in poverty and piously serving each other in charity, acquiring the necessities of life in humility, daily visiting their parish church frequently and piously by day and night as sons of obedience, assisting there at the divine service and the sermons, giving themselves to prayers and fervent meditation and that they render the works of charity to the sick, that they carry the corpses of the rich and poor to the graveyard at request to bury them, and that they practice many other works of virtue, living as good Christians, not deviating from the right faith and obeying the precepts of their superiors faithfully.[70]

Since the Cologne 1415 document contains phrases identical to the one from Antwerp it is probable that the Lungenbrüder in Cologne possessed a copy of the earlier document. Perhaps it was at the suggestion of the Cologne community, the leading house in Germany, that these testimonials were gathered together for the appeal to the Council of Constance. Though we have no evidence of the ultimate resolution of the Brothers' appeal, the council did strengthen the extra-regulars movement. The boost came as a result of an anti-Beghard assault by another Dominican, Mathew Grabon.[71] Grabon had written a treatise particularly aimed at the Brethren of the Common Life, but he applied his theories to all extra-regulars.

His argument was based on the premise that when one made the three vows of poverty, chastity, and obedience, one was removed from the world. To dwell in the world in voluntary poverty—as an extra-regular—was to engage in self-mutilation and ultimately suicide because, according to the law of the secular world, one must have property to exist. Therefore, all extra-regular communities which do not subscribe to the vows of religious orders are founded upon an immoral basis and should be liquidated. Because the bishop of Utrecht, a friend of the Brethren of the Common Life, rejected this treatise, Grabon appealed to the Pope and journeyed to Constance to defend his brief against all extra-regulars. Cardinal Pirne d'Ailly, bishop of Cambrai, and his pupil, Jean Gerson, chancellor of the University of Paris, declared the treatise heretical in a report (April 3, 1418) which was presented to the council. Grabon was condemned and imprisoned but after recanting his absurd suicide theory he was free to return to his monastery in Groningen upon the condition that he never set foot in either the Utrecht diocese or the church province of Cologne.[71] The Grabon case therefore strengthened the early Alexians and other extra-regulars as by implication their *via media* existence was generally approved by the church. Gerson was particularly impressed with the Brethren of the Common Life but harbored suspicions about the Beghards and Beguines.

Harassment remained a permanent feature of the first century of Alexian existence, a condition that they could not successfully combat other than to adopt a rule and apply for canonical status as a religious order. The city council of Cologne, for example, found it necessary once again to testify for the defense of the Lungenbrüder. On September 9, 1423 it declared that "in order to silence the slanderers and haters"[72] it verified the valuable services performed by the Brothers. As the above priests' testimonials stressed the orthodoxy and piety of these good laymen, the city council was more concerned with their various works of charity that benefited the secular commonweal in Cologne. It stated that they made "themselves useful in the city of Cologne to the citizens and inhabitants, if need be also to the pilgrims and strangers, both

during the time of pestilence as well as at any other time.
. . ."[73] The council testified that when pestilence struck down
a person, relatives and friends would flee "with horror" but
the Brothers attended the victim and "by their careful watch
. . . made for the salvation of the souls of the sick." It also
emphasized that the Brothers buried the dead "without any
discrimination."[74] Because of these services to the city and
because they led holy and praiseworthy lives, never giving
"scandal with their manner of life and their customs,"[75] the
mayor and the city council wished "to protect them from any
harm and recommend them to all whom it concerns."[76]

On August 27, 1427 the procurator of the Cologne Lungenbrüder, John of Hildesheim, assembled the foregoing documents and all the testimonials presented to the Council of
Constance, had them notarized, and initiated the first Alexian
archive at the house on the Lungengasse.[77] However, the
archive was not intended merely to preserve valuable documents for posterity but, rather, to act as a defensive weapon
against the next wave of anti-Beghard assaults.

During the 1420s the church was struggling against the
followers of John Hus (who had been executed at the Council
of Constance), a struggle which probably led to a renewal of
anti-Beghardism. Harassment against the early Alexians certainly occurred during this time, for in 1431 Pope Eugene IV
wrote a papal bull urging protection specifically for the
Brothers of the Cells. It is interesting to note that the many
historians concerned with Beghards and Beguines refer to this
bull as a stereotype decree ordering protection of innocent
extra-regulars. The 1394 bull is also referred to because it
pertains to Beghards and Beguines in general. Yet Boniface's
and Eugene's bulls contain specific references to the singular
apostolate of the early Alexians. Indeed Eugene stated that
Gregory XI's bull of 1377 was intended to protect the same
"poor persons" whom Eugene calls "our beloved sons of the
cells."[78] After quoting Gregory's bull, Eugene stated that he
had received commendatory letters which testify to the orthodoxy of the cell brothers and sisters. He referred particularly
to the sixteen letters sent to the Council of Constance by the

bishop of Worms as well as the testimonial letters of John de Cervo.[79] The Pope then listed the works included in the Alexian apostolate: "They take poor and wretched persons into their own places for the sake of hospitality, and take care of them in their illness; during the time of pestilence . . . they bury the bodies of the faithful who have died with ecclesiastical burial. . . ."[80] In spite of their good works, continued Eugene, these brothers and sisters have been "unjustly and unduly disquieted and disturbed by certain inquisitors of heretical depravity and even by some religious especially of the Mendicant orders and by others of their emissaries."[81] Because of this unjust harassment by the inquisitors he released these Brothers and Sisters from the "jurisdiction, authority, and superiorship of the Inquisitors . . . and this in perpetuity. . . ."[82] Though the Pope urged each of these Cell Brother and Cell Sister communities to elect its own superior according to canon law, he did not order them to adopt a recognized rule in order to become an acceptable religious order. As in the other bulls, Eugene's bull explicitly placed ultimate responsibility upon the local bishops for distinguishing the truly faithful Brothers from heretical impostors.[83]

It had been nearly 125 years since the Cologne Lungenbrüder had been excommunicated. Throughout that time they had frequently been slandered and persecuted, particularly, as Pope Eugene said, by mendicant friars. The city council had repeatedly responded to these attacks by testifying to their righteousness and their public services to the city. From Eugene's bull and the various testimonials it is evident that the Cellites gained great respect as a result of their work during the epidemics of the latter half of the fourteenth century. Historians of Beghards and Beguines who treat the papal decrees of 1394 and 1431 as indicative of the papacy's general concern for innocent extra-regulars are half accurate; had they known that both bulls (as well as the pressure upon the Council of Constance) originated with complaints made by Cellites, they would have altered their narratives. By the 1390s the early Alexians had spread throughout northwestern Europe and were no longer fringe communities; on the contrary they were performing services which tied them to the municipal governments. According to inquisitors such as Eyland Schoenveld and cranks such as Mathew Grabon, those laymen who adopted the life of poverty were to be anathema. The testimonies of John de Cervo and the sixteen other witnesses from cities such as Ghent, Antwerp, Haarlem, and Cologne, as well as the papal bulls of Boniface and Eugene, moved these Brothers and Sisters from the fringe to a respectable status within the church. Their way of life, their garb, and their ministries were approved by the supreme ecclesiastical authority. They were not fully accredited insiders in 1431, for they were still located on the *via media*, religious but not yet a religious order.

5

Evolution into
a Religious Order

I

When Pope Eugene granted the Cell Brothers and Sisters the
privilege of choosing their own confessors he partially removed them from dependence upon their parishes. However,
he explicitly stated that he did not wish to confirm the
Cellites as a religious order.[1] Between 1434 and 1472, the
Cellites received a series of papal and episcopal privileges
which ultimately led them from the *via media* to the *via
religiosa*. According to Aquinas, the pronouncement of the
three principal vows was the distinctive mark of a religious
community. Though the Cologne Brothers provided leadership in gaining papal protections and privileges, the movement toward professing the three canonical vows originated in
the Netherlands.

On January 3, 1458 Pope Pius II, a vigorous reformer,
issued a bull confirming the privileges of his predecessor, Pope
Nicholas V, who had granted the Brothers permission to take
the vows of poverty, chastity, and obedience.[2] Perhaps Pius II
was extending this permission to all the Cellite communities, as
he directed his letter to the Brothers of Brabant, Allemania

(Germany), and Flanders.[3] He allowed them to choose a superior from one of the approved orders who would be an official witness to the vow ceremony and to whom the vows were to be professed.[4] The superior would also function as the confessor. Almost two years later, on October 19, 1459, Pius II implicitly urged the Brothers to organize themselves into provinces when he directed each province, upon the advice and consent of three or four pastors, to choose a visitator.[5] The latter would be the ultimate authority in each province, with the specific power of punishing those brothers who deviated from the proper spiritual life and with the authority to appoint confessors to each of the houses. Pius also allowed each Cellite house to erect a chapel, preserve the Sacrament, and have Masses said by its pastor, visitator, confessor, or a priest belonging to it.[6]

Though one historian reports that the Amsterdam Brothers were the first to profess vows,[7] Huyskens contends that the Antwerp community warrants that distinction.[8] Because the Amsterdam house was permanently suppressed during the Reformation, one can say with certitude that the Antwerp Brothers are the oldest extant Cellite community in vows. In 1461 they made their solemn profession in the presence of their chosen superior, the prior of the Mechlin Carmelites.

The movement toward Cellite unity as a religious order, which was so strong in the Low Countries, evidenced itself when the other communities in Brussels, Ghent, Bruges, Tournai, Diest, and Liège followed Antwerp in professing vows in 1461 and 1462.[9] Indeed there is evidence that prior to the first General Chapter of the community in 1468, the Low Countries had already established a form of provincial organization; Peter van Lier was referred to as "Pater" of the Cellite "congregation" in 1462.[10] That same year the Rhenish houses became more tightly organized; Archbishop Dietrich of Cologne confirmed the House Rule of the Cellites on the Lungengasse.[11] Though it was not one of the officially recognized rules, the fact that it was accepted by the archbishop at the command of the papacy illustrates the general drift to the status of a religious order. Four months later the bishop of

Liège responded to the appeal of the Aachen Brothers by confirming the rule of the Cologne house for the Aachen community. When Louis de Bourbon, bishop of Liège, complied with this request and noted that the poor brothers of the Cologne house "at the lungs . . . were set over the brothers in Aachen,"[12] he revealed the evolution toward Rhenish provincial government, with Cologne as the seat of authority.

For nearly a century the Cellites developed a consciousness of their common ministries. By pursuing protective papal privileges for the poor brothers and sisters, they demonstrated their organizational skills. Permission to take vows and the formation of rough provincial lines of authority necessarily led to the first General Chapter in 1468. The choice of Liège as the setting for this historical meeting may have stemmed from Liège's central location, but Huyskens views the choice as indicative of the Netherlands Brothers' strong push toward unity.[13] Liège was therefore acceptable to all the Brothers. Of the reportedly thirty-six houses represented at the Chapter, nearly thirty were located in the Low Countries. The Cologne branch could view it favorably because the Aachen house was situated in the Liège diocese, while the Low Country Brothers could identify with Liège as a native city. The most likely reason for the Brothers' choice of Liège was that they had received such strong support from the ordinary there, Louis de Bourbon; as we will explore in a later chapter, Louis graciously allowed the Brothers of Diest and Liège to profess vows according to the Rule of St. Augustine years before the first General Chapter.[14] Though the Chapter minutes were not preserved, we do know that two major decisions flowed from the meeting: the adoption of the Rule of St. Augustine and the petition to Rome for official recognition of the Cellites as an ecclesiastical order. Because the Antwerp house *did* adopt the Rule of St. Augustine in 1461 it is evident that trends in the Low Countries were serving as models for the entire Alexian community.

The Cologne Brothers were the first German community to adopt the Augustinian rule. Ten years before the Antwerp Brothers professed vows, events in Cologne were pushing the

Lungenbrüder in that direction. In the mid-fifteenth century the prominent theologian-reformer Cardinal Nicholas of Cusa (Cusanus) was leading a drive to revive monasticism throughout Germany. He commissioned John Busch, a canon of the reformed Augustinian priory at Windesheim, to reform all the Augustinian priories in Saxony. In 1452 Cusanus, in concert with the archbishop of Cologne, Dietrich von Mors, issued a *Protokoll* (report) for the revision of all Cologne's Beguine and Beghard convents.[15] Just as Busch's task was to prod the canons to observe their vows and their rule strictly, the Cologne *Protokoll* was intended to urge Beguines and Beghards to live according to either the Rule for the Third Order of St. Francis or the Augustinian rule. Diocesan officials reported on each of the convents, including "zom Kluppel," the house of the Lungenbrüder. The report referred to the seven persons who lived in the convent without revenue or a rule.[16]

The Cologne Brothers did establish a house rule in 1427, but because it was not a prescribed rule for a religious institute, the investigators probably considered it a nonrule. There is no evidence indicating the report's immediate impact upon the Brothers. No doubt they were touched by Cusanus's reform spirit when they sought recognition for their rule in 1462. One may presume that the entire Alexian community's evolution to a religious order was influenced by this reform climate.

In 1469, the year following the Cellites' first General Chapter in which they adopted the Rule of St. Augustine, the archbishop of Cologne, Rupert van der Pfalz, approved certain amendments to the House Rule placing the Lungenbrüder under the Augustinian rule. Though Rupert's action probably encouraged the Brothers, he explicitly stated that the papal mandate from Pope Eugene (May 12, 1431) prohibited him from granting them the status of a religious order. However, he urged them to pursue the apostolic life in faith and obedience, a condition which, he said, might induce the Pope to bestow upon them additional privileges.[17]

Shortly after Rupert's January 2 approval of these amendments, the bishop of Liège, Louis de Bourbon, followed suit and allowed the Aachen Brothers to adopt the Rule of St.

Augustine. On March 13, 1469 he granted to the Cellites who lived on the "optenduppengrave" (today's Alexianergraben) permission "to bind themselves by means of the three substantial vows. . . ."[18] He also approved the traditional habit of the Brothers, i.e., a habit of black or gray made of rather coarse wool and a scapular about three hands in width made of the same color and material. The Brothers were instructed to wear this garb when they collected alms as well as during those hours when they were free from work and prayer. Their bishop urged them not to allow the profession of vows to detract them from "their humble way of living or from their visiting and treating the sick which they have done up to this time with so much mercy. . . ."[19]

Permission to profess three principal vows, the adoption of a recognized rule, and the attachment to a superior from an officially recognized community made the Cell Brothers and Sisters a de facto religious order. It was merely a matter of time before *de jure* recognition was granted.

With such sympathetic support from their bishops, the Cellites could confidently appeal to the papacy for official status as a religious order. When Rome did respond positively in 1472, it came in the form of three bulls from Pope Sixtus IV (April 25, June 5, and June 9).[20] Charles the Bold, duke of Burgundy, endorsed the Cellite appeal to Rome and was, therefore, at least partially responsible for Sixtus's favorable response. Charles may have been prompted to advocate the Cellite cause by either the bishop of Utrecht or the bishop of Liège both of whom were his relatives and owed their benefices to this Burgundian duke. Since Bishop Louis of Liège had hosted the General Chapter, he could have been the intermediary between the Brothers and Charles the Bold.

In hindsight the Alexians may be grateful to Charles and his cousin, Bishop Louis de Bourbon. If the Aachen Cellites of 1472 were closely tied to either the duke or the bishop they were running against the tide of public opinion, as both were viewed by the people with disdain. Charles was a religious (though not a pious) man who could have been vulnerable to the appeals of his cousin. Politically he reflected the famous dictum of Machiavelli: he was more feared than loved. For example, in 1468 when the people of Liège, stirred by the agents of Charles's enemy, Louis XI of France, rose in revolt against their prince bishop, Charles laid seige to the city and severely punished its citizens.[21]

The Burgundian state was at the zenith of its power, ruling over the Netherlands and expanding eastward and southward. Sixtus IV, who appears to have been a shrewd Italian prince, strengthened the secular arm of the Renaissance papacy. He was thus probably very open to the urgings of Charles; the duke had three cousins who were bishops; one was the archbishop of Lyons. Though it is entirely conjecture, it is probable that Charles's endorsement of the Cellite cause was motivated by his sense of "noblesse oblige" toward the poor Brothers mediated by his loyalty to his cousin, Bishop Louis de Bourbon. Though Louis's concern for the Brothers is well established, was he motivated by "noblesse oblige" or by the city council fathers? Only the secular authorities appear to have really appreciated the Brothers' presence.

In the first bull, Pope Sixtus IV confirmed the Cellite way of life and their adoption of the Augustinian rule.[22] They were permitted to elect a General Visitator from a reformed Augustinian monastery who, with the elders of the Cellite community, was responsible for their internal religious observances and the general spiritual health of the various houses.[23] In order to protect the Cellites from further harassment, the Brothers and Sisters were allowed to choose a prelate who would guard all their papal privileges and defend them against unjust attack. This prelate was also responsible for providing the houses with a confessor empowered to grant absolution even for those offenses normally reserved for episcopal absolution.[24] In the second bull, the Pope defined again in detail the responsibilities of the confessor and the fasting duties of the Cellites.[25]

The third bull released the Cellites from dependence upon their parishes; it granted them, on request, the permission to have their own churches and chapels with a small steeple and bell and a cemetery for the deceased of their communities. After the chapels and cemeteries were consecrated by their bishops, they were allowed to have Mass said there by either a regular or a secular priest. Pope Sixtus specified that no one was to interfere with their privilege to participate in Mass and the sacraments within their own chapel, but he also stipulated that they must respect the rights of their parish pastors.[26]

As noted earlier, the Antwerp Cellites were the first to profess the three principal vows and adopt the ancient rule. The Cologne Brothers took their vows on January 17, 1473.[27] There is no evidence revealing the specific date of the Aachen community's first profession. There are mid-sixteenth-century documents which explicitly indicate the profession of vows, but other documents imply a much earlier date of profession. In his letter of 1469, the bishop of Liège granted the Aachen Brothers permission to take vows; contained in the 1481 contract written by the archpriest of St. Mary's monastery, there is the comment that "For a long time they . . . had pronounced the three principal vows. . . ."[28] It may be presumed, therefore, that by, roughly, 1475 all the Cellites were living in vows and in conformity to a recognized rule for the religious life.

In the late fifteenth century canon law did not distinguish between a religious order and a religious congregation. The canonical requirements for religious status evolved from the promulgations of various ecumenical councils. By 1472 there were four requirements: "first, the three evangelical counsels; second, these had to be strengthened by perpetual vows; third, the vows had to be taken in a legitimately approved institute; fourth, the members had to live under a certain rule or constitution."[29]

The three bulls of Pope Sixtus do not contain a specific or explicit recognition of the Cell Brothers and Sisters as a religious order. However, the various privileges which separated the community from specific parish and episcopal jurisdictions indicate that the papacy confirmed the Cellites as dwelling in a "legitimately approved institute." Because they were allowed to have their own chapels and cemeteries, they were canonically removed from dependence upon the parish for the sacraments and for a sacred burial. The stipulations that they choose a General Visitor from a reformed Augustinian monastery attached them to an old, established religious order, while the directive that they choose a prelate to guard and defend their papal privileges indicates the Pope's intention to acknowledge explicitly that the Cellites derived their religious status from Rome. The link with the Augustinians was probably forged by the papacy's concern that a new religious order would flounder if it were not under the direction of those seasoned in the Augustinian rule and the rigors of the religious life. Had the Pope directed the bishops to appoint a General Visitor rather than grant the Cellites the privilege of choosing their own "foster superior," the community would have been governed by the diocese and unprotected from the dangers of living under an unsympathetic or apathetic visitator.

By attaching the community to Augustinians, the papacy was guided by prudence, but by granting freedom of choice the papacy illustrated its respect for the prudence of the Cellites, derived from their own rich tradition as lay mendicants for over 175 years.

The new juridical relationships between the Cellites and the reformed Augustinians came about not merely because they shared a common rule but also because of the strong spiritual relationships that had developed over the past six decades. In the chapters on Cellite spirituality and their authority structures, the Cellite-Augustinian association will be explored. Because it was such a deep filial relationship, perhaps the Cellites asked Rome to confirm legally what was in fact already a strong Augustinian influence.

In 1507 Julius II, following in the path of his uncle, Sixtus IV, issued a bull in which he explicitly confirmed the Cellites as a religious order.[30] "Therefore, desiring to give special favor to the servants of the Lord who serve him in lowliness of spirit—by our apostolic authority expressed by this present letter—We approve and confirm the rule or manor of living of the . . . Brothers and Sisters [of the Cells]."[31] Julius furthered the independence of the Cellites, removing them from all jurisdictions save those of their own superior and Visitator

General. If either religious or lay authorities would alienate the goods of the Cellites, Julius directed "the Protector [the prelate] of the Order to demand the return of all such alienated property."[32] Julius also removed the Cellites from the jurisdiction of their ordinaries, whom he forbade "to restrain, prescribe, order, or ordain anything that might prevent" the full enjoyment of the privileges granted by the Holy See.[33] Though Julius II's bull did mark the climax of the Cellites' evolution toward a religious order, it is highly unlikely that Julius himself was at all aware of the Cellite tradition. The curia was probably totally responsible for processing the bull and, in conformity with custom, the Cellites probably paid a goodly sum for the papal privileges.

II

The spirit of the Renaissance papacy from the time of Sixtus IV is cogently summarized in Outram Evennett's remark:

> Starting roughly with the pontificate of Sixtus IV, ... developments occurred which ushered in the period of maximum odium for the papal curia and which ... further accelerated the outward flow of dispensations and favours and the inward flow of money, pushing to the culmination point the secularisation and venality of the whole machine.[34]

Though some scholars have stressed Julius's good works (such as fighting heresy and reforming monasteries) as redeeming factors in his reign, Karl August Fink states that such activity "pertains to the normal work of the papal officer and the curia."[35] Fink paraphrases a famous remark on this pope when he states, "Julius II had nothing of the priest except the dress and the name."[36] The contrast between the splendor of the Renaissance papacy and the humble cells of the Cellite Brothers and Sisters is symbolic of the disparities within the pre-Reformation church. St. Francis could never have recognized the Franciscanness of this Renaissance Pope. If the church walls appeared in disrepair in the thirteenth century, by the late fifteenth century one could hardly distinguish between the walls of the papacy and those of a typical Italian despot.

Yet there were fifteenth-century Franciscan houses, particularly among the Observants, where Francis could have dwelt in peace and harmony. Indeed, many scholars of the Counter-Reformation have traced its vigorous spirituality to fifteenth-century trends in monastic reform and piety.

Evennett selects the Brethren of the Common Life as the only fresh form of corporate religious life between Francis and Ignatius.[37] The Cellites were closely tied to the Windesheim Augustinians (monastic "cousins" of the Brethren of Common Life and champions of reform). Evennett looks back at the general character of monasticism on the eve of the Reformation and sadly concludes:

> The state of monasticism in this period, however, did not cease to mirror the general state of the Church, especially it would seem, in the Fifteenth Century, that most mysterious of periods full of the most colorful and glaring juxtapositions, a century indeed of wheat and tares *par excellence*, but in which the harvest proved to be constantly receding.[38]

III

As the Cellites shifted from the *via media* to the *via religiosa* they established the most visible symbol of their newly gained independent status, the chapel. The first recorded Cellite chapel was built in Aachen. Even before Sixtus granted the papal privilege providing for such independence from the parish, the bishop of Liège granted to the Aachen Brothers the right to build a portable altar for their own liturgy. Soon after Sixtus's bulls the Aachen community erected a chapel. On January 1, 1477 Bishop Louis testified to this fact when he instructed his auxiliary bishop to consecrate this chapel which had been dedicated to Sts. Augustine and Alexius.[39] From the available documents it appears that this chapel was not an addition to the existing house but a separate building on the grounds. This was implied in a document signed by the bishop of Liège (July 3, 1481) in which he authorized the same auxiliary bishop to consecrate the cemetery adjacent to the chapel.[40] The possession of their own cemetery was crucial to the independent status of the Brothers. As a religious order they were an autonomous church community within the ecclesiastical structures. When one referred to "church" in medieval times, he meant not merely church buildings but also other property, including the cemetery. However, contained in both papal and episcopal privileges for the erection of chapels and cemeteries was the bishop's stipulation that the Cellites must respect the rights of their pastors.

Pastoral rights were referred to as stole rights, i.e., the authority to collect stipends for baptisms, weddings, and funerals. In 1481 the Aachen Brothers, who were in the cathedral parish, successfully concluded negotiations with representatives of their pastor to free them from their parish duties. The contract was quite elaborate with witnesses and notaries representing the Brothers, the pastor, and the bishop.

The archpriest of St. Mary's Monastery in Aachen was their pastor's spokesman, who granted the Brothers immunity from parish jurisdiction. In a long statement he testified to the "saintly spirited life" of the Brothers and referred to the papal permission to have their own chapel and cemetery where they could hear Mass, have the sacraments administered to them, and bury their own dead.[41] The archpriest agreed to permit these liturgies to be performed independent of the parish in return for an annual fee of 18 shillings, to be paid in perpetuity during the Easter season when the Brothers would collect the holy oils from the parish church.[42] The contract concluded with the stipulation that the Brothers were forbidden to bury the corpses of the parishes in their cemetery unless they received special permission of the competent parish authority.

In Antwerp the Brothers negotiated their independence from the parish by appealing to the cathedral chapter. On May 6, 1491 the latter granted the Cellites permission to

build their own chapel, tower, clock, and "Altaria convenien-
tis."[43] Prims notes that they also received the privilege of
burying their dead Brothers in the chapel, but he does not mention a cemetery. It may be inferred that the Cellite property
in Antwerp did not allow for a cemetery and therefore the
chapel was used for burials. For these privileges the Cellites
were, again, charged an annual fee. The contract also included
the stipulation that the Brothers were not to compete with
the parish for burials and other parochial rights. In 1493 the
new chapel was consecrated to the honor of St. Alexius.[44]

The Cologne Brothers did not erect a chapel until 1508.
Reasons for the delay are unknown, but Brother Bernhard
Giergen speculates that because the Brothers were considering moving to a new location during the 1470s, construction
of a chapel was unrealistic.[45] The Cologne Cellites did finally
erect a chapel at their original location, which was consecrated
to St. Alexius on the second Sunday after Easter 1508.[46] However, it was not until 1518 that the Brothers negotiated a contract with their pastor at Holy Apostles Church specifying
their mutual rights and obligations. In contrast to the general
restrictions placed upon the Cellites of Aachen and Antwerp,
the Cologne Brothers received a very detailed contract. For
example, they were allowed to bury members of the parish as
long as one-half of the money offering for the remembrance
and for the candles be granted to the parish. If the Brothers
gathered offerings on the four major feasts, i.e., Easter, Pente-
cost, Christmas, and the Assumption, they were to give part to
their pastor for each of these days. Upon the death of one of
the Brothers the pastor was to receive a specified donation and
out of the general donations to the chapel the Brothers were
to pay an annual fee.[47] In return the pastor granted the Cellites
their autonomy and promised not to meddle in the internal
affairs of the community. The superior of the Cologne house
and the pastor of Holy Apostles turned to the papacy for
confirmation of their agreement, since this took place after
the bull of Julius II that explicitly recognized the Cellite
independence from the bishops. Noting the sense of justice
and charity that motivated the Brothers and their pastor, Pope

Leo X granted his confirmation of the contract on August 23, 1518.[48] By choosing St. Alexius as their common patron, the Cellites gradually adopted their modern name, Alexian Brothers.

The establishment of their own chapels and cemeteries marks the completion of the evolution from the *via media* to the *via religiosa*. Their canonical status as a religious order emanated from Rome and was confirmed by local ecclesiastic contracts. Their social status had obviously changed from the Beghard days when they dwelt on the suspect fringe of society. Because they were now considered vital to the general welfare of the community, the city councils acted as safeguards of their stability. Economic advantages flowed from the Cellite services; donations of property and money allowed them to improve their houses, to erect chapels, and to provide for the general continuity of their ministry. Though they were now cemented to the ecclesiastical and secular establishments, their ties with the reformed Augustinians and other sources of reform seems to have protected them from becoming too secular.

The Brothers were now canonically cemented to the religious life, but they rededicated themselves to a life on the graben. It was not that they were Brothers without priest membership which prevented them from earning ecclesiastical prestige, nor was it because they were uneducated. On the contrary, they were not placed on the fringe; they had chosen again that location as a sign of their calling. From their Beghard-Lollard origins, they were men of the graben administering to those persons who had been placed at the furthest limits. Daily dwelling with those whom society had exiled, the Cellites lived in quiet inconspicuousness. As they performed their ministries to the plague victims and to the dead they seem to have nurtured anonymity. Their founders were anonymous; one of their ministries was to those declared anonymous; their spirituality stressed humble anonymity; to be an insider in the church would have been a contradiction of their charism, their religious raison d'être.

PART TWO

+

COMMUNAL AND SPIRITUAL LIFE

Introduction

In the preceding narrative there is an emphasis upon the cultural setting in which these early Alexians evolved from a spontaneous *pauperes Christi* movement of the early fourteenth century to a self-conscious religious institute of the late fifteenth century. The 175 years from folk Beghard-Lollard to Cellite status led the Brothers across a constantly shifting cultural landscape. In 1300 the papacy appeared to be very stable, the Albigensian and Waldensian threats appeared to be subsiding, and the friars provided an alternative path between the parish and the monastery. Christian spirituality was gradually entering a revival of mysticism, while Meister Eckhart's utterances revealed a strong scholastic foundation. Urban economies had experienced a century of sustained growth and the urban classes were maturing into roles of real social, political, and economic dominance. Though feudal lords were compelled to make certain adjustments, feudalism, like Scholasticism and the imperial papacy, gave the appearance of a stable social order. Now visible to historians, but hardly perceptible to the historical participant, are the shifts in the cultural landscape and the weaknesses of the religious and political edifices, which by 1300 were combining to make broad cultural changes.

During the fourteenth and fifteenth centuries, famine, plague, and war were the catalytic agents profoundly affecting the process of transition from the "high" to the "late" Middle Ages.

The actions of the original Alexians form a sort of epilogue to the *pauperes Christi* movement of lay spirituality which is related to the making of the high Middle Ages. Gregory VII's pontificate was a watershed through which passed those streams of medieval idealism infused into the imperial papacy, the Crusades, monastic reforms, and the scriptural refinement of lay spirituality. *Pauperes Christi* Beghard and Beguine groups were spawned in those streams of idealism, which by 1300 were rapidly diminishing to a trickle. The Lungenbrüder of Cologne, the Brot-Beghards of Aachen, and the Lollards of Antwerp were dependent upon the tradition established during the two previous centuries, but the cultural supports for such groups were by 1300 undermined by cultural changes, i.e., urbanization, secularization of religious and political attitudes, economic decline, the plague catastrophe, and the complex political and business arrangements that were replacing the simpler instrumentalities of feudalism and the guilds.

In short, by 1300 medieval culture had begun to pass from community to society. The first century of Alexian history reflects the persistence of the old community folk culture; such community life was characterized by orderly world-views that were woven into the entire social fabric to form predominately religious patterns. Traditional symbols, rituals, and folk customs mixed together to form beliefs that provided individuals with the means of grappling with the unknowns of nature and supernature. Birth, marriage, sickness, death, and the cycle of nature were viewed as events in a grand mystery drama in which individuals coped as members of communities. Even the literate men of the day who possessed sophisticated concepts of natural causation with refined categories of time, space, and culture would wear amulets to ward off demons.

Unlike modern man who dwells in an ever changing open-ended culture, traditional man was unaccustomed to change. We have noted how war, famine, and plague had accelerated the cultural change from the "high" to the "late" Middle Ages. Huizinga describes how western European society coped with these threatening changes by formalizing the traditional rituals to the extreme.[1] It is almost as if society sensed the decay of the medieval and, rather than face the unknown future, it exaggerated the past in order to live more securely in a precarious present. The indulgence crisis that set off Luther's attack upon the "good works" path to salvation illustrates the thesis: men sensed the disintegration of culture and frantically searched for secure recipes (indulgences) for salvation. Though many historians view the Renaissance of the fifteenth and sixteenth centuries as the dawn of the modern era there is a recent trend among some cultural historians to focus not on the rising sun of the scientific-humanist modern but the persistence of the dark-night images of the medieval. A collection of essays entitled *The Dark Vision of the Renaissance* suggests that the ideals of medieval culture remained normative until the late seventeenth century;[2] though they were shadowy ideals they did not die out until the high noon of the modern era when science and reason finally toppled the authority of tradition.

The preceding chapters have noted the reciprocity between cultural trends and the Beghard-Lollard evolution to religious-order status. During those 175 years the Cellites successfully grappled with plagues and with persecutions. Part One is primarily a historical narrative of the Alexian foundation. Part Two, an analysis of the historical significance of this foundation, is divided into three topics: Alexian Body, Alexian Spirit, and Alexian Expression. Because such an analysis is based upon the prior narrative some repetition is unavoidable.

These portions of the Alexian story will focus on the three major components of a religious institute, its structure, prayer life, and ministries. To explore prayer one must penetrate the Brothers' religious perspectives as they affected their experiences, their aspirations, their goals, and their authority structure and ministries. Because of the undocumented basis of much of early Alexian prayer life, cautious inference may compensate for the lack of explicit literate sources. Since authority is grounded on the permanence of the written word, there is abundant documentation on the evolution of the authority structures, particularly when the Beghard-Lollards move toward Cellite religious-order status. This process illustrates a cultural trait; as they entered Rome's orbit these oral lay mendicants were juridically absorbed into the literate culture of the papacy.

Though many documents testify to the Brothers' nursing and burial ministries, there are no sources that give witness to their attitudes toward these ministries. Through an examination of specialists' works on attitudes toward sickness, death, and funeral customs, and by one's own reflections on limit-situations, one may visualize the Brothers' perspectives on their unique Alexian expression. Just as the Black Death acted as a catalyst in cultural change, so it played an identical role in the body, spirit and expression of the early Alexians. Though the Brothers represent an epilogue to the *pauperes Christi* drama of the high Middle Ages, they survived for the next six and a half centuries because they evolved with the culture and remained relevant to the needs of society.

The Veurne Alexian Seal depicting St. Alexius under the stairs.

An ancient Eastern depiction of St. Alexius.

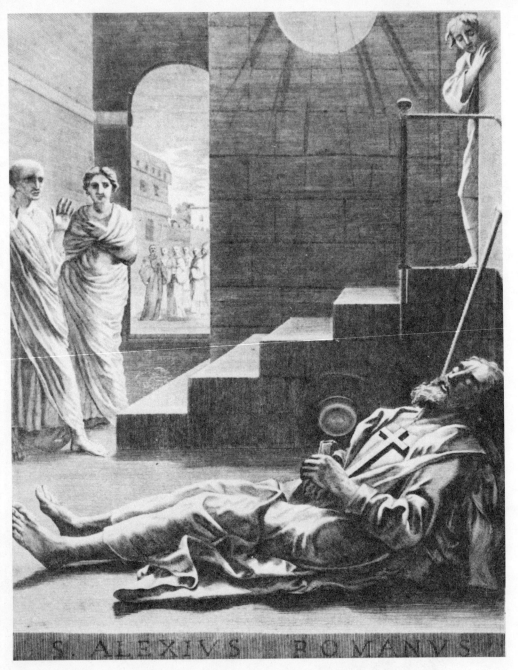

St. Alexius's family discovers the beggar's true identity.

The Papal Bull
of Julius II, 1506—
a notary's copy.

Cologne Cellites
minister to plague
victims (ca. 1605).

The Alexian chapel
in Aachen,
erected in 1683.

The Alexian house
and chapel in
Veurne, Belgium.

6

Organization
of the Community

I

Brother Paul, our fictional ideal-type Alexian, was a participant
in a religious movement and not a religious order. He was
swept into the *vita apostolica* by the tides of lay spirituality,
which had gained momentum during the twelfth and thirteenth
centuries. Paul's oral-folk perspective did not include a specific
constitutional design with detailed rules and regulations on
governance structure and on the role of the various Brothers.
Brother Paul absorbed the word of God as a real happening;
the Jesus of the past became present and Paul's notion of the
future was limited to the end-time rather than the evolution
of his Alexian community as a continuing institution. Thus
his evangelical character was in a sense antithetical to rigid
institutionalization.

But the everyday practical concerns did require some form
of organization. When the Brothers were wandering mendicants without the stability that a permanent residence provides,
a primitive organizational feature such as a prayer leader or
spiritual father may have been the extent of their governance

structure. When the Brothers in Cologne were given a house, they referred to their leader as *procurator*. This office could have been borrowed from the Franciscans and directly tied into their life of voluntary poverty. Because hospital "administrators" were also referred to as procurators, the term may have derived from their ministerial contacts with nursing. Upon entering the community, Brother Paul gave all his possessions to the procurator, who was responsible for holding them in common for the community. When he returned from a period of begging "Bread for the Love of God" his collections were also turned over to the procurator for common distribution.

We may also assume that there were specific initiation rites and a probationary period before Paul would be considered a full Beghard-Alexian. When Paul first appeared at the Lungenbrüder house, he would no doubt have been asked by the procurator and the elders of the community why he wished to enter their family. Paul's likely response would have been "By renouncing all worldly possessions, by begging for my bread, and by ministering to the dying and dead to unite myself with the poverty, passion, and death of Jesus." Before experiencing the entrance rites Paul would probably have lived with the community for a brief time. He would perhaps have worn a simplified habit and been placed under the guidance of an older Brother who would introduce him to the family's way of life.

The entrance rite would include the entire community. Brother Paul would be led into a circle of Brothers where he would utter a specific formula and perhaps include his own words of confession—as community confession was common among *pauperes Christi* groups. The formula may have contained a commitment to the evangelical counsels—poverty, chastity, and obedience; chastity and obedience to the procurator may have been implied in the vow of poverty rather than explicitly stated. Evangelism and mysticism, so common to the spiritual climate of the day, may have been expressed in a community prayer during the ceremony. Clothing Paul in the gray-black garb of the Beghard-Alexian must have been rather elaborate—perhaps Paul extended his arms to assume the posture of the Crucified Christ; sacramental symbols such as candles, holy oils, and holy water, as well as community song, could have been included in the ritual. Paul thus ritually passed from the profane to the sacral world.[3] The sacral-folk community did not distinguish between symbol and reality; the Beghard Alexian family viewed themselves as apostles, and as Paul entered through the ritual he immersed himself in the passion of Christ. Evangelical poverty was the sacral life that invoked the presence of the impoverished Jesus who lived among the outsiders of Hebrew society.

The relatively primitive internal structure of the Beghard Alexian house must have been determined by the demands of their ministries. No doubt they opened and closed their day with those prayers memorized by the laity, *Aves* and *Pater Nosters*; they may have at an early stage introduced some or all of the psalms included in the funeral chant, particularly the *De Profundis* and the *Miserere*. Because their nursing ministry took them into the homes of the critically ill, it would seem that they did not view their life as strongly monastic.

There may have been some rudimentary division of labor according to the specific talents of the community, but there was no written constitution specifying the offices of bursar, porter, etc. The procurator was probably an elected superior with no designated term of office. In the early phases the procurator likely presided rather than governed as superior. He may have demanded obedience but his decisions were made in counsel with at least the elders of the community. As superior of a community frequently referred to as "Brothers of Voluntary Poverty," it would seem that he would be chosen superior on the basis of his inspirational leadership rather than his organizational skills. We know that as soon as the Brothers in Antwerp settled in Suderman's house, they were placed under a board of governors. Such an arrangement was very appropriate to the Brothers' spirit, as it meant that they would not experience a conflict between property ownership and the evangelical counsel of poverty.

Each house was an autonomous religious-social unit. The

term *family* is an appropriate description for the form of association within each house. The Beghard-Alexian family tended to be *Gemeinschaft*, the famous ideal-type term coined by the sociologist Ferdinand Tönnies: an "intimate, private, and exclusive living together is understood as life in Gemeinschaft (community)."[4] Tönnies's description of the *Gemeinschaft* of "friendship" could be applied to the Beghard-Alexians. Friendship bonds are forged from "similarity of work and intellectual attitude." Common religious values and goals urge the "brethren of such a common faith [to] feel . . . everywhere united by a spiritual bond and the cooperation in a common task." Members of the *Gemeinschaft* dwell in a "tacit" understanding; "real concord cannot be made by agreement . . . cannot be artificially produced."[5] Tönnies implies the oral-culture characteristics described above when he states: "In the same way as the general use of a common language, making possible understanding through speech, brings nearer and binds human minds and hearts, so we find a common state of mind which in its higher forms—common custom and common belief —penetrates to the members of a people (Volk)."[6]

When a religious community is still in its foundation stage (for Alexians, roughly the first century of their existence, 1300–1400), it is dwelling in its original charism. This charism is usually embodied in the founder of a religious order, such as Francis or Dominic. Without a known founder the Beghard-Alexian *Gemeinschaft* was bound together by the Brothers' *pauperes Christi* ideals. The community did not impose contracts upon its members; the charism of radical poverty and the evangelical ministry to those on the limits of existence, the dying and dead, circulated through the community precluding the need for institutional contractual arrangements among the members and between the sacral community and the ecclesiastical structure or the secular authorities. As we have seen, throughout the first century of Beghard-Alexian existence a series of events occurred which compelled the Brothers gradually to adopt institutional structures and contractual arrangements with secular and church authorities.

The Cologne Lungenbrüder were obviously moving in this

direction. In 1427 they codified their traditions into a rule and took a solemn promise to live according to its regulations.[7] Over the next few months nineteen brothers vowed, for the course of their common life together, poverty and obedience toward their prelates.[8] The question concerning common property and the exclusion of private ownership was regulated in more detail. In order to provide for peace and order, the Brothers bound themselves in charity to obey the procurator of the house in all things. No one could enter the house without his approval. Upon entering, a man should bind himself to the procurator, the majority of the Brothers, and, with a notary present, promise to obey the ordinances of the house. If a Brother violated the rule and did not mend his ways after being admonished by the procurator or a majority of the Brothers, then he would be removed from the house. A Brother who left the house for whatever reason or died within the house had no claim on the property of the house (nor did his heirs). A person who joined the community must renounce all claims and rights for himself, his heirs, and his offspring.[9] Although the rule places grave responsibility upon the procurator, the frequent mention of "the majority of the Brothers" illustrates the relatively democratic character of the rule. The strong stress upon poverty harks back to their *vita apostolica* origins.

The city council of Cologne assisted the Brothers in their efforts to establish a firm rule. The council resolved on February 20, 1428 the following ordinance:

1. All those that do not live in the house "dzo der lungen" or have left it, are not allowed any more, to wear the garb of the brothers of the City of Cologne.

2. He who in the house is not willing to observe the good ordinance according to the document which is in possession of the brothers or whoever without the knowledge or will of the brothers leaves the house, is forbidden by the city council of Cologne under penalty to continue to wear the brothers garb in the City of Cologne:

3. Since all property shall be common the Brothers according to the said document, the city council threatens every brother with penalty who takes something from the house without the knowledge and consent of the brothers. . . .[10]

The Cologne rule was gradually adopted by the Cellite houses in other towns. The Trier and Coblenz houses were particularly close to the Lungenbrüder of Cologne. Documents concerning each of these houses reveal that they were subject to the Cologne house in a sort of mother-daughter relationship. Cologne's role as chief advocate for the Cellites, particularly evidenced at the Council of Constance, distinguished her as the preeminent community in the northwestern section of Germany.[11]

The Aachen house was also dependent upon the Cologne community. For example, on September 17, 1434 Eugene granted the poor sisters and brothers living in the vicinity of Cologne permission to have their own confessor. The Lungenbrüder who had successfully petitioned Eugene for this privilege were contacted by the Aachen Brothers and on May 25, 1435 they received a copy of this privilege so that they too might have their own confessor.[12] Aachen's dependency on Cologne does not appear to have been as deep as was that of Trier and Coblenz; it was a matter of deferring to Cologne's ascendancy as the most influential and prominent house in the Rhineland. Though the status of a religious order was not conferred until 1472, the Cellites had obviously evolved far beyond their Beghard-Lollard origins. The "tacit understanding" and the implicit "familial ties" of the Beghard *Gemeinschaft* were by necessity made explicit through the rules and regulations of this first phase of the Cellite institutionalization. As the entire Cellite family moved in the direction of religious order with an organizational structure, it assumed some of the characteristics of what Tönnies calls a *Gesellschaft*, a society, an aggregate of individuals, vis-à-vis a community.[13] Brother Paul, our folk Alexian, was not disturbed by this process. Though his ties with his immediate religious family were placed on a legal footing and though his day may have been subjected to an explicit schedule, family life could have been just as vibrant as previously; the body may have been more explicitly organized but the original Alexian charism and *Gemeinschaft* character were sustained by the continuing ministries to those on the limits of existence. He would no longer be the object of suspicion or abuse; his way of life was respected by both secular and church authorities. Perhaps the Cellite of the early fifteenth century no longer possessed the resilient pioneer qualities of the Beghard-Alexian founding Brothers necessary in an earlier day. A century of adversity witnessed the forging of strong traditions in which the Alexian life of sacramental ritual for the dying and the dead became a permanent feature in the everyday life of the townspeople in Cologne, Aachen, and Antwerp.

Though the Antwerp Cellites were the first to enter the religious life formally (yet to be officially approved as a religious order) a document concerned with structure was intended for the Cell Brothers "who resided in the towns Ghent, Bruges, and Alderney in the Diocese of Tournai."[14] Written by the vicar general, the representative of Tournai's bishop, this document is entitled "Statutes and Mode of Life of the Religious Institute Commonly Known as Brothers and Sisters of the Cells."[15] Like their Antwerp Brothers, the Tournai Cellites adopted the Rule of St. Augustine, but that rule is characterized by general precepts and does not stipulate concrete rules and regulations. Since the vicar general stated that the request for "Statutes and Mode of Life" came from the Brothers and Sisters, one may infer that these statutes were a written form of what tradition had etched upon the Cellite way of life. In short, the Brothers and Sisters probably had the customs written, and the vicar general merely certified them in legal form with specific guarantees for the bishop's prerogatives; or the bishop could have merely derived these Cellite constitutions from an established religious order, perhaps the Augustinian. The "Statutes" are the first detailed record of the early Cellite way of life. The vicar general also stated that the Brothers and Sisters had presented to their bishop "certain documents concerning . . . [their] case . . . which with good reason have influenced us."[16] He was no doubt referring to copies of the various papal bulls, perhaps that of Gregory XI but more likely those of Eugene IV and Pius II.

After prefacing the "constitution" with these remarks and others concerning the edifying plague ministries of the Cell

Brothers, the first statute contains the mandate that they must "continue to live under the obedience and ordinary subjection"[17] of their bishop. Though there was no specific reference to provincial authority structures, this was implicit in the directives on election of house superiors. They were to be elected by a simple majority after the celebration of a "Low Mass in honor of the Holy Spirit."[18] The official visitators, assisted by the pastor, were to examine the ballots, and the person with the most votes "whether he is a member of this community or another"[19] should be confirmed as the new superior. Thus the houses must have had some sense of congregational unity, or else the possibility of electing a person from another house would never have been mentioned. Perhaps the Antwerp house was, like the Cologne house in the Rhineland, a seat of provincial authority. Toward the end of the statutes, when the vicar general confirmed the papal privilege granting the Brothers and Sisters their own confessor, he notes that if their own superior "be a priest" then he will also be authorized to hear confessions.[20] There are two ways to interpret this remark. One, when it was stated that a person "from another community" was eligible for election as superior it might have meant a priest from an Augustinian house. It also could have meant that priests did enter the Alexian community, and that since it was not uncommon for the superior of a male house also to be the Sisters' superior, there was no need to specify the Brothers' community when it was stated "if he be a priest." The former is more likely the accurate interpretation, for lay institutes of the day, particularly sisterhoods that were not officially religious orders, did frequently have priests as superiors.

The superior was told to call a chapter of faults at least four times a year, if necessary more frequently. The vicar general specifically stated the penances to be imposed according to the offence:

> Likewise, those who hold a chapter should know in what manner each kind of offence is to be punished.
> Below there follows what is considered a condign punishment for each kind of offence: that is, the penance will consist of taking dinner

on the floor in the presence of the whole community, a fasting dinner of bread and water, and also take the discipline or perform other works of reconciliation according to the discretion of the superior.

Also, anyone who talks during times of silence and outside of time for meals or eats without permission, will do penance for one day.

Likewise, anyone who speaks in insulting or haughty manner to another brother or sister, or who grumbles about the food or drink or clothing or anything else, or who leaves the house without permission, he will be subject to penance for three days.

Also, no brother or sister is to hold a conversation with someone of different age or sex in a private room unless the door be kept open, to avoid any suspicion. Anyone guilty of the contrary conduct and when admonished does not amend his ways, he is to do penance for five days. Likewise, anyone who has sworn disgracefully by God or His saints, or one who has refused to accept the penance imposed upon him by the chapter, or one who has struck a brother or sister companion without however shedding blood, or one who has been known to have or convicted of having his own supply of money, or one who has quarrelled either with friends or with someone outside the house, in all such cases occurring within the house—such a one is to be bound to perform penance for twenty days.

Likewise, it is our wish that the present rule and prescribed statutes do not bind under pain of sin, but oblige only to performance of the prescribed penance as expressed in the previous articles.[21]

This rather rigid set of rules was apparently a codification of Alexian custom. To "take the discipline" meant that the offender was to flog himself. The vicar general instructed the Sisters to "take the discipline" three days a week during Advent and Lent and every Friday during the rest of the year. In keeping with the bias toward male moral superiority, the Brothers were not directed to impose the discipline upon themselves in any regular way.[22] However, both Brothers and Sisters were told to abstain from meat and fast on Fridays and most of Advent and Lent, and not to sleep on beds or wear linen nightshirts[23] (until into the twentieth century some Alexian Brothers slept on straw mattresses and were not allowed to wear linen nightshirts). According to church law of the time, every Brother and Sister was required "to let blood four times a year," on the advice of their physicians.[24]

The statutes concerned with the "novitiate" were very specific: "... no brother or sister is to be admitted to the community unless [he or she] be of use to the House and without physical defect and no brother is to be admitted to profession unless he has completed his twentieth year and no sister unless she is eighteen years of age and has gone through a probation of one year or longer."[25] Upon entering the community, the aspirant was to be examined by "three outstanding Brothers" who would "inquire into [his or her] morals, and piety and manner of life"[26] after which they were to report the results to the superior and the whole community. Ultimately the authority to accept or reject the aspirant resided in the "conscience" of the entire community. When the aspirant was accepted he or she was formally received into the community according to a specific formula. The aspirant, prostrate before the superior, would be questioned as to what he or she was seeking, and should respond, "Father, I beg God's mercy and your favor." The superior would then direct the "recipient" to rise and be instructed in the "strictness of the profession or rule." If the recipient would agree to all that is required as a member of the institute he or she would state: "May the Lord who has begun this good of himself, be willing to bring it to completion." Whereupon "the bystanders ... respond: Amen." Assuming that the recipient met all the qualifications (be single, at least twenty-one years old, free from debt and from any other religious order), the person was assigned to a "master" who would "teach him the rule or regulations of the house, and also correct him by word or sign for any defect."[27] Humility was the theme of the novitiate: "novices ... are in no way to regard their own will, but are to defer voluntarily in obedience to the will of the superior." When the Brothers and Sisters professed their vows they were to use this formula: "I, N., a brother or sister, promise to God, to the Blessed Virgin Mary, to St. Augustine, and to all the saints of God perpetual chastity, and to live without personal spending money, and obedience to my Lord, the present Reverend Bishop of Tournai and to all his successors who will be canonically appointed to this See, and also to you father and to all your successors who will be legitimately elected as superiors to this community."[28] The document concluded with an explicit statement on the authority of the bishop, who had the sole power "to correct, change, interpret, and if need be, improve these . . . statutes. . . ."[29]

This 1461 constitution for the Cellites of Tournai illustrates the widespread movement toward a monastic life within the Belgian "province." In 1462 the Cellites of Diest also received a constitution from their ordinary, the bishop of Liège, Louis de Bourbon.[30]

In his preface, the bishop gives us a glimpse of the Brothers' eagerness to achieve the status of a religious order. After noting the humble and holy lives of the Brothers (unlike the vicar of Tournai, he never mentions Sisters), he stated that he had heard from the "Master" of the Diest house "that it is continually and happily growing in numbers."[31] The strong relationship between the Alexians and the Augustinians (embodied in the reformer John Busch) was made explicit. The Diest Brothers had bound "themselves by vow to the three substantials of the rule or order of Saint Augustine" because they were "passionately desirous of a more severe life."[32] "Severe" should be interpreted as a more routinized monastic life grounded in solemn vows. These Brothers not only came under the direct influence of the Augustinians, but according to this document they were eager to be absorbed by the Augustinian order. "They have persistently begged us to deign to erect their community into a conventual house of their order and to provide them with suitable favors and constitutions to ensure the stability of their rule. Therefore, since we are favorably inclined toward such requests by present letters we do erect and establish this community as a conventual house of said order of St. Augustine. . . ."[33] Because Bishop Louis also refers to the statutes of Cellites of Liège as a precedent for his decision to attach the Diest Brothers to the Augustinians, perhaps this affiliation was widespread.[34] The natural affinity between the two religious groups is well documented. Besides sharing a common rule, which was adopted by many religious institutes, the Windesheim reform movement was the most compelling factor in cementing a strong Cellite-Augustinian alliance. We have already referred to the reform concerns of Nicholas of Cusa and John Busch as the likely stimuli motivating the Cellites toward the status of a recognized religious institute. Though with hindsight we can trace this drift to the early fifteenth-century Cellite appeal at the Council of Constance, the Augustinian reform movement emanating from Windesheim appears as the immediate cause for the Cellite pursuit of permission to profess the three cardinal vows.

If a Cellite superior was anxious to secure stability and permanence, and if he was in touch with the religious trends of the mid-fifteenth century, then he would have been struck by the Augustinian model. The major goal of John Busch and the Windesheim reformers was to revive the central meaning of monasticism contained in a strict observance of the vows, the rule, and the ancient spirit of the founders. Though the Cellites had traveled the *via media* of their founding Beghards for almost two centuries they had suffered from their precarious status. Because reformers were circulating throughout the Low Countries and the Rhineland in the mid-fifteenth century clamoring for a return to the regular religious life, the Cellites probably viewed the *via media* as no longer fulfilling their need to carry on as a religious foundation.

Until Rome recognized the Cellites as an independent order, the wish to profess vows could only be satisfied by affiliation with canonically approved communities. In contrast to the Tournai statutes those of Diest were very brief, the bishop logically assuming that the Brothers would live according to Augustinian customs. Bishop Louis did specify that the Brothers could choose either a prelate or a prior as their official visitator "in matters concerning approved order and regular observance."[35] After witnessing the profession of vows, the visitator was instructed to appoint a Brother as rector "according to his knowledge and with the advice of the more prudent members of the community."[36] In spite of their near Augustinian status, the Brothers were told that they must continue in their ministries to the sick and the dying. Resembling the Tournai statutes, the Diest rules contained directives to pray *Pater Nosters* and *Aves* as a substitute for the Divine Office, to fast and abstain according to the monastic regulations, to hold a chapter of faults "in the monastic manner" each week, and to confess every two weeks. Bishop Louis also granted them permission "to set up a chapel with an altar in it, having a portable altar stone where they can hear Mass."[37]

The Liège Cellite community, which was also a conventual Augustinian House, was made guardian to the Diest Brothers. Bishop Louis instructed the Diest rector to visit "the house of his brothers of the Cell; which we have some time ago erected in our city of Liège ... lest the remoteness of these communities from one another be an impediment to maintaining conformity in manner of life and in monastic discipline, and the [rector] can then discuss with them the progress of the order and the observance of discipline and other such suitable matters in the manner of a chapter."[38] They were to continue to wear the traditional garb of the Cellites and were permitted to "gather alms according to their custom from Christ's faithful."[39] Since the Cellites of Liège and Diest were allowed to carry on their unique traditions and their traditional name, Brothers of the Cell, the affiliation with the Augustinians was merely juridical. Though they were not absorbed into the canons, the strong natural affinities between the two groups during the reform period urged the Cellites to view the Augustinians as guardians or counselors in their new life under vows. Perhaps Bishop Louis knew full well that it was merely a matter of time before the papacy would place the Cellites on the canonical footing of an independent religious order.

II

During the same year that Bishop Louis confirmed the Cell Brothers of Diest Augustinians he granted the Aachen Cellites permission to adopt the rule of the Cologne house because the latter was "set over the brothers in Aachen"[40] (October 8, 1462). Bishop Louis had become the major episcopal spokesman for the Cellites. As the ordinary of Liège, he "hosted" the first General Chapter in 1468. On March 18, 1468 he fulfilled the wishes of the Aachen Brothers who, according to the mandate from the first General Chapter, appealed to Louis for permission to profess vows. This approbationary letter is in content identical to the one he wrote to the Diest community with the exception that he did not confer on the Aachen house the status of a "conventual house" of the Augustinian order.[41] Perhaps the Aachen Brothers had already developed a filial relationship with a Windesheim Augustinian Priory which had been founded in Aachen. It is also probable that the first Cellite General Chapter precluded Louis's concern explicitly to attach the Aachen house to an established religious order.

The Cologne house, which had formulated its own rule in 1427, also fulfilled the General Chapter's mandate by asking Archbishop Rupert to confirm certain amendments to their 1427 rule. On January 2, 1469 (seven months after Louis's March letter) Rupert confirmed these amendments with the understanding that the Brothers were to continue to live honestly in obedience to the church and respectful of the rights of the archbishop and local pastor.[42] Besides the adoption of the Augustinian rule, the amendments included the new manner in which vows were to be professed. The professing Brother had formerly vowed poverty, chastity, and obedience for "as long as I shall remain in this house or in this congregation" (*congregatio*).[43] Instead he simply professed according to the Augustinian rule and the house rule "before the father of the house (*Paterfamilias*) whom they call Procurator. . . ."[44] The prior procedure with its time limit indicates that promises were entailed rather than canonically approved vows. When the latter was permitted they seem to have shifted from temporary to final vows.

The Cologne Brothers juridically tied themselves to the reformed Augustinians when they stipulated that their visitator must be "a religious of a reformed monastery of the said rule" (Augustinian). The following lists the duties and responsibilities of the visitator.

The visitor shall be permitted and entitled to visit the said house, head and members of it, every two years at least and as often as it seems opportune, aided by good and exemplary companions, i.e., a dignified priest and a "procurator" of the similar houses chosen by them, and he shall punish excesses according to the rule and the order of the house and according to the decisions of the holy fathers. In case that some one, which God forbid, would be disobedient and would stubbornly not cease his wrong doing or would refuse to undergo punishment, the procurator and the brothers should call on the civil authority, in order to put the incorrigible one into the episcopal prison until adequate atonement.[45]

Bishop Louis de Bourbon's "statutes" for the Aachen Brothers also included stringent measures for Brothers who violated the rule. One could infer that this rather harsh attitude stemmed from actual experiences with recalcitrant Cellites. Because the Cellites were so deeply influenced by the major reform movement embodied in John Busch, it is likely that the Brothers were anticipating the possibility of a decline in monastic observance rather than reflecting such decline. Indeed their spirituality was at a very intense level during this period. The Cologne amendments stipulated that the new house and Augustinian rule applied to all "the brothers that live outside the house within or without the diocese of Cologne and who are subject to the house. . . ."[46] This could refer to the Aachen Brothers who, their bishop said, were under the Cologne Brothers, thereby implying that provincial authority resided in Cologne. However, since Louis de Bourbon granted the Aachen Brothers their own "constitution," it may be that the Cologne rule applied to those Lungenbrüder who were engaged in either long-time begging or nursing outside the house. Since these "house Constitutions" for the Tournai, Diest, Aachen, and Cologne Brothers were formulated before the Cellites were constituted as a recognized religious order, they dwelt as sort of an Augustinian "third order" with episcopal Congregation status. The three bulls of Sixtus IV elevated them to a papally approved religious order with rights and privileges which removed them from the direct governance of their ordinaries.

Subsequent to the conferral of religious-order status the Cellites established an appropriate authority structure. At the top was a general who was elected by the General Chapters.[47] The following houses, which hosted early chapter meetings, indicate the four Cellite provinces, Rhineland, Brabant, Flanders, and Holland: Bruges 1469, Cologne 1470, Haarlem 1478, Cologne 1473, Liège 1475, Ghent 1476, Aachen 1478.[48] The exact powers of the general and provincial were primarily visitorial. In an early eighteenth-century codification of tradition, i.e., "constitution," the superior general was directed to visit each of the houses at least once a year in the company of two other Brothers.[49] The role of the non-Cellite visitator was obviously diminished, probably called upon only in crisis situations.

Each house elected its own superior whose title changed from procurator to pater; his assistant was called vice pater. The pater of the Cologne house was the provincial for the Rhineland, which included Aachen, Neuss, Trier, the Cellite Sisters of the Holy Trinity in Cologne, and the Sisters in Düsseldorf and Düren.[50] Apparently this was according to tradition rather than constitutional prescription. The other provinces appear to have elected their provincials with no consideration for the candidate's membership in a preeminent house. The election of provincials may have occurred either at the General Chapter or provincial chapters.

With roughly two hundred years of house autonomy we may infer that this structural arrangement provided a new layer of authority which was relatively remote from the governance of each house. Even in the eighteenth century the principle of monastic stability was strong. Though the general could transfer a Brother, this appears to have been the exception. For example, if a Brother successfully requested a transfer he would lose all seniority when he moved to a different house, with the obvious implication that when he entered a Cellite house he was expected to reside there for life.[51] Because each Cellite house did develop its own customs, particularly in the ways in which it related to the city council and to the people, this principle of stability (*stabilitas loci*) appears to be appropriate to the perpetuation of Cellite diversity.

Cellite governance had evolved from simple communalism to a highly structured organization with clear lines of authority and practical directives for community life as well as a structured prayer day. E. K. Francis distinguishes between a community of religious (*religiosi*) and a religious order by imposing a sort of *Gemeinschaft-Gesellschaft* dichotomy. "The Community of religious represents an intimate face-to-face group which, in the extreme case, performs practically all the functions of the natural family short of biological procreation. . . . By contrast, the religious order tends to substitute more impersonal, segmental, and abstract relationships among the members of its local establishments, more properly called 'convents,' that is, gathering places rather than communities."[52] Though the Cellites adopted the terms of abstract relationships in the gradual changes from movement to order, there are three reasons why one should not rigidly apply Francis's dichotomy. Firstly, *stabilitas loci* remained, with some qualification, a continual feature within the Cellite way of life. Francis considers the breakdown of "stability" as evidence of the *Gesellschaft* character of a religious order.[53] This characteristic does not apply to the Cellites, as each member of the order was grounded in a primary family. Second, though certain titles represented the shift from personalist "community" to abstract "society," the title for house superior experienced a reversal of this trend—procurator to pater. Thus, "pater" and *stabilitas loci* strengthened familial ties among the Brothers. Third, and perhaps most significant, the charism of their Beghard-Lollard origins was sustained by their continuous service to those on the limits of existence. Their ministry evolved along lines similar to their spirituality, i.e., from spontaneity to routinization, but the individual Cellite was still encouraged to engage in a personalist and sacramental witness illustrative of a Cellite continuum from the origins. The Cellites were institutionalized but the process did not yet seep down drastically to alter many of the mendicant and ministerial characteristics of the Cellite way of life.

III

Dom Jean Leclercq points out that when a member of a religious order takes vows his act of profession is "not to a rule alone, but according to three elements, among which there exists a hierarchy and which complete one another."[54] The first is the "Rule of Charity" followed by the particular rule, i.e., Augustinian; while the latter "retains permanent value," the third element, the institution, "represents the changeable . . . and can modify the rule on certain points."[55]

There has been a long-standing scholarly dispute on the various texts of St. Augustine's rule. Four texts have appeared over the years but there is a consensus that the rule adopted by various religious communities of men and women is derived from a letter written by the saint to a troubled community of nuns that he had founded. By the twelfth century it had evolved into a rule for men, the one adopted by the Cellites.[56] The various orders which adopted the rule had also added amendments appropriate to the character of their own cloister and apostolic life.

In contrast to the Benedictine rule, that of Augustine is far more general and easily adaptable. When the Brothers adopted the Augustinian rule at their first General Chapter it is likely that they followed the rule as it was later printed for the Brothers in the early eighteenth century, which is almost identical to the contemporary rule. The contents of both rules follow roughly the same lines: introductory remarks about communal life and prayer followed by chapters on fasting, celibacy, care of the sick; on prudent association with women; on proper dress; on the acceptance of gifts; and on the need for obedience to supervisors and for weekly recitation of the rule.[57] The Alexians are still living according to the Augustinian rule qualified by the changing needs of the time.

The communalism of the Cellites' *pauperes Christi* was suitable to their spontaneous founderless origins. As they experienced a quantitative growth subsequent to the plague crises they experienced qualitative changes and the tensions which accompanied these basic changes. Encounter with crisis accelerated that pace of change. The new spirituality of the *Devotio Moderna* was democratic in that it was intended to revive popular piety, but as it expressed itself in monastic reform it encouraged a strict observance of the rules. As the Brothers were absorbed into the reform movement they were driven to pursue vows, a rule, and full recognition as a monastic community with well-defined authority structures. The amorphous communalism of their origins could not withstand growth and continuous crisis nor could their original spirituality be fully expressed within such critical conditions. Their fifteenth-century spirit and expansion drove them to construct new means of government. Every "modern" religious order possesses such instruments of government, but the Cellites are unique for they form the only surviving Beghard remnant as it evolved in the late Middle Ages.

7

From Meister Eckhart
to Thomas à Kempis

The founders of religious orders are identified with the formation of the various "schools" of spirituality. By examining the founder's writings and the testimony of his disciples, scholars may trace Franciscan or Ignatian spirituality from its charismatic sources, and thereby form a criterion for evaluating the spiritual trends of succeeding generations of Franciscans or Jesuits. Without a founder and the documented witness of the Alexian pioneers, the Alexian Brothers' spirituality does not have the distinctive imprint of identifiable individuals. From its origins their spirituality was orally expressed, collectively conceived, and eclectically nurtured. When they were moving toward religious-order status the Cellites were directed by their bishops to observe a regular prayer life; these directives are documented.

John Busch, an Augustinian champion of the *Devotio Moderna*, provided posterity with a singular witness to the Cellite prayer life of the late Middle Ages. Because Counter-Reformation spirituality (1550–1650) was partially dependent on the *Devotio Moderna*, the Cellites were probably lively participants in the spirituality of the era. However, the Cellites of the early seventeenth century were unable to journey back to their thirteenth-century foundation via the written word and perceive the distinctive spirituality flowing from the charism of their origins. To impose order on the flow of Cellite spirituality the historian is therefore compelled to penetrate the general climate of spirituality and with the tools of logical inference develop the story of the shifting spiritual perspectives of the Cellites, from their origins to the Reformation.

I

The spiritual ancestry of the original Cellites appears, as we have seen, in diverse religious families: the *pauperes Christi* lifestyle, Franciscan ideals of poverty, Beguine spirituality with a strong Cistercian flavor, Dominican mysticism of Meister Eckhart. Their *pauperes Christi* lineage stretches back to the twelfth century. Their notion of the mendicant life was related to the Franciscan ideals of the thirteenth century. When we first view the Beghards of Cologne, Franciscan spirituality, particularly in its development from a core commitment to poverty, was passing through an acute crisis. After Francis's death, interpretations of his doctrine of absolute poverty gradually led to a polarization within his own order.[1] The Conventual Franciscans reconciled their founder's doctrine with the expansion of Franciscan wealth on the grounds that their vow of poverty was limited to renunciation of *dominion* over property; their opponents, the Spirituals, identified poverty with "total restriction of all *use* of property."[2] As the polarization developed, extremists on both sides gained leadership and the controversy went beyond poverty to such central doctrinal issues as the nature and mission of the church. Many of the rigorists were imbued with an apocalyptic vision of the imminance of the end of the world. Influenced by the twelfth-century Cistercian Abbot Joachim of Fiorre, who prophesied the culmination of history in an age of the Holy Spirit, some

Spirituals and their supporters identified absolute poverty not merely as a vow for Franciscans but as the sole means for church reform in anticipation of the Age of the Holy Spirit. When the Spirituals were challenged by the papacy their tendency was to reply that the institutional church was working contrary to the will of God.[3]

The Spirituals who had gathered a strong following among the Beguines in southern France were investigated at the Council of Vienne and ultimately suppressed (in 1323) by John XXII, a strong opponent of poverty-extremism both within the Franciscans and among their Beguine followers.[4] Though the internal development of the Franciscans led to a peaceful solution with the formation of the Friars Minor of Strict Observance as orthodox heirs of Spirituals, the latter influenced many lay groups committed to Francis's ideal of absolute poverty and frequently viewed as heterodox. Like the Franciscans, the original Alexians conferred the title of procurator upon their superiors. They probably did not engage in deep speculation on the problem of renunciation of dominion and/or use of property, but the Franciscan ideal was implicitly present in the Brot-Beghard mendicancy. Though poverty may be viewed as their eighth sacrament they were apparently protected from extremism of the cult of poverty not only by the rigors of their ministry but also by the quiescent Beguine mysticism that touched many Beghard communities. The Beguines of the thirteenth century were more numerous and more influential than the Beghards. Cistercian spirituality, particularly as expressed in the mysticism of St. Bernard, was very popular among Beguine mystics of the Rhineland and the Netherlands. Marie d'Oigines (d. 1213), Juliana of Cornillon (d. 1258), Beatrice of Nazareth (d. 1268), and Hadewijch of Antwerp (d. ca. late thirteenth century) are the most noteworthy of the Beguine mystics. According to Marie's biographer, Jacques Vitry, she longed to adopt the *pauperes Christi* life of begging: "She often thought on the poverty of Christ, who was born without a shelter, who had no stone on which to lay his head, no money to pay tribute, who lived on alms and the hospitality of others."[5] Because the *vita aposto-*

lica stressed the humanity of Christ it is not coincidental that Beguines such as Marie and Juliana of Cornillon enthusiastically promoted the institution of the Corpus Christi feast, a devotion which is still very popular in the place of its origin, Belgium and the Rhineland.

Beatrice of Nazareth and Hadewijch represent the Beguine mysticism derived from St. Bernard but very influential upon the Rhineland spirituality of the fourteenth century.[6] Hadewijch's utterances closely resemble those of Meister Eckhart: "For God the Soul is the free and open way, into which he can plunge from out of his furthest depths; and for the soul, in return, God is the way of freedom, towards the depths of the Divine Being, which nothing can attain save the depths of the soul."[7] Meister Eckhart preached to Beguines and apparently learned as much from them as they learned from him. Stressing the divine simplicity of the mystical union with God, his sermons appear as inspirational utterances for the many groups along the *via media*, including the Cellites.

If indeed the Beghard-Alexians absorbed the climate of Beguine-Eckhartian mysticism it would seem to have strengthened their existence midway between the parish church and the monastic cloister. Grounded in a personalist covenant with God they would be less dependent upon the ecclesiastical paths to grace, which demanded total withdrawal into the monastery. Indeed, we may conclude that one of the reasons the once disparate Brot-Beghards gathered into single communities was to regularize their prayer life. We have no record of this prayer life for the first hundred years of their existence, but it is very likely that they were influenced by Beguine and Eckhartian mysticism, which accented a life of detachment and uncomplicated identity with the scriptural Jesus. There were no great Beghard mystics. Because some beguinages represented a cross-section of society, they contained many literate Beguines who could develop their spirituality in a sophisticated style. Beghards appear to be drawn mainly from the lower classes and therefore illiteracy obstructed such development. Yet, since the Brethren of the Free Spirit were obviously schooled in mysticism we can conclude that these lower-class

Beghards reflected the spiritual climate of mysticism in their prayer meetings.

The popular piety of the day, which stressed veneration of the saints and contained strands of superstition, must have also had an impact upon their spirituality. Perhaps as they gathered in prayer the Cellites represented traditional spirituality by reciting *Pater Nosters* and *Aves*, popular piety by invoking their favorite saints, and an Eckhart-like mysticism by uttering their reflections on the roles of poverty, detachment, and ministerial immersion in Christ. Because their active nursing ministry was, according to modern nursing standards, only custodial the Brothers' primary concern was to bring prayer to the bedsides of their patients. As spiritual guides to the sick and dying and as active participants in the burial rites, the Cellites were constantly in touch with the transient character of human existence.

As we have noted, the early Beghard Alexian did not view his life as divided between prayer and apostolic work. Brother Paul's life of poverty extended from the community house to the skid rows as a continuous bond of witness. Nursing the dying and burying the dead were active ministries through which Paul's evangelical spirituality touched those on the limits of existence. Because he nursed in homes rather than in a hospital, Brother Paul's spirituality was expressed in a personalist setting. Father David Tracy has elaborated on limit-situations and limit-language as a condition and form of expression which discloses a religious dimension, a sort of ontological closeness to the Divine Source of all being.[8] Brother Paul's religious world was ordered by poverty and his folk absorption of the varieties of mystical breezes in his climate. His ministries situated him on the boundaries where he not merely brought spirituality to his "patients" but must have partially formed his spirituality from those limit-situations. Two spiritual currents flowed through Paul's religious life—the general lay mendicant stream reflecting variations of culture and that stream which flowed from the subterranean depths of limit-situations. The encounter of "limit-spirituality" in his ministry appropriately blended with his mystical and evangelical character, which were also grounded in "limit-situations." His spirituality would likely be expressed in simple proverblike statements that were easily stored in his only reference source, his memory.[9] After reflecting on events in his life and how they affected his beliefs perhaps he would have said: "The people have departed from the word of God but the Lord touched the apostles and they dwelt in community. I too have been touched by the word of God and must be one of his apostles and, like them, seek my poverty community among the people. In my town are men who have been touched by this word and who bring the word to bedside and graveside. I have died in the Word; the world seems to be consumed by the worms of evil; I became a Beghard-Apostle to beg for bread as my poverty prayer. We Beghards have heard the preachers and Beguines who have also died in the Word and who utter his Word. Meister Eckhart has said it is better to bring a sick man broth than to dwell on the words of St. Paul; we bring broth and St. Paul to the sick and chant the words for the dead. These are harsh times, the Lord is calling for righteousness, he may soon come again. I hear his call from the lips of holy men and women, from my brethren in our Beghard house, and from the dying and the dead. *Ave . . . Pater Noster. . . .* Here is broth, listen to the Lord."

II

In the charismatic foundation periods of all religious orders the element of personal and cultural crisis is at least implicit. Benedict, Francis, Dominic, and Ignatius Loyola were translating their call to sanctity into the language of crisis, particularly since all of these founders identified their own personal sanctity with a particular medium (e.g., mendicant) through which the teachings of Christ would extend more deeply into their particular cultures. I have already suggested that the founding Alexian Brothers sensed a cultural crisis similar to Francis's vision of the walls of the church. Perhaps the original

Alexian lay mendicants envisioned their asceticism as a medium for society's religious regeneration. When they settled into their specific ministries they were apparently responding to the need for religious witness to the dying and dead who dwelt in urban poverty.

Because the ministry chapter contains an elaboration of this need-response situation, it is appropriate here that we limit our focus to the spiritual implications of this ministry. As nurse-ministers attending to the physical and spiritual needs of the dying and providing the dead with the prescriptive burial rites, these Beghard-Alexians were obviously dwelling in daily crisis situations.

As I noted earlier, the ministry was fulfilling a critical need, one recognized by prominent citizens of Cologne, Aachen, and Antwerp. In contrast to other religious men who were teachers, scholars, preachers, these dying and death ministers were called to "the limit" on a daily basis. When the Low Countries and the Rhineland were beset by famine, wars, and plague, the death motif began to dominate culture, and when the Black Death struck (1347–1350) the Cellite death ministry became crucial to the general welfare of the towns. This catastrophe was a profound test of their spiritual mettle. Obviously the Cellites had more than a sense of human daring; their "crisis-limit" spirituality compelled them to carry on their ministries throughout catastrophic periods.

Zeigler and Lea have stated that the Cellites were fellow travelers of the heretical flagellants.[10] Without specifying place, time, and particular flagellant group (there were various types) such statements cannot be taken seriously. It is certainly not impossible that as a group of flagellants wandered into Cologne, Aachen, or Antwerp, and publicly scourged themselves in the town square, one or two of the Cellites joined the group for the required 33½ days of penance. Perhaps they were in harmony with the anticlerical tendencies of these extremists. Richard Kieckhefer doubts the extent of heresy among the flagellants and has disproved the "Free Spirit" contagion within the movement. He concludes: "It is true that some of the sources speak of the flagellants as associating with 'beghards' or 'lollards.' But in the late Middle Ages these terms were commonly used as abusive terms for religious enthusiasts of all sorts; without specific evidence, it would be rash to assume that a 'beghard' was in fact a heretic of the Free Spirit though many historians tend to equate the terms."[11] Considering the penitential character of the Cellite ministry, it is logical to assume that they may have sympathized with aspects of flagellant spirituality, but because they were so vitally needed in the towns it is highly improbable that the Cellites would have participated generally in any itinerant movement.

The growth of the Cellites subsequent to the Black Death is well documented. The waves of plague that engulfed Europe in the second half of the fourteenth century led the Cellites to assume a primary character as plague-victim ministers, and we must presume that as plague ministers they were considered "outsiders," shunned by those who feared contagion. They seemed to have immersed themselves in the sacred and with a sort of apocalyptic enthusiasm infused the sacred into the profane world. Continuously encountering the social/cultural crisis of the Black Death and their personal crisis of harassment by church officials, their existence as a viable group was characterized by insecurity.

They were, therefore, groping for a communal spirituality in harmony with their original ideals and yet engendering the stability and respectability which would bring an element of routine into their prayer life. Because their ministry was so active any tendency toward a mystical prayer life was blunted, and this necessitated the need for a systematic prayer schedule. This growth and expansion also compelled them to seek practical forms of communal life through which they could protect themselves as permanent ministers to the dying and dead. And with expansion came property and all its potential conflicts with their poverty ideals.

In search of a way to reconcile these crises (ca. 1400–1460) they were touched by a fresh breeze of spirituality, the *Devotio Moderna.*

After Meister Eckhart's death in 1327 Rhineland mysticism

continued to flourish. "The Friends of God," particularly John Tauler (ca. 1300–1361) and Henry Suso (ca. 1300–1368), mark the continuity of Eckhartian spirituality. In the Low Countries, John Ruysbroeck (1293–1381) is an important spiritual light of the fourteenth century. Though some historians view him as the founder of a new school of spirituality in the Low Countries, Dom François Vandenbroucke sees him as "a disciple of the Rhineland mystics."[12] Thus, the spiritual climate similar to that which permeated the Cellite houses in Cologne and Aachen is also found in Antwerp. Scholars have noted the various distinctions between the Beguine mystics of the thirteenth century and those who followed Ruysbroeck in the fourteenth century, but with regard to the Cellites such distinctions were probably not manifest. The *Devotio Moderna* stressed such themes as contemplation of Christ's passion, the joys and sorrows of Mary, and meditations on the Our Father and Hail Mary. Gerard Groote (1384), as well as his famous disciple Thomas à Kempis, viewed the practical aspect of contemplation as the quest for perfect charity. The "imitation of the humanity of Christ" was achieved by detachment, contemplation of the divinity of Jesus, and the *vita caritatis*.[13]

The most vigorous practical church reformer of the Windesheim community was John Busch. As he stated in his *Liber de Reformatione*, "I have journeyed through and covered, since I took my vows [1427?], more than 6,000 miles, with 520 miles for the reform of divers monasteries, unto almost 100 cities, besides the villages lying around or between, and to more than 30 castles."[14] The fifteenth-century church desperately needed reform. Many religious houses had generally departed from any semblance of observance of the three principal vows. John Busch commented in the epilogue of his *Chronicon Windesheimse*:

> In our land, desert and barren and unfruitful, there was formerly no place for refuge, where [one] could be saved and could work [one's] own salvation, whether in the world or in Religion. For men and women, old and young, commonly trod the broad and easy way that leads to perdition. Few orders, save the Carthusians and a few

Cistercians, were then loyal to their Rule and their constitution; but rather, in almost every religious house, there were open transgressors ... of the Three Substantial Vows.[15]

Busch traveled throughout northern Germany and the Low Countries, frequently armed with secular power to aid him in compelling monasteries and nunneries to reform themselves according to the Windesheim ideal. During the 1450s he worked closely with the reform efforts of Cardinal Nicholas of Cusa.[16] The latter was not only concerned with reform in the religious communities but also in popular piety, forbidding certain popular devotions which were tinged with superstition.[17]

This monastic reform movement, which urged a strict observance of the vows, detachment from worldly goods, and a harmonious blend of contemplation and active apostolate, no doubt influenced the Cellites in their pursuit of religious-order status, the profession of vows, and the adoption of the Augustinian rule. John Busch, the first visitator of the Cellite house at Hildesheim, has left us a remarkably long and detailed account of the entire Cellite way of life. Because it contains a singular witness to Cellite existence of the fifteenth century it is worthy of quoting in its entirety.

All those brothers are laymen, unlearned and without education, unless one has learned how to read or to write before he joined the Order. For all of them were shoemakers, or tailors or practiced some other craft before. This is why they have no priest or father with them in the house, but they select one from their own community as their superior, whom they call procurator everywhere. He has the right of a father to give orders to all as to what they should do or omit. They promise him obedience according to St. Augustine's rule. The procurator provided each one with all things necessary for clothing and living subsistence. There are no revenues on account of their being voluntary poor; they have no money or property, but they live from the alms of the faithful, begging from door to door. For daily they go through the streets of the town two by two, one day these streets the other day other streets, begging from door to door. They do not enter the houses, but remain outside [saying] in German "Brot um Gottes Willen" [Bread for God's sake]. Often they get something often they do not, in which case one hears "Gott berate euch" [May God take care of you]. Often they take the gifts cheerfully and often shamefully, if they have entered the Order recently.

But in this manner and in all the other actions they learn to deny their own will, to control their nature and get rid of their false shame. The gifts thus collected they consume with gratitude to God in common in the refectory. The citizens as a whole have much affection for them and show them many favours, since they sit up with the sick of all kinds of infirmities, waiting on them by day and night until death, rendering them the services necessary, comforting them in all good things and assisting them in their agony against the attacks of the devil. They dress the corpses and embellish them, providing everything necessary for the burial; they carry the corpses to the grave and bury them. On account of their care for the sick and the dead and their provisions for the funeral, they are of great help in the cities. Although they render such works of mercy to all by whom they are requested, they live in their houses and churches according to very strict regulations. For they rise after midnight for morning prayer which each individual says silently with the Lord's prayer in their fashion in the little chapel of their house. All kneel down straight without leaning against something. After the morning prayer they make their meditation on the life and passion of our Lord Jesus Christ; for almost two solid hours they remain on their knees unless they stand up a little while for relief. After the meditation they return to their cells and go to bed for a little rest. Between four and five o'clock in the morning they rise again and betake themselves to their mother church, i.e., the church of the secular canons, in order to assist there at Matins. They take their seats in the rear of the church under the tower at the place assigned to them and pray there the little hours, i.e., a fixed number of Pater Nosters. For two or three hours they assist at Matins, the Masses, and the other canonical hours kneeling all the time on their knees. Then they resume their meditation on the life and passion of our Lord Jesus Christ, where they interrupted them during the night. Without reluctance and distraction of mind they meditate on these mysteries and shape their life accordingly. By doing that they find great joy of heart, knowledge of God, tranquility of all emotions, tranquility and peace of the conscience. It seems marvellous that they are able to devote themselves to meditation in the throng of people, kneeling daily upright without leaning back, and yet not suffering from headache or exhaustion of the body. Their spiritual exercises are not written, but one learns them from the other, and yet they are everywhere the same in Cologne as well as in Saxony. They have abandoned the love of this world and everything dear to the world. To meditate on those things, they think it worthless; on the contrary they meditate on God, on their good spiritual exercises without real distraction. They are able to do so, because they are simple lay people without education, and because their heads are not filled with all kind of things and ideas. They do not worry about the next day, because the good Lord provides for them and will never allow that they should lack anything. For clergymen or learned men it is impossible to concentrate on one subject in this manner and for such a long time every day and every night without fatigue, much less to dwell on one and the same point with the greatest joy of heart, as these simple lay people do, who are despised by the world and despise the world and everything belonging to it for the love of God. This is why they obtain from God, the remunerator of all good deeds, undoubtedly a magnificent crown of victory due to their extreme poverty and purity of heart, their faithful and voluntary service rendered to their neighbors in their dire distress. At the end of the spiritual exercises, for which they remained in the church, they go home together. Then the procurator will tell them through which particular street they should go begging, appointing the individuals, because today they walk through one street or two, tomorrow through others. When they arise in the morning they do not yet know what they will have to eat at breakfast or supper, only that the Lord will provide. After breakfast the brothers apply themselves to manual labour, which they practice at home, except for those brothers who have to wait on the sick in the town. At the time of Vespers all go again to the mother church and say Vespers with a Pater Noster and spiritual exercises. After an hour or two they return home again and get ready for supper. This will be taken in silence, which they also observe at breakfast, and after a short spiritual reading in German and when the procurator after a little while gives the sign, those who are able to do so, say their night prayer in the chapel each one for himself. There they remain a full hour devoting themselves to their usual spiritual exercises and meditations, all the time kneeling straight without leaning back. For in their chapels they do not have seats, footstools or pews. At the sign of the procurator all arise and go to sleep, in order to rise again at midnight for the praise of God. When going to church they do not leave behind anybody to guard the house, since they possess nothing save their clothes and furniture. Detached from the world and without unnecessary solicitude, they are able to devote themselves entirely to their God and Lord during the divine service.[18]

R. R. Post, who has done extensive research on the *Devotio Moderna*, confirms the general reliability of Busch's report, "although he [Busch] was not ... above a certain distortion in his own favor."[19] Busch does seem to have painted a rather idyllic picture of the Cellite way of life. Even if he does exaggerate, his writings nevertheless contain an extremely valuable survey of Cellite prayer and work. Their traditional "Brot durch Gott" mendicant prayer was still their "trademark." The stress on poverty was present but because of its routinization into a schedule its evangelical character appears to have been restrained. Their original stress upon poverty was indicative to Busch of detachment and he seems to regard the nursing ministry as secondary to Cellite spirituality and rule observance. He testifies to their personal nursing in the homes of the sick as well as their participation in the funeral and burial rites, ministries which had gained the respect of the communities. In contrast to his extensive commentary on Cellite spirituality and the observance of the rules and customs of their rule, these remarks on their ministry appear introductory tidbits of information. A strand of anti-intellectualism, slightly characteristic of the *Devotio Moderna*, surfaces in Busch's remarks on the inability of "clergymen or learned men" to meditate joyfully on one subject. He seems to idealize the "simplicity" of the Brothers in a rather paternalistic tone. The Brothers dwelt in quiet, in prayers, models of uncluttered devotion.

Busch was in accord with the "learned ignorance" theology of Nicholas of Cusa, which stressed man's incapacity to journey rationally through the divine world of mystery. As a paramount leader in the New Devotion, Nicholas also admired the "childlike" vision of those who sought God unencumbered with theological baggage. E. F. Jacob views this attitude as characteristic of the *Devotio Moderna*. "This attitude of Cusanus is extremely significant. It illustrates the fact that the leaders of the Devotio Moderna ... strove to escape the formulae of the schools, and to resort, not to the application of normal dialectical methods to the problem of religion, but, without any underrating of the intellect, to the practice of a deep intellectual humility. ..."[20] Jacob places this drive for intellectual humility within the Eckhartian tradition and implicitly provides a clue as to why the Brothers may have unconsciously sensed some continuity between Eckhart and the New Devotion. To substantiate his parallel, Jacob quotes Eckhart's advice to those who had difficulty comprehending his sermons: "To understand my sermons a man requires three things. He must have conquered strife, and be in contemplation of the highest good, and be satisfied to do God's bidding, and to be a beginner with beginners and naught himself, and be so master of himself as to be incapable of anger."[21]

III

The first record to confirm Busch's testimony of Cellite community prayer life appeared in the 1460s and 1470s when the bishops of Tournai and Liège imposed "constitutions" upon the newly professed Brothers. Louis de Bourbon, who brought the Aachen Brothers under his authority in 1469, directed them to follow specific rules for prayer. Instead of Matins and Vespers each Brother was to recite fifteen Our Fathers and Hail Marys and instead of Prime, Terce, Sext, None, and Compline, seven Our Fathers and Hail Marys should be said for each of these canonical hours: at Prime and Compline one *Credo in Deum* and *Credo in Spiritum Sanctum* should be added to the regular prayers.[22] The substitution of *Aves* and *Pater Nosters* for the Divine Office stemmed from the practices common to the *converso* lay brothers of the larger religious orders such as the Cistercians.[23] It is interesting to note that when the Hospitallers of St. John of God, which was an order of nursing lay brothers founded in late sixteenth-century Spain, adopted a regularized prayer day they also substituted *Aves* and *Paters* for the Divine Office.[24] One should avoid imposing contemporary attitudes toward rote prayers upon these oral-culture Cellites. The *Ave* and *Pater Noster* were absorbed into their memories as sacred utterances which were capable of invoking the presence of God and Mary in a much more profound sense than they would for today's literate person reciting the rosary. The oral-folk perspective did not contain a strong sense of time and space. The *Ave* and *Pater Noster* were not devotions but rituals.

The *Devotio Moderna* frequently emphasized stringent observance of rules and constitutions as if they were ends in themselves. Busch tended to such extremism when he commended the rigid posture of the Cellite contemplatives at prayer as if it were a sign of sanctity. The *Devotio Moderna* was so dedicated to the proper methods of developing the interior life that many of its exponents omitted the sanctity of the exterior ministerial life. Thomas à Kempis, the most famous example of the new *Devotio*, wrote of the conflict between the world of mental prayer and the created world. "If you look at creation, the Creator withdraws from you."[25] Perhaps this explains why John Busch's description of the Cellite way of life conspicuously deemphasized the nursing and burial ministries, as if this work were a mere sideline for the Brothers.

The Brothers were considered heroic because they came into contact with that most feared phenomenon, the Black Death. Their ministry may have also compelled them to grope for a spirituality suitable to withdrawal. It is impossible to discern which of these came first: a spirituality of withdrawal into cloisters with a rule and the profession of vows, or the practical organizational problem of forming viable structures. It is very likely that the two occurred simultaneously and that they shifted from the *via media* to the *via religiosa* as a response to spiritual and temporal crises.

The temporal crisis is embodied in the question "How does one persist as a poverty-community in the condition of expansion?" while the spiritual crisis expresses itself in the question "How does one persist as a 'poor of Christ' minister in the face of so much criticism from church authorities?" The answers gradually emerged: by professing vows, regularizing prayer life, gaining recognition by Rome, withdrawing into a contemplative cloister, and carrying on the ministries with detachment and moderation. This shift from a religious movement to a religious order implied a profound transformation of their spirituality and their temporal way of life. Their original commitment appears to have been to permeate the profane world with their sacred *pauperes Christi* ideals and ministry, apparently guided by an apocalyptic vision of the imminence of the Second Coming. The plague ironically seems to have verified such a vision at the same time as it resulted in their expansion. They ultimately reconciled this and the harassment crises by suppressing the apocalyptic vision in favor of explicit withdrawal into monastic enclosure. In that they no longer were driven by the *pauperes Christi* idealism of radical poverty, they were tacitly accepting the world on its own terms and withdrawing into monastic enclosure where their personal covenant with God could be nourished in regularized prayer. The original zeal to place the sacred into the profane may still have been a strong motivating factor in the ministries, but the sense of urgency was no longer present.

They had avoided the cloister because it appeared to be founded on a decadent compromise with worldly possessions. Theirs had been an existence wrapped in evangelical mystery. Post-plague problems compelled them to compromise their original *via media* ideals, but as they embarked on this new path they were refreshed with a new spirituality, one which stressed the *vita apostolica* foundations of the religious life and one which was a development of their original Beguine-Beghard élan. The continuity of their origins was symbolized by the persistence of their mendicant and ministerial activities. A routine prayer life and the personal-piety character of the *Devotio Moderna* imposed at least potential restraints upon many of their original characteristics, i.e, their spontaneity, their evangelism, and their uncomplicated identification of slum dwellers as their community. Perhaps the intensification of their self-consciousness as individuals withdrawn from the town community was the most significant break with the past. The Beghard immersed himself into a *pauperes Christi* mystery-existence; the Cellite joined a religious order and, though "mystery" was a vibrant dimension of his way of life, directives from Windesheim accented the common problem of individual dedication to religious life. One receives the impression from Busch's commentary that he was not referring to the Cellite corporate community. On the contrary, he seems to view the Cellite spirituality as an aggregate of individual piety.

In a very real sense the spiritual evolution of the Cellites from their *pauperes Christi* Beghard origins to Cellite religious-order status reflects the evolution of culture from the high to the late Middle Ages. The profound adversities of the fourteenth century—war, famine, plague—generally intensified the consciousness of the precariousness of existence. Death motifs dominated the fifteenth century and produced a quest for new forms of security. The *Devotio Moderna*, with its simple directives for piety and meditation, illustrates one aspect of this quest. Certainly, the struggle for Cellite survival motivated the Brothers to secure moorings as a religious order. Popular piety on the eve of the Reformation was partially characterized by a frenzied search for recipes of salvation in traditional pilgrimages, indulgences, and cults of the saints. The late Middle Ages appears as a time of "confusion of tongues";[26] there were diverse alternative paths for security proposed, all unified by the general gloom pervading the era.

IV

In the late fifteenth century, when the Cellites were dedicating their chapels to St. Alexius (particularly the Aachen Chapel), the Brothers were first called Alexian Brothers. The stories of St. Alexius reveal a thread of Cellite spirituality which was appropriate to the general pattern of the fifteenth century.

The relationship between St. Alexius and Cellites appears to hark back to the community's origins in the *vita apostolica*. The story of St. Alexius the beggar, the man of God, had strong appeal to those voluntarily poor brothers who begged "Brot durch Gott." Until recently the most commonly accepted narrative of the saint's life placed his birth in Rome during the fifth-century reigns of emperors Honorius and

Arcadius.[27] His parents, Euphemian and Algas, had been child-less. When he reached the age to marry, his parents chose a princess to be his wife. Immediately after the wedding cele-bration, when normally the bride and groom would enter their nuptial chambers, Alexius took flight from Rome and sailed to Syria. He then journeyed to Edessa in Syria where he assumed the life of a beggar at the door of a church dedicated to Mary. Though his father's servants traced him to Edessa they did not recognize him among the city beggars. Apparently years went by before his identity became known; a voice came from the image of the Madonna directing the church custodian to "see to it that the man at the door come in. He is worthy of the kingdom of heaven; the spirit of the Lord rests upon him, and his prayers have ascended like incense in the sight of the Most High." Humbly, Alexius shunned the notoriety; he began a journey to the city of St. Paul, Tarsus in Celicia. However, Providence intervened in the form of a storm which directed the ship to Ostia, the nearest port to Rome, whence Alexius made his way to the Aventine Hill, where his parents lived. He met his father but Euphemian did not recognize the ill-clothed sickly beggar as his son. Euphemian did respond to Alexius's plea for alms, brought him to his house, presented him with a room under the stairs, and employed him as a servant. After seventeen years of hard work and inconspicuous humility Alexius died. Immediately the bells of Rome tolled for his death and a voice from heaven uttered, "Seek the man of God, that he may pray for Rome." From St. Peter's Basilica these words resounded throughout the city and guided the Romans to the room below Euphemian's palace stairs where Alexius lay dead holding a scroll on which he had written an account of his mendicant life. Hearing the news, Alexius's parents and wife burst into tears. He was granted a saint's burial; his body placed first in St. Peter's Basilica and many centuries later brought to the Church of St. Boniface on the Aventine Hill.[28]

The oldest account of the *Mar Riscia*, i.e., the man of God, is of Syrian origin. Written in the sixth century, this story tells of a wealthy Roman who on his wedding night set out for

Edessa, became a beggar, and died there during the episcopate of Bishop Robbula (412–435); when the church custodian heard that the holy man had been buried in Potter's Field, he urged the bishop to grant him a proper burial. Opening his grave, they discovered that the man of God's body had been miraculously removed. There is no mention of the Roman's name; he was called merely *Mar Riscia*.[29]

Within a few centuries another similar story appeared, one which was developed in Byzantium. John was a rich young Roman who met a Byzantine monk, a guest in his parents' home. Later John secretly left Rome to enter a monastic community. Though he was accepted by the monks, a heavenly voice urged him to seek the blessings of his parents before he died. His superior sent him back to Rome and John appeared at his parents' home dressed as a beggar. They did not recognize him but charitably provided him with a small hut (Calybe). There John lived and shortly before he died he revealed his true identity. After his death a large church was constructed on the spot where he had lived a beggar's existence, and St. John Calybite was buried there.[30] Because the various Alexius stories contain a blend of both the *Mar Riscia* and the St. John Calybite story, some scholars conclude that Alexius is a legendary figure whose appearance in the West can not be accurately dated before the tenth century. From the tenth through the fifteenth centuries, narratives of the life of St. Alexius appeared in every European language, some deriving their origin from Greek sources, others from the Latin. The Bollandist authors of the eighteenth century, who did not note the great divergences among the narratives, wrote the life of St. Alexius according to the common story, i.e., St. Alexius under the stairs. Modern scholarship is divided on the proper interpretation of the various Alexius texts: the Syriac, the Byzantine, and the Western Greek and Latin. Among the recent scholars only Father Louis Zamborelli holds to the traditional account found in the Bollandist writing, stating that oral tradition would never have successfully passed on the story had it not been grounded in durable fact.[31]

C. E. Stabbins, who has done the most recent research on

the origins of the legend, concludes that it probably originated in Greece. However, he calls for further research into the exact origin of the story which, because it has attracted so many scholars, illustrates the "eternal vigor" of "L'homme de Dieu."[32]

Monsignor A. P. Frutaz, who authored the "St. Alexis" article for the 1967 edition of the *Catholic Encyclopedia*, sided with those who question the authenticity of the popular Bollandist-Zambarelli interpretation. Monsignor Frutaz stated in a 1967 letter to the superior general of the Alexians that, of the various legends, the Syriac is the most reliable. Based on a sixth-century manuscript, this account "speaks of an anonymous person who left Rome the evening of his wedding to go to Edessa where he led an ascetic life under the episcopacy of Robbula (415–435). For myself, this man of God [who later had been baptized 'Alexius'] existed. It is not the question of a mythical person."[33] Because the sainthood of Alexius was based upon unreliable oral tradition, the Vatican removed him from the Roman hagiography. If we assume that the "man of God" did indeed exist and lived a saintly life, then this patron of the Cellites appears to be more in harmony with their tradition than the popular St. Alexius under the stairs.

The vast popularity of the legend during the period that witnessed the proliferation of so many *vita apostolica* groups iluustrates the close relationship between the layman saint and these apostolic lay communities. According to tradition, Peter Waldo, the poor man of Lyons who was ultimately excommunicated, was converted to a life of poverty after hearing a minstrel sing a ballad of the life of St. Alexius (ca. 1170). Indeed the spirituality of the *vita apostolica*, particularly that of the Cellites, contained many themes in common with the legend of St. Alexius. The self-styled mendicant existence of the ancient "man of God," his anonymity, and his utter detachment from the luxurious life of Rome have blended to form the model for the Cellites.

Aachen was particularly devoted to St. Alexius. On his feast day, July 17, pilgrims from all over would flock to a festival held in the Aachen cathedral square. Thus, when the communities of Cologne, Aachen, and Antwerp took St. Alexius as the patron of their chapels they had developed a strong devotion to him long before they had become a religious order. It is fitting, therefore, that Alexius, a man of God, should travel for centuries with those who choose his life—one of anonymity, dependence upon God, and charity alone for livelihood.

8

Ministry to the Outsider

Before launching a long narrative of Cellite ministries, we should have a grasp of the scriptural and early Christian roots of the term "ministry." We are accustomed to the traditional church dichotomy—clergy and laity, as if the layperson's only distinction is not to be clergy. Robert McAfee Brown has pointed out that *kleros* and *laos* are used in the New Testament *"to describe the same people*, the whole people of God."[1] *Diakonio* originally referred to a person who waited on tables but "gradually came to mean one who serves others, one who ministers."[2] Just as *kleros* and *laos* in the New Testament converged to mean the people of God, so in the early church every Christian dwelt in *diakonio*, in the ministry of the church. Brown employs Hendrik Kraemer's phrase "the Church is ministry."[3] This ministry manifests itself through the clergy and through lay ministers. *"There are not two different ministries. They are two forms of the same ministry."*[4] Brown refers to 1 Corinthians 12:4–7:

> Now there are varieties of gifts, but the same Spirit; and there are varieties of service but the same Lord, and there are varieties of working; but it is the same God who inspires them all in everyone. To each is given the manifestation of the spirit for the common good.[5]

By the time the Beghards and Lollards entered the scene, this identification between church and ministry had been replaced by the notion that the church possesses ministry and that only the ordained clergy exercise that ministry. The original Alexians who responded to the gospel invitation to ministry appear to have been self-consciously departing from this dichotomy between laity and clergy.[6]

I

The theme woven throughout the narrative of the Beghard-Lollard origins is that these oral-folk Brothers were scripturally and charismatically motivated to witness to Christian poverty. Though their begging and nursing were objectively nonsacramental activities, the charism of the founding Brothers seems to have directed them to identify their total *pauperes Christi* existence as a sacrament. Thus, to say that the original Cellites were social workers is to impose the modern upon the medieval. To conclude that they merely adopted nursing as a well-rationalized apostolate is to impose the literal upon the oral. To see them as nascent members of the urban proletariat is to make the social the determinant of the religious. The evangelistic, mystical, and communal traits of the *vita apostolica* lead one to conclude that the oral-folk Brothers were primarily ministers.

The development of the Cellite ministries is best understood by applying the challenge-response theory to the first century of their existence. Because there is no definite Cellite birthday, it is necessary to trace their ancestry by examining those earlier *pauperes Christi* groups that responded to challenges in an analogous way. The *pauperes Christi* movement, as we have seen, originated in the Gregorian reform period (late eleventh to early twelfth centuries) when the laity in general became more actively involved in the service of the church. Hans Wolter succinctly describes their motivation: "Prominent among the motives of the *vita apostolica* was the example of Christ as healer and helper: the *pauperes Christi* wanted to become poor in order to succour others in their necessities."[7]

The social consequences of the Crusades, ranging from "disabled veterans" to the utterly destitute, provided a major challenge to these healers and helpers. A variety of groups responded to the critical challenges, which were compounded by the growth of towns: Canons Regular and the Norbertines (Premonstratensions) sponsored many forms of charity; hospital confraternities under the direction of these and other religious orders sprang up; military orders such as the Teutonic Knights Templar, the order of Lazarus and the Hospitallers, founded many types of health-care institutions; and some *pauperes Christi* formed themselves into communities and attached themselves to hospitals and almshouses. As towns developed communal organization they established municipal charity institutions. Though the latter were frequently administered by town authority, the role of the church was preserved through diocesan responsibility for the spiritual care of the patients and through the religious who cared for the sick. The original (pre-Black Death) Cellites were in the tradition of the *pauperes Christi* healers and helpers, particularly in their commitment to a radical notion of poverty.[8]

After the Black Death these Beghards and Lollards were engaged in a variety of ministries, but the most common and unifying ministerial expression was the care and burial of pest victims. This leads one to wonder whether in the pre-plague days these early Brothers had already been administering to those people whose diseases marked them as untouchable. Their *pauperes Christi* ideals implicitly clashed with the ecclesiastical structures and marked them as outsiders. It is not surprising, therefore, that they gravitated to helping and healing the diseased outsiders. No doubt, plague victims were treated as lepers. The latter were isolated into colonies—of which there were over two thousand in thirteenth-century France. There was a refined ritual for the leper's passage from his community to the colony:

> The unhappy man, dressed in a shroud, is carried to the Church on a litter by four priests singing the psalm, "Libera me." Inside the church the litter is set down at a safe distance from the congregation. The service for the dead is read. Then, again singing the psalm, the

143

clergy carry the leper out of the Church, through the streets, out of town, to the leper colony. He is given a pair of castanets, a pair of gloves, and a bread basket. After the singing of the "De Profundis" the priest intones, "Ses mortuus mundo, vivens iterum Deo" (Be thou dead to this world, living again to God), concluding "I forbid you ever to enter a Church or a monastery, a mill, a bakery, a market, or anyplace there is an assemblage of people. I forbid you to quit your house without your leper's costume and castanets. I forbid you to bathe yourself or your possessions in stream, or fountain, or spring. I forbid you to have commerce with any woman except her whom you have married in the Holy Church. I forbid you if anyone speaks to you on the road to answer till you have placed yourself below the winds."[9]

II

Those early documents that refer to the Beghards in Cologne and Aachen and the Lollards of Antwerp provide pieces of information which suggest their particular *vita caritatis*. We have seen that after the archbishop of Cologne closed the Lungenbrüder house (1307), identifying its members as *apostolici* heretics, members of the town nobility successfully pressed for the reopening of the Beghard house, recognizing their valuable services to the community. The Cologne Brothers first appeared at the end of the thirteenth century living in the cemetery of St. Mauritius' Church. In 1306 a priest, John of Krefeld, purchased a home on the Lungengasse as a gift to the Beghard Nicholas. An earlier document refers to a priest and a Beghard as procurators of a hospital in Cologne,[10] which could have been Father John and Beghard Nicholas. Because the office of procurator was a salaried position within the city administration, perhaps through savings and money gifts they were able to purchase their home in 1306. It is also likely that this penetration of the Cologne "welfare system" allowed the Beghards to assert some influence among the town patricians, who pressed for the reopening of their house in 1308. Regardless, it is very probable that the Beghard who was procurator of the hospital was a Brot-Beghard later of the Lungenbrüder community, and that other Beghards cared for the sick of that hospital, and perhaps in the town pest houses as well as in the homes of the critically ill or diseased "outsiders."

The earliest document referring to the Aachen Brothers is a notice of alms in 1334.[11] Some time after 1343 when a former castle was taken over by the Aachen city council for use as a hospital, four Brothers were assigned there as nurses to the "Pestkranken"[12] (plague victims). It seems, therefore, that the relationship between the city council and the Aachen Brothers may have preceded the Black Death and that the Brothers were more or less official city nurses, particularly to the outsiders.

When Henry Suderman gave his house to the Antwerp Lollards in 1345 he placed them under the control of the city council. Though these Lollards appeared as a threat to the church establishment, the secular authorities even before the Black Death absorbed them into their charity system.

Recognition by the town councils in the form of monetary support (Aachen, 1334), moral support (Cologne, 1308, etc.), and legal support (Antwerp, 1345) illustrates that from the earliest period the Brothers were not merely respected but were, in various ways, the responsibility of these political authorities. Each of these three communities had established residences, thereby removing themselves from the "floating" population. A house provided them with solid links to the town. From the bishops' chanceries these pious lay mendicants may have appeared as threats to orthodoxy and stability, while the city hall recognized them as members of a house of charity. This conflict between church and secular authorities first surfaced in Cologne in 1308. One may recall the problems of the Cologne house in 1326 when the Brothers asked certain patricians to assume the role of procurator. Asen interpreted this as indicative of the Brothers' need for protection against church harassment.[13] Neumann disagrees; she maintains that the house had probably fallen into debt or was in some way inefficiently carrying out its responsibilities to the city—actions which demanded the city council to take a direct hand in the management of the Brothers' affairs.[14] Regardless of which interpretation is correct, the fact that the city council was directly involved in the governance of the house (analogous to Suderman and the city council of Antwerp) indicates the then current trend in municipal government toward overseeing all forms of charitable work. Though town administrations were primitive by today's standards, the Brothers were semi-officials of the local government.

Perhaps by listening to our fictional Brother Paul as if he were appearing before the Cologne or Aachen city councils or before Henry Suderman, his Antwerp patron, to express his gratitude for this support, the life of the pre-Black Death Brothers may be clarified.

"Before we settled into our home we journeyed from town to town. We had heard the gospel words and those of Francis to live a life of poverty and to dwell with and serve the poor. We bring the words of Jesus to the sick and the dying; we urge them to repent; we pray with them as we bring a cup of broth and try to make them more comfortable. We are dead to the world; when people die sometimes we are called to prepare the body for burial and to participate in the burial rites. Some of us go to the hospital, and pest houses; others go to the homes of the sick. We have heard the word and have no other choice but to live the word. The poor people trust us because we are poor and we ask nothing from them. We are not church people but gospel people. We live together as Brothers; we bring the love of Jesus to our poor brothers, and we await the coming of Jesus.

"Some church people fear us because they do not understand the gospel. You have helped us because we try to help you to help the poor. We are not heroes; we thank you for your gifts but remind you that you too must repent. These are troublesome days—famine, wars, men without work—we do not understand the ways of God but we have heard that the Kingdom of God is near."

III

When the Black Death struck, it appeared to many as the end of the world. "Witches' " graves were opened to appease revenging spirits.[15] Belief in demons prevailed throughout fourteenth-century society in "normal" times (theologians and popes testified to powers derived from witchcraft).[16] How much more credible were such *incubi* and *succubi* in plague times. George Deaux remarks: "In describing the plague, the chroniclers of the Church repeatedly write at length about demons as well as mysterious markings on walls, voices from the grave presaging disasters, and improbable celestial phenomena, many of which must have been the result of the sort of delirium the plague sometimes induces."[17]

The moral decline of the fourteenth-century church is no longer a controversial issue. There are numerous documents evidencing simoniacal abuses of episcopal authority, clerical concubinage, and monastic violations of the three evangelical counsels. One chronicle of 1348 contains this bitter criticism: "Simony has become so prevalent among the clergy . . . it looks as if the Lord had not driven the buyers and sellers from the Temple, but rather invited them to remain there."[18] The satirical tales told by Boccaccio and Chaucer expressed the popular attitudes toward the clergy's pastoral irresponsibility. The flagellants represented extreme atonement for the sins which caused the plague, but they also frequently engaged in anticlerical protest. G. G. Coulton examined twenty-two chroniclers for evidence of clerical behavior during the Black Death; only a few comment on the bravery of some friars and nurses and even these are mixed with criticism of the parish priests. The vast majority are "frankly and sometimes violently unfavourable."[19] Though the clergy were probably just as irresponsible as their secular counterparts—town counselors, doctors, bureaucrats—the testimony contained in the chronicles represents the popular anticlerical attitudes of the day. The following quotations from the chroniclers illustrate the general behavior toward plague victims.

"Many were buried for money by vile persons, without priests, without candles" (*Chron. Padua*, 626). ". . . Neither priest nor friar went with them [the dead], nor was funeral service said" (*DiTura*, 123). "And the sick were abandoned by servants, doctors, notaries, priests, and friars, so that the plague-stricken wretches were neither tended nor healed, nor could they make their wills nor die confessed or absolved" (*Parma Murat* XII, 746).[20]

Among the heroic nurses and burial sisterhoods and brotherhoods only the Alexian Brothers were so clearly marked by their ministries during the plague. During the century after the Black Death the Brothers expanded to form a network of at least thirty-six houses and in almost every town they were designated as burial Brothers, with particular rights of burial for the pest victims. This could never have become their unique feature had their service during the Black Death not been widely and popularly acclaimed.

The evangelistic and apocalyptic tendencies of many groups in the *vita apostolica* may have touched the Brotherhood and prepared them to face what appeared as the end of the world. Prior to the outbreak of the Black Death, the Brothers must have had many experiences with funeral and burial customs as ministers—participants and religious witnesses. If we are to penetrate the religious folk-view of death and their ministries to the dying and dead, it is necessary to examine popular theological notions, folk beliefs, and customs which form a rough picture of the way they may have coped with the problem and mystery of death.

Judeo-Christian belief, based on the sin of Adam, has persistently viewed sickness and death in terms of the consequences of sin. Though by the fourteenth century the theology of redemption had been well refined, popular devotion, the hell-fire sermons of the typical preachers, and the superstition of the day veered away from the redemptive Christ and stressed instead the God of final judgment. If one were to judge popular attitudes by the preachers' sermons, one would assume fear and trembling among the people. However, for those who have studied the death-notions in art and literature, a different image emerges.

Walter Rehm has traced the evolution of the concept of death, and has distinguished between high medieval and late medieval ideals and sensibilities. In the high Middle Ages the concept of death was articulated as suprapersonal; it was considered a fact of *collective experience*. There was a fear of second death in eternal damnation, but death itself was accepted with little or no rebellion. Laymen viewed death as a loss of earthly goods but did not perceive it as a private affair. Rather, it was an event within the drama of community existence. Nor did the layman form an abstract notion of death; instead he regarded it frequently in benign terms. The monastic ideal was embodied in Pope Innocent's *Contemptus Mundi*: "Life is death and death is the beginning of life." The mystical ideal stressed a longing for union with God, not an embrace of death. In general, according to Rehm, death was thought and felt to be the inevitable collective experience within the dogma of the church.[21] Phillipe Ariès refers to this attitude as "Tamed Death." He describes the traditional death scene as public, with specifically prescribed rites—"death was familiar and near, evoking no great fear or awe."[22] The tameness of death was symbolized in the social-religious events which took place in the *atrium* of the church, that area later referred to as the cemetery.[23] This intermingling of the living with the dead appears to verify Rehm's stress upon the collective, communal notions of death. The fact that there were many common graves—particularly among the poor—also supports a collective rather than a private and individualized modern concept of extinction. "As yet unborn was the modern idea that the dead person should be installed in a sort of house unto himself, a house of which he was the perpetual owner or at least a long term tenant. . . ."[24]

Rehm shifts to the late medieval ideas and feelings toward death, and in contrast to the unifying element of the previous period, he says that the fourteenth and fifteenth centuries were characterized by diversity. Though death was still expressed in harmony with church dogma there was a growing disunity. The Black Death was the catalyst of these changes. Experiences with the horrors of the pest encouraged the conceptualization of death. The daily encounter with so many plague-stricken people created callousness; a sense of indifference prevailed. Death as personal Lord and Warrior gave way to an anonymous Mr. Death. Late medieval culture, characterized by its extreme formalism, was expressed in death-thoughts, i.e., traditional church dogma mingled with the modern private-individual notions of the "last moment." Mysticism evolved from a flight to the Beatific Vision to the embrace of death, i.e., the posture of St. Francis and Dante (the latter imagery gained popularity in the postplague period). The conflict between the mystical embrace and the layperson's callousness toward death strengthened the view of the late medieval period as one of extreme tension. Rehm concludes that the unifying element amid this diversity was the didactic character of the preachers and of contemporary religious art and literature. Death was no longer a respected event in the community's mystery drama—it tended to become an abstract problem to be solved by the individual.[25]

Ariès refers to the beginning of modern attitudes during this period in his chapter appropriately titled "My Death." To illustrate the evolution toward the postmedieval portrayal of death as an individual, private happening, Ariès examines the changes in the artist's conception of the last judgment. He contrasts the tomb sculpture of Bishop Agilbert (ca. 680), which depicted the Last Judgment as the collective resurrection of all Christians, with the art of the twelfth and thirteenth centuries, which focuses on the Divine Judge scrutinizing the individual's *liber vitae*—book of life—before meting out eternal justice. Though "my death" notions do not prevail until much later, Ariès views the thirteenth century *liber vitae* symbol and its supportive eschatology as the point of origin of such notions.[26]

Speculation on early Cellite attitudes toward death includes a review of their spirituality as the first step in understanding the ideals of their ministries. It has been suggested earlier that Beguine and Eckhartian mysticism flowed through the Brot-

Beghard and Lollard communities. Meister Eckhart's eschatology is more easily understood by what he didn't stress than by what he actually said on divine judgment. His view of holiness was never associated with the avoidance of sin because of fear of God's wrath; he stressed neither purgatory nor hell. Rather Eckhart emphasized the continuous flow of God's mercy:

"Indeed, if you could in a short time renounce sin so vigorously, with such true disgust, and turn so whole-heartedly toward God, even if you had committed all the sins that had occurred since Adam's time and those that are yet to come, it would be completely forgiven you together with the punishment, so that if you were to die now, you would go into the presence of God."[27] This vision of God's forgiveness would seem to run contrary to the *liber vitae* symbolism that was gaining momentum during Eckhart's lifetime. His view of the redemption, which he considered an ever present reality rather than a historical event, could have had a strong appeal to those committed to the *vita apostolica* who viewed their *pauperes Christi* ideals as invoking the sacramental presence of the Redeemer. Eckhart stressed the collective consequences of redemption. "You can also remember that God was the common Redeemer of the whole world. I owe him much more gratitude for this than if He had saved me alone."[28] Men should never allow themselves to consider their distance from God. Whatever a man does or wills to do, "God never goes far; He always remains standing near and if He cannot remain within, He still does not go farther away than just outside the door."[29]

The original Alexians probably shared the layperson's perspective on death as a collective experience. Though, unlike ordinary laity, they had renounced all property, they probably did not have a concept of "my death" but, rather, saw death in concrete terms as Lord or Hunter of all men. They could have possessed a more intensely Christian awareness of how death opens the door to a collective sharing in the redemption, but as they wandered through a cemetery they may have had the common folk sensitivity that the living and the dead form their own Christian communities. If they had that sense of the final apocalypse so common to many *vita apostolica* groups, then they saw death in cosmic terms; "my death" would have been consumed within the vision of death as the final collective act of human history. If it was more particularly expressed in the prophecies of Joachim of Fiore, then they would have meshed their notion of death into the imminence of the age of the Holy Spirit.

From the time of the early church to the eighth and ninth centuries, anointing the sick was supervised by the church and frequently administered by laymen. With the Carolingian reform came the elevation of anointing to the status of a sacrament, thereby restricting its administration to priests. The sacrament was then linked with penance of the sick and Viaticum. Penance of the sick was in the early church a public penance and if the penitent recovered he was obligated to wear the garb of the penitent and abstain from meat and from sexual intercourse for the rest of his life.[30] According to Bernard Poschmann, as late as the fifteenth century lay people would put off requesting the holy oils because they associated it with penance of the sick and entailing all the foregoing obligations.[31] Thus the term "extreme unction" designated anointing as a sacrament of the dying.

When the original Alexians first appeared in the lanes of the urban poor, the church's ministries to the sick were in corrupt condition. Poschmann lists the reasons for this situation: "Laziness and indifference often kept priests from visiting the sick and the faithful from troubling about the sacrament. Matters were made worse by the custom which soon developed of remunerating the priest for his services and what was at first a free will offering became in a very short time a considerable burden for the poorer people. Significant of this state of affairs is the admonition frequently addressed to priests that they should require not only the rich but also the poor to receive anointing."[32] In the thirteenth century priests extended their "stole rights" to include fees for linen sheets and candles, which were used during the administration of the sacrament. An anonymous writer from Passau (1260) said that because "unction required many priests and twelve candles, only a man worth two cows could afford the sacrament."[33] It seems, therefore, that the original Alexian Brothers were responding to this challenge (as well as others) in the church's ministry to the sick and the dying; attempting to fill a sacramental void which threatened the spiritual life of the sick, particularly those who were poor.

Perhaps Beghards and Lollards knew of priests who were sympathetic to the plight of the poor and at the critical moment would call upon them to minister the last rites. Indeed, since it had been reported that some Beghard houses had priest members, it is possible that they would be the official minister to those poor requesting the last rite. It is certain that the Brothers religiously responded to the Black Death catastrophe, and it is also logical to assume that they responded to those caught in that catastrophic moment when death demanded to be tamed by traditional rituals. Their attitude toward death was probably formed by their folk notions on the collective character of death, by their closeness to the *vita apostolica* sense of detachment from all but the love of God and humankind, and by Beguine and Eckhartian urgings to consider Christ's redemption as an eternal happening infused into their lives.

Before the plague "Brot-Beghards," "Lollards," and "Matemannen" were generic terms not specifically designating those Brothers later called Cellites and Alexians. Even after the Black Death they were called such names as *Rollbrüder* (Burial Brothers) and *Seelbrüder*.[34] The latter is literally translated as "soul Brothers." Because a *Seelfrau* was an elderly woman who laid out the dead and *Seelmissa* are masses for the dead, the term *Seel* vis-à-vis corpse connotes the religious themes surrounding death. In fourteenth-century Aachen the Brothers were called *Zielbrüder*. Though a literal translation is "purpose (end, goal) Brothers," Zielbrüder in Dutch means "soul Brothers."[35] This could have been corrupted into *Cellbrüder*. Zielbrüder as "goal Brothers" could also be appropriate if "goal" meant the termination of one's earthly pilgrimage. The Brothers were not, therefore, medieval pallbearers, but soul Brothers entrusted with the traditional ritual from the moment of death to burial in the cemetery.

The oldest document specifying the ministries of the Brothers is Pope Boniface IX's protective bull of January 7, 1394: ". . . They shelter in their houses poor and miserable persons who ask for it, and practice other works of charity, as far as possible visiting the sick and, if need be, taking care of them in their illnesses and waiting on them, of course at request, and giving an ecclesiastical funeral to the bodies of the faithful departed in their home town at request."[36] "Poor and miserable" are the key words depicting their "outsider" ministry. As was mentioned earlier, at the turn of the fifteenth century the Brothers mounted a massive defense effort against the attacks from various inquisitors by gathering sixteen testimonials, which they presented as evidence of their orthodoxy at the Council of Constance. Though the intention of these documents was to verify the good faith and morals of the Brothers, three of them included comments on their ministries.

In 1405 John Bitegod, pastor of St. Catherine's Church in Mechlin, said that the Brothers were "looking after the sick, bringing the corpses [souls] of the rich and the poor of the whole town into the parish churches, doing the same to the bodies of those who die outside the town, if called upon. . . ."[37] The pastor of St. Mary's Church, Antwerp, also referred to the burial ministries of the Brothers for the "whole city, after being requested."[38] The pastor of the Lungenbrüder at Holy Apostles church said that they "carried the corpses of the rich and poor to the graveyard at request to bury them."[39] Another Cologne document of 1423 contains the city council's commentary on the general orthodoxy of the Cellites, who were "making themselves useful to the City of Cologne to the citizens and inhabitants, if need be, also to pilgrims and strangers, both during the time of pestilence as well as at any other time, when they are afflicted with pestilence or some other fatal illness to such a degree that often even relatives or friends fled them with horror, by their careful watch and by *their salubrious exhortations made for the salvation of the souls of the sick* always having in view the eternal life or the eternal punishment. Without any discrimination they carry the corpses of the rich and poor, if called upon, at the funerals and bury them. . . ."[40]

Each of these five documents dating from 1394 to 1423 is primarily a deposition for the Cellite plaintiffs. Though each refers to their ministries to the dying and the dead, only the Cologne laity seem to have been struck by the spirituality infused into these ministries. Pope Boniface's bull and the parish house letters relate the lives of the Brothers with moderate praise; the city hall brief emphasizes their heroic plague efforts. Over a hundred years had passed between the time when the Cologne Brothers established their house on the Lungengasse and 1423 when the Cologne city fathers had written the edifying account of the Cellite way of life. During that century when the Brothers experienced continuous adversity their foundations were firmly established. Their characteristic features were developed out of a religious and social milieu abundant with similar apostolic groups, some of which engaged in administering to the sick. As we have seen, during and after the Black Death the Brothers distinguished themselves from their companions in the *vita apostolica* by their particular response to the diseased outsider, the pest victim, as well as their widespread participation in burial rites. Religious communities had been traditionally responsible for attending to the dead as one of their many duties; only the Cellites were so thoroughly marked as *Seelbrüder*. It appears as if we have now discerned the full charism of the founding Brothers. John Carroll Futrell, S.J., says that any charism is "a gift of the Spirit to an individual for the good of others."[41] To apply his thoughts on specific charism to the Cellites it is necessary to recognize not an individual but a collective founder, that is, the Brot-Beghards, Lollards, and Matemannen. "A specific Charism is given at certain moments in the history of the Church to a person whose manner of reading the multidimensional gospel portrayal of the life of Jesus brings him to focus on some particular aspect of Jesus' life, leading him to follow Jesus and to serve others for his love in a particular way."[42] The original Cellites appear to have been struck by the example of Jesus and the first church in Jerusalem as principal helper and healer. Since other *pauperes Christi* groups had also attempted to adopt that principle as the model for their ministries, the development of the specific charism of the Brothers can be discerned only by examining their early experience.

To explain why the Cellites, unlike the other groups that did not evolve into religious orders, blazed a particular path from the helper-healer gospel theme, one is dependent upon inference. The founding Brothers were outsiders who were frequently harassed by various enemies, e.g. archbishops of Cologne and regular mendicants. As they worked out their apostleship during these crises they seem to have identified with the care of the impoverished sick and those exiled by disease. When the Black Death struck, their dedication to the most wretched of all possible outsiders—the dying and dead of the plague—marks the climactic appearance of their specific charism. The following decades witnessed their phenomenal expansion concurrent with periodic confrontation with the inquisitors. From their origins they responded to a variety of helper-healer needs; the Black Death firmly established their burial ministry, but their original flexibility in responding to various needs led them into many ministerial expressions.

As major participants in the taming process, the Cellites engaged in sacred ritual prescribed by the church and tradition. The term *Seelbrüder* suggests that when the Brothers washed the body, wrapped it in linen, and "watched" during the nights until burial, they were not practicing the mortician's trade but were performing rites for the souls etched by tradition upon the folk beliefs of the day. The folk imagination conjured up images of the soul wandering the world and appearing to relatives. The scriptural resurrection-basis for the funeral on the third day nourished popular speculation about the location of the soul from the first to the third day of death.

The term "funeral" is derived from *funis*, torch. The *Seelbrüder* would probably be responsible for keeping the candles lit next to the "reposed soul," symbolizing the light of faith; or as a late seventeenth-century French writer, K. Muret, stated, ". . . to put all the powers of darkness to flight, and to show that Christians have never had any fellowship with those infernal Spirits, which endeavor to hide all their actions."[43] Muret's translator said that the candle lights were "tapers to scare the evil spirits from invading the defenseless sleeper."[44]

Because an individual's death was considered a public event, the body was frequently placed near the front door. Such a tradition supports the notion that death was a collective experience, a natural event in the community's existence. The Brothers were probably regular participants in the vigils for the dead, reciting customary prayers, rosaries, and litanies of the saints as they watched throughout the night. The belief in demons, black magic, and haunting ghosts led to many bizarre customs at such vigils. The Council of York (1367) forbade "those guilty games and follies which transformed a house of tears and prayers into a house of laughing and excess. . . ."[45] To provide Cellites at the "watching" was a guarantee that such follies were likely to be prevented as well as ensuring the maximum prayers for the soul. On the morning of the funeral the body would be carried to the front door of the church. Along the route, the procession would frequently resemble a pilgrimage as it stopped at shrines and gathered great crowds. One historian relates how the funeral also "stopped at taverns 'to wet the lips' of the 'thirsty souls' who carried the corpse."[46] When the procession arrived at the church the priest would meet the coffin at the front door, a symbol of his civil-law responsibilities to discover whether the death was caused by any foul play. He would then begin the "Dirge" from *Dirige*, the first word of the antiphon for the office of the dead.

The consecration of the body during the funeral was in the form of three circles around the coffin. The candles made one circle and the priest circled the coffin twice, blessing it with holy water and incense. Though some would interpret this as symbolizing light, refreshment, and peace, Louis Bouyer interprets it as popular belief: "Care was taken to erect a triple barrier about the corpse so that the soul, forced to renounce its stay in its familiar haunts which could be distressing to the living, is constrained to quit the earth."[47]

After the funeral the cortège proceeded to the church burial grounds with the priest and religious leading the way, followed by the Brothers carrying the coffin. If it were the burial of a rich person many mourners would join the procession with candles, as the poor would be given alms for such service. The burial had two major parts: the priest blessed the site of the grave, using holy water, and then etched a cross in the earth. The second part consisted of the actual grave digging as psalms were said. According to tradition the corpse would be buried with its feet to the east, ready to rise at the Last Judgment. A cross, symbolizing absolution, would remain in the coffin and as it was lowered into the grave the priest recited the collect for forgiveness. The mourners returned to the church chanting the Seven Penitential Psalms.[48] That the *Miserere* (Psalm 129) and the *De Profundis* (Psalm 50) eventually became part of the regular prayer life of the Cellites may have derived from their roles at graveside.

This brief digression on medieval funeral liturgies is meant to accent the ritualistic character of the Brothers' death ministries. The emotional expressions of grief at funeral and burial liturgies frequently reached a high peak. The Brothers must have been enthusiastic in their expression, as in Cologne they were referred to as *leyrbrudere*, lamenting brothers.[49] This nickname was of fifteenth-century origin and in a sense reveals the era's obsession with death. As Huizinga puts it, "Primitive custom demanding that the dead should be publicly and loudly lamented still survived into the fifteenth century. Noisy manifestations of sorrow were thought fine and becoming, and all things connected with a deceased person had to bear witness to unmeasured grief."[50]

As regular participants in the mourning process, that which "gives grief its form and rhythm" and "transfers the actual life to the sphere of drama,"[51] the Brothers were like late medieval actors in a mystery play whose prayers and lamentation were prescribed by tradition and expressed by religious dedication.

During the remainder of this chapter we will explore the

general mood of late medieval culture, particularly those portions that appear to relate to the Brothers' attitudes toward their death ministries. Such an exploration leads us to consideration of Jean de Gerson (1363–1429), sometime chancellor of the University of Paris and a major theological voice at the Council of Constance (to which the Brothers made the first general appeal for recognition), and of Nicholas of Cusa, the great reform cardinal who was indirectly responsible for urging the Brothers to take vows and whose ideals on piety were reflected in the Brothers' spiritual posture.

Gerson was a church reformer of a conservative mold. When he attacked the worldliness of the church it was to justify its traditional authority. His theological work *De Mystica Theologia* (1408) stressed mystical love of God as the path to knowledge of God more than did the theology of Scholasticism.[52] However, he qualified his moderate approach by warning against the tendency of mysticism's devolving into a mere celebration of the sensuous. Gerson's writings on death reflect the dominant mood of the fifteenth century. Theodore Spencer says, "It is hardly an exaggeration to say that in Northern Europe the whole fifteenth century was frenzied about death. Emphasis upon death seems to have mounted like a rushing tide."[53] Sister Mary Catherine O'Connor views Gerson's *De Arte Moriendi* "as the chief source" of a new literary genre, the literature of preparation for dying which flourished throughout Europe from the fifteenth through the seventeenth centuries.[54] Gerson's *De Arte* was translated into the vernacular probably because it was meant to provide laypersons with a practical bedside guide for the proper disposition toward death during time of pestilence. Because Gerson's work reads like a catechism and was, according to the mandates of many bishops, to be the basis of sermon instruction for the laity, O'Connor concludes that it was "sort of a laymen's ritual to be used at the bedside of a dying friend."[55] *De Arte Moriendi* contained a rudimentary sketch of basic beliefs apparently intended to supply the totally ignorant with a summary creed. Gerson's *De Arte*, like the *Ars Moriendi*, stressed man's fundamental solitude at death. The dying person, Moriends, ". . . is presumed . . . to be a lone warrior, unsupported by family, friends, or Church. . . ."[56]

This solitary concept of death substantiates Ariès' views on the shift from the preplague idea of death as a collective experience to a subsequent emphasis upon one's own death. The basically didactic character of both Gerson's book and the entire *Ars* genre substantiates Rehm's conclusion that didacticism was a major unifying factor among the diverse death feelings and ideas in post-Black-Death Europe. Because the recurring waves of pestilence decimated the parish clergy, death without a priest had become common by the early fifteenth century. As death ministers, particularly to the plague victims, the Cellites were thus responding to the priestless death scene.

Like the *Ars*, the *danse macabre* strand appeared throughout Europe largely through the diffusion of woodcuts and verse. Though the origins of the dance have evoked an impressive scholarly discussion, the basic themes have been traced to twelfth- and thirteenth-century writers who stressed ". . . the omnipotence of death, its coming at an unexpected time, its equalizing power, its lack of respect for the strong and the weak, the wealthy and the poor, the powerful and the serf."[57]

The *Ars Moriendi* and the *danse macabre* reflect the didactic approach to death. Whereas a gloomy pessimism shrouded the culture in general, these two literary and artistic expressions did not stress the wormy corpses and hell-inflamed flesh images. Indeed, death is portrayed (in the *danse macabre* usually as an anonymous skeleton) as the fact of life. At the opening of the Basel *Todtentanz*, one may read: "Many of those who sleep in dust,/shall wake again; God says, they must arise and at His Judgement seat/Receive what for their works is meet: Some life eternal, others grief/and endless pain without relief. /Those who are wise shall brightly shine/in heavenly light and joy divine;/and they, who many souls have taught/and wanderers back to God have brought/shall like the stars in glory be/made bright to all eternity."[58]

The *Ars Moriendi* centers on the struggle for the soul of the dying person, with the battle lines clearly drawn between devils and angels. The physical pain of death is not stressed; rather, it is placed into the context of a penitential rite for one's sins. The chapter on temptation "is clearly the high spot of the treatise,"[59] in which the temptation to give up hope is countered by faith in Christ's redemption. This triumph of optimism leads O'Connor to conclude that the *Ars* "is a complete and intelligible guide to the business of dying, a method to be learned while one is in good health and kept at one's fingers' ends for use in that all-important and inescapable hour. . . . In spite of its purpose the *Ars Moriendi* is not a doleful book—no clarion call to repentance. There is little stress upon hell, only hope of heaven. . . . The *Ars Moriendi* is no more intended to frighten and depress than is any medieval book on hunting and hawking or on table manners for children."[60]

The *danse* and *Ars* may not be in expression all that frightening but were nevertheless derived from a basically morbid sentimentality. Huizinga considers the death motif as the "great cultural idea"[61] of post-1400 Western Europe. He states that a "new and vivid shudder was added to the great primitive horror of death."[62] One poem contains a reference to the dying person with the "smell of putrefaction"; another, "Death makes him shudder and turn pale."[63] The stress upon physical decomposition, whether in nonfrightening or in gruesome terms, reveals the cultural preoccupation with the death event and is characteristic of the "my death" theme that was replacing the notion of death as a collective experience. Indeed, the *Ars Moriendi* origin appears to be linked to the breakdown of traditional rituals for taming death, and constitutes a substitute for them.

The passion and death of Christ is a central theme for meditation and the core of the Eucharistic celebration. However, the spirituality of the *Devotio Moderna* interwoven with the death motif of the day had for its focal point the physical agony of the passion. The community at Windesheim—where John Busch was trained—modeled the daily prayer exercises on "The Letter on the Life and Passion. . ." supposedly written by John Vos and found in John Busch's *Chronicon Winde-*

sheimse. The following selection urges the *devoti* to penetrate the wounds of Jesus:

> What is sweeter, more comforting, more pleasing to God, more salutory for the simple dove than to dwell in the cleft of a rock, that is, in the wounds of our Lord Jesus Christ? May your sweet Lord and lovable bridegroom grant you the favour not merely to dwell there daily and to repose in joy but also to die daily, while still alive; in the same love with which he accepted wounds and death.[64]

The spirituality of Thomas à Kempis also accented the lessons to be drawn from identification with Jesus' physical dying: "Ah, Lord God, how deeply the points of the thorns extend into thy most holy head: how cruelly they tore the tender skin of Thy flesh with the bones and nerves; so that from the wounds they made streams of blood flowed down Thy neck, down Thy eyes, down Thy ears and face. . . ."[65]

Probably the Cellite death ministers pursued their services for the dying and dead with a mixture of old and new attitudes. Serving the poor wretched outsiders was the core of their original charism. Though an "our death" sensibility must have prevailed along with their roles as ritualizers of grief, within the traditional religious setting they were set apart from town society by their communalism, their voluntary poverty, and their outsider ministry. They were probably not intimately affected by the rise of the gruesome death motifs of the late Middle Ages. The "my death" focus with its stress upon the macabre must have affected the way in which townsfolk viewed the services of the Brothers. Thus the *Seelbrüder* could have become more respected as ritualizers of death, as living symbols of the *Ars Moriendi* and the *danse macabre* theme.

As late as 1634 E. Binet, S.J., wrote:

> . . . They [the Cellites] offer their services to those afflicted with the plague, and to all those who are seized by infectious diseases. Day by day, they are exposed to the danger of falling victims to the same diseases themselves; thus standing on the edge of their grave every day. To live amongst the dead, without fearing death, which otherwise strikes terror into people, is really a valiant calling, which would have extorted admiration even from a Caesar or an Alexander. These servants of God bury the dead and pay them the last tribute of respect, being filled with true divine compassion and leaving

nothing undone to console the sick and to assist the dying. It may be absolutely maintained that they are there as representatives of Divine Providence and that it may be said of them, as we even say of God: "The poor are confided to Thee; Thou are a Protector and Helper to the orphans...." The Alexian Brothers are so secluded and surrounded by the dead, by coffins and pest-stricken that the remembrance of their merits also seems to be buried and forgotten with the dead. But the day will once come which will bring to light the value of these noble-minded and glorified warriors of Christ, who have waged the battle against death, against the plague and against the most incurable diseases."[66]

Binet viewed Brother Tobias as the founder of the Cellites. Tobias's picture, along with pictures of thirty-four other founders of religious orders, hangs above the choir stalls in the Benedictine Abbey of Liessies in northern France. In this portrait are the symbols of the Brothers' death ministry: the skulls, the sarcophagus, the coffin, the spades, the funeral candles, and the processional torches all framed in a dramatic baroque style. Hence the artist's depiction of Tobias appears in accord with the *Seelbrüder* way of life as tamers of death.

PART THREE

✝

THE DECLINE OF
THE MEDIEVAL
CELLITES AND THE
EMERGENCE OF THE
MODERN ALEXIANS

Introduction

The history of the Cellites from the Reformation to the French Revolution is the story of the decline of the medieval Cellites and the origins of the modern Alexians. Chapter IX traces the apparent continuity between the spirituality of the Cellite foundations as a religious order and the dominant religious ideals of the following 150 years by contrasting the themes of the *Devotio Moderna* with those of the Counter-Reformation. Ironically, some of the very documents which chart the idealism and the asceticism of the Brothers' prayer life during this period also contain specific references to abuses that were endangering the Cellite spirit. Chapter X opens with a discussion of the expansion of the Brothers' status and wealth because evidence suggests that there were violations of poverty and a general drift away from strict observance of the rule.

The story of the departure from the purity of their foundations is not one of continuous descent from the heights of communal poverty to the depths of individual self-aggrandizement. On the contrary, as Chapter XI clearly illustrates, decline cannot really be charted on a continuous slope. The Cologne Brothers were accused of abuses at the opening and close of the seventeenth century, but in the 1660s they again served the plague victims with selfless heroism. There is no evidence of decline in the Aachen house until the eighteenth century, while it is only by inference that one can conclude that the Antwerp Brothers had also deviated from the spirit of their rule.

The writing of a constitution in the early eighteenth century was motivated by the fear of general decline throughout the order. Because the subsequent eighteenth-century history of the Brothers suggests that this reform movement never gained noticeable momentum, one is compelled to conclude that on the eve of the French Revolution the Cellites were floundering: they were then almost completely under the governance of their bishops; the Aachen house had broken away from the order to form a separate Cellite faction; and the consciousness of abuses lingered on without the appearance of effective reform leadership. Their ministries were "profitable" but it appears as if their medieval idealism was fading.

Chapter XI appears almost as a contradiction to the theme of decline as it charts the continuity of the Cellites' ministries to the outsider. Regardless of their occasional abuses of poverty and their inability to reform, the Cellites continued to respond to the diseased outcast. Though one particular ministry, the care of the mentally ill, did not originate until the sixteenth century, it is characteristic of the Continental Alexians of the twentieth century. Thus this volume concludes when the medieval plague and burial Brothers are waning and the modern Alexians with their large institutions for the mentally ill are on the ascendancy. Only with hindsight can one detect their perseverance in the ministry to the outsider.

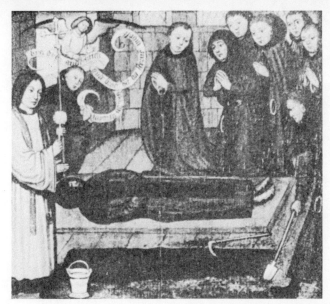

Cellites of Cologne taming the death of their brother—from a picture in the Cloister's necrology book.

A last Judgment scene—Cellites are disinterring the bodies.

Cologne brothers brought
this cross to the
scaffold of those
to be executed.

A baroque portrait
of Brother Tobias,
the apocryphal founder
of the Alexians.

AVCTOR FRATRVM

Laicorum, qui Cellitæ, et Alexiani vocantur, Tobias
assignatur. Incertâ regulâ, fundatione, confir-
matione, mortuis, furiosis, pestiferis inseruunt.

Brother Jan van der Linden,
Pater of the Antwerp house
(1618–1638) and Provincial of the
Brabant Alexians (ca. 1621–1633).

Brother Reutger Linden,
Pater of the Aachen house
(1633–1642).

The funeral procession
in Cologne of
Jean-Baptiste de Tassis,
who died at
the siege of Bonn in 1588.

A close-up of the preceding
illustration. The Cellites
appear in their role as "soul
brothers," tamers of death.

An 18th-century depiction
of the Alexian asylum
in Braunschweig,
cornerstone laid in 1552.

9

Spirituality and the
Counter-Reformation

The Protestant Reformation profoundly affected the development of the Cellites. The Dutch houses were dissolved and many Belgian communities suffered temporary crises. Of the three houses that concern us, only the Antwerp community was deeply involved in the profound religious controversies that rocked the foundation of Europe.

The Reformation in the Low Countries involved not only the conflict between Catholics and Protestants—particularly Calvinists—but also struggles between, first, Hapsburg imperialism and the Netherlandish political self-determination, and, second, between Spanish economic interests and the interests of the thriving towns of the Low Countries. Thus religious, political, and economic forces contributed to the revolt of the Netherlands, which broke into an intense eighty-year war against Spain in 1566. Though all seventeen provinces of the Netherlands participated in the revolt at one time or another, the seven northern provinces were eventually successful in permanently separating themselves from the Spanish and Roman Catholic orbits. As the most prosperous province, Brabant assumed leadership at the outset, and Antwerp as its major city became a rallying place for religious and political revolt.[1] As a great cosmopolitan center numbering some

100,000 people, Antwerp absorbed various national groups, many of whom were sympathetic to the new reform sentiment. Because the revolt opened with Catholics and Protestants allied against Philip II, the energetic Spanish champion of the Counter-Reformation, Antwerp at first dwelt in hostile coexistence between Catholics and Protestants, a condition frequently marked by anti-Catholic demonstrations. From 1578–1583 Antwerp was the capital of the rebellion. During that period when Catholics were persecuted, Cellite survival there was tenuous at best.

Eight years before the revolt, in 1558, the Antwerp city council agreed to send the sick to the Cellite house where the Brothers cared for them "at 2.5 [pennies] daily."[2] There was to "be a seemly number of brothers to serve the community"[3] during a condition of pestilence as well as normal times. In the spring of 1571 when the plague struck there an incident occurred which illustrates the continuing "outsider" character of the Cellites. Because the Brothers transported the pest victims through the city to their house, many of their neighbors were angered and some Brothers were attacked. Though the city council took them under their protection, such anti-Cellite incidents were not uncommon in Antwerp.[4]

By the beginning of the 1580s the anti-Spanish alliance between Protestants and Catholics had virtually disintegrated. Antwerp became a major Calvinist stronghold. By a decree of 1580 the Cellites, along with all other Catholic religious, were compelled to wear "worldly habit" when they engaged in their burial and nursing duties. A decree of July 1 proscribed the practice of Catholicism, but the Cellites were permitted to use their entire monastery "provided they are of use and necessary to the city."[5] The Cellite house, which had become, like the other houses of the community, a hospice for the sick and pensioners, was transformed into a refugee station for Protestant families who had escaped from the ravages of war. At one point the city council ordered as many as twelve families to be lodged in the Brothers' house.[6] Prims reports that many of the Cellites converted to the reformed religion. We know of three such Brothers, each of whom demanded continued residence and service with the Brothers after he had converted and married. For example, on April 28, 1583, the city decided that William Janssen, a former Brother turned Calvinist, would be allowed "the accommodation and use of the possessions [in the Cellite house] just as the others [Brothers] if he does a decent service."[7] It is difficult for us to appreciate William Janssen's point of view. Brother Lauries von Looms, who was pater of the Antwerp house from 1582 to 1617, considered the return of one of the former Brothers who had married a bad example as well as dangerous, since the couple would reside in a house frequently subject to contagious disease.[8] Janssen probably considered the Cellite religious order in Antwerp to be synonymous with a communal guild in which he was entitled to a share of the property and the "right to work."

Without the privileges of Mass, Holy Communion, and permission to take in novices, the Antwerp Cellites diminished in numbers and spirit. On January 21, 1584, the city council, at the request of the chaplains and "deacons" and because "most of the *Cellebroeder* either died or left the monastery,"[9] established an organization of burial bearers to which the first to be accepted would be the remaining Cellites and the pallbearers of the reformed churches. The group was to be responsible for transporting the sick and the dead. Eight members, including some Brothers, were specified as plague-victim bearers and were paid a higher wage for this dangerous work. The superior of the Cellites was stationed at the "little house of our Dear Lady's Cemetery and enjoys an extra salary of 50 gd." (guilders).[10] This group was short-lived due to the Catholic reconquest of the city, which ultimately meant the revival of the Brothers and their old privileges.

The Cologne and Aachen houses were not internally divided by the new wave of religious reform. Though they were located in cities which had experienced Protestant-Catholic conflicts, these Cellite communities appear to have defended their faith by clinging to the *Devotio Moderna* spirit infused into their origins as a religious order.

In his essay on "Piety in Germany around 1500," Bernard

Moeller writes: "The willingness, and indeed the desire to sanctify the worldly life within the framework of the institutions, created by the Church and with the help of the treasures of grace she offered were hardly as generally widespread at any other time in the Middle Ages and have never been more clearly visible."[11] Moeller notes two apparently contradictory "tendencies or moods" within the German church. The first tendency was toward "wild and whenever possible violent excitement, an inclination to simplify and vulgarize the holy. . . ."[12] Mass pilgrimages to honor a saint who had miraculously intervened in human events, the veneration of relics, and a general craving for concrete symbols to verify salvation characterize this dimension of popular piety. The other tendency or mood "is a tender individualism, a propensity for quiet inwardness and devout simplicity."[13] This quiescent piety, embodied in the *Devotio Moderna*, was probably the dominant characteristic in the Cellite spirituality of the day. However, Moeller points out that by 1500 the religious writings which were influenced by the *Devotio Moderna* were "lacking in originality and also frequently in depth."[14] The Cellites were more touched by direct involvement in Windesheim spirituality with its simple directions for a quiet personal form of piety than they were by published books on spirituality. They were still too close to their origins to have drastically departed from the spirit of the *Devotio Moderna*. They were thus not subject to the growing anticlericalism.

Such anticlericalism was not limited to the intellectual elites; one may turn to a list of grievances and demands drawn up by the common membership of the craft guilds of Cologne during a period of revolution in 1513, four years before Luther nailed his ninety-five theses to the cathedral door at Wittenburg. The following are just a few of their demands, relating to the wealth and conduct of the clergy:

13. Every cleric, secular or regular, young or old who has committed a misdemeanor or felony against the council is to be taken to the dean of the Cathedral Chapter, who should punish the cleric as though he were a lay person.

28. The Beguine nuns should be gathered into a few houses where

they may occupy themselves with spinning and sewing until they die. Their most valuable houses should be sold.

32. Clerical persons should from now on bear the same civic burdens as burghers.

107. Let the council attend to the problem of real properties willed by testament to the regular clergy. Such properties are required to be sold by the monks within a year and a day, but the following subterfuge is common among them. Having taken a lay citizen as a boarder into their monasteries, they sell him pro forma all properties willed to them; he, in turn, wills these properties back to them, and so on and so forth in perpetuity. In this way the monks hold on to their worldly goods, legally and permanently.

147. The Council should instruct the preachers of the four regular orders to preach nothing but the pure word of God and to utter no lies or fables, rather to be silent altogether and say nothing.[15]

Though these sentiments were expressed in a politically polarized situation, they do represent the "common person's" views of the abuses within the church as well as the laity's desire to hear the "pure word of God." Thus in a very real sense, the success of Martin Luther's message is related to late medieval strivings, particularly the Christocentric focus of the German mystics and the *Devotio Moderna*. Like the mystics, Luther viewed the sacrifice on the cross as the central salvific act in human history, one which transforms the lowly believer into a redeemed Christian. However, his formulation of this traditional doctrine, which was based on the total inadequacy of humanity to participate in a life of true holiness, was a radical departure from the mystics and one which struck at the heart of orthodox beliefs in the efficacy of good works, and at the total commitment to Christ found in the monastic ideals.[16]

Some scholars have traced early Lutheran spirituality to the *Devotio Moderna*. Though there is a certain resemblance between the two approaches to spiritual life (indeed Luther admired Thomas à Kempis), the *Devotio Moderna* was so thoroughly orthodox in its interpretation of the traditional vows for religious and of the efficacy of charitable works that the resemblance is confined to their common Christocentric focus. When Martin Luther denied the theological basis for the religious life, he found some support from those cloisters that were intellectually in harmony with his views on faith and Scripture. Perhaps there were some Brothers who were converted to the new theology, but they were the exception to the general Cellite rule of orthodoxy. The Cellites in Aachen and Cologne were not very vulnerable to Lutheran spirituality and theology because, first, they were probably still tied to the Windesheim influences and were thus strongly clinging to their newly developed traditions as a religious order. Second, their active ministry was so intimately bound up with their raison d'être that Luther's "justification by faith alone" was not appealing to the Cellites. And, third, though Cologne and Aachen contained Protestant communities, Catholic majorities jealously protected their own rights and privileges.

The *Devotio Moderna* spirituality was influential in the formation of the Counter-Reformation spirituality.[17] Like the New Devotion, Counter-Reformation spirituality is characterized by its emphasis on the sacraments, on simple practical techniques for meditation and devotion to the Eucharist, on the active apostolate of good works, and on the drive toward individual sanctification. John Busch's description of the early Alexians stressed these very characteristics, with the exception of the active apostolate, because "good works" had yet to be theologically challenged by Luther and there was no need self-consciously to defend the traditional path to salvation. By clinging to their fifteenth-century traditions the Alexians were, therefore, harmoniously dwelling within the dominant force of the Counter-Reformation of the sixteenth and seventeenth centuries.

The earliest extant written constitution of the Cellites did not appear until 1686. Until that time oral tradition sustained the customs of the community. Those chapters which touch upon spirituality appear consistent with the traditions of the late medieval Cellites. The rules of the Novitiate could have been written by John Busch two centuries earlier: "The novices must be instructed, in detail, as to the true meaning of the words of the Our Father, the Hail Mary, the Apostles Creed, and the Ten Commandments. . . . They must be taught to meditate, especially on the life of Jesus Christ."[18]

The chapter on "Exercises of Piety and some other Observances" is quite similar to Busch's description of the fifteenth-century Cellite prayer schedule. "The Brothers are to arise at midnight, make the sign of the cross and proceed to the oratory for Matins, and remaining in prayer [mental prayer] for one hour. If through sloth a Brother fails to be present, he should be given a penance and also have one meal less than the other Brothers on that day."[19] The morning began with Mass at 4:00 or 4:30, depending on the season—and the day ended at 8:00 P.M. The Brothers were allowed to read spiritual books procured by the superior, but only in their cell or in church and only with the permission of the superior. Besides rather stringent fasting regulations, every Friday during the year, every Monday, Wednesday and Friday in Advent, and those days before receiving Communion, the Brothers were expected to keep silence from the evening time when the sign was given until 5 o'clock the next morning.[20]

Because "silence is a protection," it was also to be observed in the refectory, sleeping quarters and chapel. The Brothers were to go to confession at least every fourteen days while they ". . . receive Holy Communion on Sundays, with the permission of the confessor and the Superior."[21] There are many more regulations which are concerned with deportment and the Alexian apostolate, but they are thematically better related to other chapters. Although the multitude of regulations reflects the impact of the Council of Trent and other Counter-Reformation directives aimed at strengthening the religious life, the style of spirituality is close to the community's *Devotio Moderna* origins. The stress is not upon the medieval communal Benedictine ideal of life and worship but upon individual piety and sanctification, which is characteristic of both the *Devotio Moderna* exemplified by John Busch and the Counter-Reformation exemplified by Ignatius Loyola.[22]

The Brothers structured the prayer day on the recitation of the Office of the Holy Cross. Thomas Simmons, who has studied the York "Hours of the Cross," states that the devotion should not be "confounded with the older office of the cross or the *Cursus de Sancta Cruce* mentioned by Udalric. They do not appear to be earlier than the beginning of the four-teenth century."[23] Yet the *Tierce* prayers of the tenth-century "office," the fourteenth-century York "Hours" and the twentieth-century Alexian "office" contain identical passages. Udalric was an eleventh-century Cluniac monk—prior of Telle —who compiled the liturgical customs of the Cluny abbey. His *Cursus de Sancta Cruce* includes psalms which were incorpo-rated into the Divine Office and are indeed distinctive from the Little Office, York Hours, and Alexian Office of the Cross. Ironically, the earlier Little Office included collect antiphons for the concern of the sick which probably by accident never found their way into the Alexian Office of the Cross. According to Jungmann the Brüderschaften (Congregations of Brothers) were responsible for embellishing the office beyond its tenth-century form.[24] There is no evidence involving the Cellites in this process, nor is there any evidence as to the exact date that the Cellites adopted the Little Office. The earliest document evidencing the Brothers' recitation of the office is a 1601 prayerbook of the Antwerp Brothers, but they had no doubt recited the office for some time before that date.[25] Regardless of the time of its adoption, the Office of the Cross contains the themes of the death and passion of Christ that penetrate Alexian spirituality from at least the early fifteenth century.

Gabriel M. Brasso traces a continuum from the *Devotio Moderna* of the fifteenth century to the spirit of the Counter-Reformation of the sixteenth and seventeenth: "Actually the *Devotio Moderna* opened a chasm between the individual ideal of Christian perfection and the liturgical life of the Church. Its characteristic note is *individualism*, and for that reason it finds itself diametrically opposed to liturgical spirituality, which is essentially ecclesiastical and communitarian."[26] The new forms of devotion in which "the individual has come to be the principal center of interest" and in which "self-knowledge and self-analysis are put at the basis of perfection"[27] eventually prevailed over the older communal tradition.

According to Evennett, "The central position of the in-dividual in the practice of counter-Reformation spirituality was, admittedly, radically different both from the moral view of his position in the purely humanist ideology and from the theological view of his position in the Protestant scheme of things."[28] The humanist viewed the ideal person as an autonomous self-determined individual, while the Protestant viewed the ideal Christian as totally dependent upon God's salvific will. The practitioner of Counter-Reformation spirituality stressed the individual's own efforts buttressed by "systematic precepts and counsels representing accumulated wisdom and experience" of the church. One was indeed at least partially responsible for one's own salvation. Persons must battle and conquer the concupiscence found in self in order to achieve personal sanctity but, as Evennett points out, that was "only half the story."[29] Individual salvation was achieved through the circularity of God's response to the person who responded to God.

Cellite spirituality was primarily monastic in the sense that Cellites structured their communal prayer life according to the canonical hours, Prime, Matins, etc., with the Office of the Holy Cross as a substitute for the Divine Office. It seemed to be permeated with *Devotio Moderna* themes, which were in accord with the thrust of the Counter-Reformation. Outside this structure, the Cellites venerated their patrons, St. Alexius, St. Augustine, and beginning in the mid-seventeenth century, St. John of God (d. 1550), who in the previous century founded the Order of Hospitallers. The John of God Brothers and the Cellites shared a nursing and mendicant tradition. Gabriel Russotto characterizes John of God spirituality as strong, apostolic, and joyful. He expands on these characteristics by referring to the writings of St. John and those of the early Brothers who knew him. John's stress upon the passion of Christ, his asceticism, his mystical tendencies, and his concern for the sick and the poor must have struck the Cellites as being in harmony with their own ideals.[30]

The two orders also shared the Rule of St. Augustine and prayed Little Offices during the specified canonical hours.[31] The John of God Brothers prayed the Office of Our Lady. Since the tenth century, devotion to Mary had grown in popularity; its growth spurted in response to Protestant attacks upon it.

Though it is difficult to gauge the subjective approach to Mary, Jungmann concludes that "in the consciousness of the people, Marian mediation was in a certain sense a substitute for the mediatorial role of Christ which was no longer clearly understood."[32]

The major distinctions between the John of God and the Cellite traditions appear to flow from the founderless basis of the Cellites. Unlike the John of God Brothers, who have a popular hero at their origins, the Cellites could not look for inspiration from *the* "charismatic Cellite." Their spontaneous origins, their outsider experiences, the harassment by church officials, and their ministries to the outsider are the distinguishing marks of the Cellites. The Cellites also did *not* develop large health-care institutions, as the Hospitallers did, until modern times. Though there are parallels between the two communities, the Cellite plague-burial and home-nursing ministries blended with their late medieval tradition of anonymity to place the Cellites far from the Hospitaller tradition.

10

Abuses and Reform

I

The Cellites possessed their own authority structure, but the bishops and city councils tacitly shared in their governance. Thus it is necessary to explore the ways in which the Brothers related to these three forms of authority, as well as to examine the economic conditions of the house where "decline" situated itself. In this process of exploration one should note that the term "abuses" was frequently used imprecisely by those in authority. When church, city, and Cellite authorities refer to decline and the need for the Brothers to return to the path of strict observance, they seldom reveal the entire story. Because one must rely entirely on the administrators' point of view, which may be frequently distorted by an inflated sense of authority, one should be reluctant to consider the references to abuses as containing the whole truth. Another hazard in interpreting "decline" is contained in the localized character of the order, which was so variegated that it defies accurate generalization.

Stabilitas loci was the most significant principle of Cellite authority, and one which harks back to the communal origins of the Cellites. Unlike other religious orders, the Cellites cannot refer to the writings of their founder nor to the correspondence of the first-generation Cellites for guidelines and procedures. Without a central person, place, or document from which they could mark their origins, they naturally followed the traditions established by each house. They also shared the principle of local autonomy before they became a religious order. Thus, at the first General Chapter dozens of independent houses seem to have committed themselves to provincial and general lines of authority, but it appears as if they intended to establish a loose confederation rather than a unitary system of governance. This arrangement must have also stemmed from certain practical considerations. In terms of their economic stability the Cellites were almost completely dependent upon the local town government, with which each house had entered into a contractual agreement. Thus there was no central Cellite "treasury" from which the central authority could derive the power to control the development of each house, and it would have been unreasonable to transfer Brothers who were tacit employees of the city council. (For example, in Antwerp, Brothers were frequently appointed "pestmasters" with specific duties and an annual salary.)

Local character was so strong among the Cellites that each cloister had its own coat of arms, which was frequently a blend of the city's symbols and a ladder, symbolic of their common patron, St. Alexius "under the stairs."[1] The organization of Benedictines may be analogous to the rural feudal manor, the Jesuits to the cosmopolitan national state, and the Cellites to the strongly autonomous towns of the Rhineland and the Netherlands.

The centralized structure, which was erected at the first General Chapter (1468), lasted for only a century.[2] The politico-religious wars in the Netherlands during the second half of the sixteenth century drastically reduced communication among the Cellite provinces, preventing the calling of general chapters and the election of a superior general. The Calvinist ascendency in the seven northern provinces of the Netherlands meant the dissolution of the Cellites' Dutch province. Because these wars created a vacuum of Cellite authority, the local bishops stepped in to fill the void; the Brothers in Flanders were so absorbed into the diocesan authority

structures their provincial authority was dissolved. The Cellites of the province of Brabant successfully struggled against
their bishops, and their provincial structure remained intact.
Hence at the opening of the seventeenth century there were
only two Cellite provinces, Brabant (including Brothers in the
district of Liège) and the Rhineland, with Cologne as the
provincialate. General chapters and the elections of superior
generals were never revived. Though the lengthy wars appear
to have almost destroyed their autonomy, those Tridentine
decrees, which extended the authority of the bishops over
exempt orders, contributed to the final demise of the Cellites'
centralized structure. The two provinces held individual chapters, but the Cellite religious order had devolved into a
diocesan congregation. The houses in Flanders such as in
Ghent, Veurne, and Brussels were de jure diocesan congregations.[3] The houses in Brabant and the Rhineland had some
measure of autonomy from their bishops, such as the right to
choose their own visitator and provincial, to accept novices
without the prior approval of their bishops, and to manage
their own financial affairs. However, as will be explored later
in this chapter, there were instances in which some of these
rights were suspended. Prior to the establishment of centralized authority structures, the Cellite houses had developed
very durable local traditions. Hence they were able to survive
the breakdown of their religious-order status. But without a
General Chapter and a central superior each of the houses
was weakened in its negotiations with its bishop. Though the
absence of a superior general may not have directly caused
the decline in their religious life it certainly diminished the
effectiveness of remedying abuses and initiating a general reform movement.

II

Traditional European society was hierarchically structured,
with many distinct levels ranging from the royal court to the

lowliest serf. Individuals were identified by their membership in a recognized group, each of which also tended to be hierarchically structured. At first, the Beghards, Lollards, and *Matemannen* appear to have been unattached *pauperes Christi* groups, sort of floaters or vagabonds. They gained stability in Cologne, Aachen, and Antwerp by settling into a legal residence. With stability came their official recognition as members of a charitable organization. One may recall that at this time town government was asserting its responsibility for organizing charity tasks. For example, in the Low Countries the trend was to establish "tables of the Holy Ghost" for the poor residents of the town; and for those poor who could not meet the residency requirement, i.e., pilgrims or vagabonds, the "Tables of the Heesrparnen" (tables of those who had no roof over their head) were established. Each table had its own organization and account books administered by "*magistri* and *gubernatores*."[4] Though this is a fifteenth-century trend, there is evidence of some tables formed earlier. As *pauperes Christi* laymen, the Brothers had no corporate privileges like those of religious orders that would have set them apart from the town hall. With no legal charter and with no means of livelihood other than begging, the Brothers' ministries came under the authority of city councils; unattached charity groups were unheard of. Because these relationships between the Brothers and the town councils occurred during the foundation period of the Cellites, they became an essential aspect of the Brothers' ministerial expression. Today these relationships may be viewed as a dangerous dependency on secular authority, but the Beghards were lay people and the city councils were aware of their own religious responsibility.

Once they were established as viable communities, particularly with religious-order status allowing them chapels, it was inevitable that certain lay people would show their appreciation for their ministries by giving them land and money bequests with requests for prayers. Of the three houses, Cologne appears to have been the most wealthy. Its ties to the city council were equally strong. On June 5, 1481, the city gave the Lungenbrüder a house, "zum Leopard," located near the new market adjacent to their other house on the Lungengasse.[5] Three years later (November 8, 1484) the Brothers received one-half of the house "zum Kluppel," which was next to "zum Leopard." The other half they had received on the same terms in 1336.[6] Brother Bernard lists the various donations to the Cologne Alexians, many of which came from priests and laity who specified Masses and other prayers for the repose of their souls.[7] It is interesting to note that Brothers in the Cologne and Aachen houses also donated money to their communities. Brother Philip Neidler bequeathed his house to the Aachen community in 1595.[8] In 1616 Brother John Humpel of Linden donated two altars and an iron choir screen to his confriars in Aachen.[9] In 1637 Brother Friedrich of Kler donated a "red satin vestment" which, according to Brother Ignatius, is still used today.[10] The Aachen community also received money donations; their property was not a gift from the city but from private benefactors, including Brothers. In contrast to the moderate wealth of the Cologne and Aachen Brothers, the Antwerp community appears to have been relatively poor during the sixteenth and seventeenth centuries.

The Cologne house amassed great wealth very early. According to Brother Bernhard who depended on Paas's extensive research of the Cologne city archives, the Lungenbrüder managed their wealth by very diligently investing in annuities. On August 14, 1490 Pater Peter von Nettisheim bought an annuity from the city of Cologne which cost two hundred Rhenish gulden and paid an annual premium of eight gulden. In 1537 and again in 1550, the Brothers purchased more annuities, with a total investment value of 1,350 gulden.[11] Other documents reveal the purchase of annuities from the Cologne Cathedral Chapter.[12] On at least one occasion, the Cologne Brothers made a private loan to a married couple for four hundred talers at 4 percent interest.[13]

In spite of their early accumulations and investment of capital, the Brothers were occasionally compelled by dire economic circumstances to appeal to the city council for financial aid. In 1546, after the Brothers had registered two pleas for help, the city council provided a necessary grant.[14] In 1549, because of increasing debt, the Brothers once again successfully appealed for aid. Yet their condition worsened.[15] In 1566 many Brothers left the house on the Lungengasse to live in private homes, apparently because the community was too poor to provide for them. The city council responded to these "desertions" by instructing the "justice of the peace" to direct these Brothers either to return to their Cellite house or leave the city. Ultimately this crisis was resolved by the city council granting about one thousand gulden for the Brothers' debts, in return for the right to supervise the economic conditions of the Brothers. Four citizens were appointed as provisors of the house on the Lungengasse.[16] In the late sixteenth century the city council even interfered with the elections of paters because of complaints of poor management.[17] In the early seventeenth century conditions apparently improved, as the Brothers were allowed to purchase a house in 1609, and in 1629 two houses were granted to the Brothers because the owners defaulted on mortgages that were held by the Lungenbrüder.[18]

In the late seventeenth century, because the council suspected the Brothers of cheating on burial fees, they ordered an investigation of the books.[19] In November 1695 the council terminated the Brothers' privilege to bury the dead. Because it concluded that their economic behavior had improved, the council decided on March 25, 1696 to return the burial privileges to the Brothers.[20] Since the late fifteenth century the Cologne Brothers had supplemented their income by operating a public wine tap. Though there were early complaints that the Brothers had actually established a tavern in the cellar, the city council did not take action against the Brothers until 1662, when it forbade them to operate their wine pub. Before this could be implemented a Cellite/city council struggle ensued, culminating in a 1701 decree to close the Brothers' wine cellar.[21] (The Aachen Brothers had a public beer tap that went uncriticized.)

Brother Bernhard concludes that although by the opening

of the eighteenth century the Cologne Cellites were dwelling in prosperity, they were still not as wealthy as in the early sixteenth century and were almost completely dependent upon the city council.[22]

During the sixteenth century the Aachen house also grew in wealth and prospered. One may presume that such wealth could have led the Brothers to deviate from strict observance of the rule, but the Thirty Years' War (1618–1648) imposed many serious hardships upon residents of the city of Aachen, including the Brothers. At first the war affected only the economy of Aachen, then in 1632 it began to involve the entire city militarily. Various armies representing both the Catholic Hapsburgs and the Protestant princes at one time or another occupied the city, demanding tribute and frequently going on looting and robbing rampages.[23] With the city debt skyrocketing and business in a deep depression, the Brothers, who may have invested in annuities that were declared valueless, were forced to borrow money for the first time.[24] Cash was needed to complete their building program (the construction of a new chapel), but even after that had been achieved they still needed money; they sold their brewery in 1650.[25] The great Aachen fire of 1656 destroyed 4,500 houses, of which eleven belonged to religious. Though the Alexian houses were not totally destroyed, they did experience some damage and the Brothers' financial situation obviously deteriorated.[26]

In accord with the general prosperity of Aachen during the eighteenth century, the Cellites enlarged their wealth. Many wealthy noblemen were pensioners in their houses. Donations for their funeral and burial services during the eighteenth century varied according to the means of the families. The general fees were six, eight, and twelve florins, with the very wealthy paying twenty-four and thirty-three florins in burial fees. Eight Brothers carried the corpse of Mayor Weispen, for which they received sixty-six florins. A glance at the following chart illustrates the extent of the funeral services of the Brothers.

During this fourteen-year period the Brothers served at

	Funerals in Aachen 1748-1762[27]	
Year	Total, Adults and Children	Number Performed Gratis
1748	948	310
1749	1034	260
1750	983	253
1751	750	210
1752	875	215
1753	724	168
1754	1044	288
1755	746	203
1756	732	244
1757	902	309
1758	1071	397
1759	1087	308
1760	1244	472
1761-62	830	238

12,970 funerals, of which 3,875 were "for the love of God," i.e., gratis. Brother Ignatius points out that the Brothers were so prosperous during the period 1748–1772 they loaned a total of 4,300 talers from their cash at hand.[28] Abuses were apparent in that period of prosperity, but in contrast to the richly documented story of the decline of the Cologne Brothers, we gain only a shadowy image of a general decline.

The Antwerp house revived and gradually stabilized after reaching its nadir during that bitter period of persecution (1578–1583). Because they appeared to have been permanently dwelling in debt and because the guilds in Antwerp were threatening their livelihood from burial services, the Antwerp Brothers were continuously appealing to the city council for financial aid and a redress of grievances. In 1551 and again in 1676 the Antwerp city council issued a decree stipulating the burial privileges of the Cellites and the fees to be paid to the Brothers.[29] These identical decrees were prefaced by a lengthy description of the poverty of the Cellites that compelled them to transfer Brothers to other communities where decent board was guaranteed. The city council responded favorably because it realized the city's dependence upon the Cellite plague and burial services. Brothers and certain guildsmen engaged in such a conflict over burial rights that in 1689 a decree was issued which allowed the Brothers to bury persons of any trade who had expressed this wish in their will.[30] The Cellites appear to have been so financially desperate that they appealed to the court of Charles VI at Brussels for a redress of grievances related to burial fees.[31] The Brothers complained that some Antwerp citizens paid only one guilder instead of the two required as the burial fee. They pointed out that the guildsmen who buried the dead were paid two guilders while the Brothers buried six hundred to seven hundred poor people annually on a gratis basis. They contended that even two gulders was not enough to support their community because eight Brothers were compelled to remain at home caring for the sick with little financial compensation. Charles decided in favor of the Cellites' major complaint and set a two-guilder minimum fee for their burial services.[32]

On the evidence of these decrees, the Antwerp house appears to have been rather poor. Some of these documents contain references to city hall investigations of the Cellite financial situation which verify the Brothers' case. During the eighteenth century they seem to have improved their condition but there is no evidence of abuses among the Antwerp Brothers. Neither city nor church authorities suspected them of grossly violating legal, canonical, or moral laws. This was certainly not the case with the Cologne Brothers.

The Reformation dramatically exposed the deterioration of clerical and monastic life. The Council of Trent was deeply concerned with many of the reforms earlier sought by Nicholas of Cusa and John Busch. Schema 20 of the council (November 1563) was passed with the intention of restoring the communal poverty "that had been almost completely abandoned in monasteries."[33] Bishops were empowered to correct and punish all exempt religious orders and they were frequently buttressed by papal nuncios. Duke Ferdinand of Bavaria convened a commission in 1601 when he was coadjutor to Archbishop Ernst of Cologne. Pope Clement VIII granted him authority to inspect all the exempt monasteries in order to pursue the Tridentine reform mandate.[34]

On February 28, 1601 this commission declared that the Alexians should be reprimanded for their conduct at funerals because their behavior annoyed the pastors. Without specific information on this charge one might infer that the Brothers had been soliciting funds during the funeral procession.[35] The official visitator of the Lungenbrüder was the prior of the Crosier house, who successfully sought permission for a commission to help him put an end to the "spreading abuses in the Lungenbrüder monastery."[36] A subsequent report of March 1613 stated that only the removal of the superior would stem the tide of corruption within the Alexian house.[37] The story ends on a consistently vague note: the commission reported that since they could find no one to take his place the superior was allowed to serve another year with the admonishment to improve conditions.[38]

Though it was not until the beginning of the eighteenth century that corruption became blatant, the German province seems to have attempted to reform itself by the new constitution of 1686. Originating in the Provincial Chapter of 1648, this document is one of the first extant complilations of what Dom Leclercq calls the Rule of the Institution, i.e., the changeable customs of the community. The immediate cause for the codification of these customs seems to have been the need for monastic reform, but we may presume that many of these statutes were derived from oral tradition preserved for centuries. A reform statute in chapter V of the constitution—"Accepting Candidates"—includes the words that "they must not be accepted merely because they have means."[39] Though the dowry practice was commonly accepted and confirmed by the Council of Trent, it appears contrary to the original Alexian spirit.

The traditional local house authorities, pater and vice pater, remained as before but their responsibility to punish offenders was elaborately described in the four chapters dealing with penalties and punishments. For "Minor Faults" such as frivolity or wastefulness the superior was directed to give the offender one or more *Pater Nosters* and *Aves* as a penance.[40] For greater faults but not serious offenses—lying, use of profane language—the superior was to impose a day's diet of bread ("usual allotment of beer is allowed") and one *Pater Noster* and *Ave* upon the offender.[41] For "serious faults" such as concealing a gift, obstinate disobedience of a superior, or inflicting blows on another Brother, the offender was "given a severe discipline [the whip] right at the chapter [of faults] in the presence of all."[42] Following is the punishment, quoted in full: ". . . at the Refectory he is to eat his meals in a kneeling position; three days a week he is to be on a bread diet (the usual drink permitted); in the refectory he is to prostrate himself on the floor and let all the Brothers step over him, duration of some of these penances will depend on circumstances."[43]

Chapter XXVI, "The More Serious Faults," included the punishment by confinement in the "community prison" on a bread diet for obstinate refusal to perform required penances and for starting a serious fire.[44] If a Brother "falsely accuses another Brother before others" or "commits an impure action" then "proper penances will be imposed upon him"[45] with no exact specification of the type of penance. If a Brother refused to go to confession he could not be buried in the community cemetery and if it was discovered that a deceased Brother "had been a source of scandal to seculars,"[46] his body was to be exhumed and buried in unconsecrated ground.

Obviously these "faults" represent common injuries to the Cellite community life, while the punishments represent legal remedies. The code also protected the community against a too lenient superior. We may conclude that the Brothers responsible for this constitution were reformers who were conscious of the then current deviation from the monastic idealism of "the old days" and were demanding strict discipline according to their notions of the purity of Cellite foundations.

During the late seventeenth century the Brabant houses were also on the decline. According to a letter written by the archbishop of Mechlin, Alphonse de Bergues, to a superior of the St. John of God Brothers, the Cellites were vulnerable to attack.[47] Dated May 9, 1672, the letter was a response to an appeal that the St. John of God Brothers absorb the Cellites. Archbishop de Bergues addressed himself to the three presuppositions for such a merger made by a Brother Joseph of the

Holy Cross. The latter based his appeal on the premises that the Cellites were in need of reform, that they were vagabonds without a superior, and that a merger would be facilitated by the fact that the two religious communities shared the same rule. The Mechlin archbishop responded negatively, stating that since the Cellites were not vagabonds but had a provincial their absorption into the St. John of God community was unnecessary. Though this letter substantiated the regular status of the Brabant Cellites, the archbishop may have been motivated by his own episcopal interests in maintaining authority over the Brothers, for in 1707 Brother Provincial Hendrik Kerkhoff demanded that the archbishop of Mechlin confirm the ancient privileges of the Cellites, which exempted them from specific episcopal prerogatives. Though the outcome of this conflict is unclear, according to Clement XI's papal bull of August 31, 1709, the Brabant Brothers successfully appealed to Rome for confirmation of their statutes.[48] Clement was vague on the question of authority; the bull contains no specific reference to exemption from episcopal jurisdiction, nor does it refer to the bulls of Popes Sixtus IV and Julius II. Other than extending his general "favors" and graces and confirming the statutes, Clement XI "discharged" the Cellites "of all excommunications, office suspensions and prohibitions and other ecclesiastical verdicts. . . ."[49] However, because the first statute refers to the authority of the Cellite superior general, Clement did tacitly confirm the exempt status.[50]

On May 5, 1710 the Brabant Brothers opened a provincial chapter in which the delegates decided to publish a Rule Book containing the Augustinian rule, the statutes of the Cellites, and the bull of Clement XI. The Rule Book also contains a rough historical sketch of the community and a long letter by Brother Hendrik Kerkhoff dated May 15, 1710. It seems that Brother Hendrik and the delegates were anxious to unite the two provinces under a superior general. This is evident not only from the first statute on the authority of the superior general but also from Brother Hendrik's reference to the Cellites of Flanders, Brabant, Liège, and Germany.[51] However, from the wording and tone of his remarks, Brother

Hendrik was primarily concerned with religious reform rather than the restoration of ancient privileges and central authority structures. He opened his letter with this remark: "The Holy Ghost compares a monastic order to a well ordered army drawn up in battle array, which is fearful to the demons of hell (Book of Psalms, fourth chapter)."[52] Such an army could not stand firm without rules or when superiors and "common soldiers do not keep the rules."[53] Brother Hendrik quoted a letter from St. Bonaventure in which he said that the reason abuses creep into a religious community is because the rules are not respected and the transgressors go unpunished.[54] The pater provincial reminded superiors that they will be compelled to give an account of their service on "the day of Judgment."[55] Brother Hendrik stated that the rule and statutes "as they have been practiced from the beginning . . . without the least change shall be printed and distributed to our different monasteries."[56] Later he quoted St. Augustine to support the conservative position when he said "that change of laws or habits disturb by their newness even when they are profitable."[57] He also quoted an "experienced statesman" who wrote, "It is better for a society that the laws although bad, stay unchanged, than that they be changed very often." Brother Hendrik concluded his defense for the preservation of the ancient rules and customs by remarking that ". . . all changes are subject to hate and controversy and that the Statutes and rules of our forefathers are sufficient, if they are kept."[58] His peroration was:

In order to do my duty regarding this, I admonish earnestly and from the deepest of my soul, yes, I vow by the blood of Jesus-Christus, that all the Pater Superiors of the monasteries which are in my care that they themselves must keep the Rule and the Statutes so carefully and so strictly that their behavior will be an example to the Brothers as to how they shall be kept; to that purpose I warn them that they shall punish the breakers of our Statutes without exception, so that the punishment will keep others from transgression. Whenever I find in my visits that transgressions have been left unpunished, and, that such has occurred because of weakness or faintheartedness of the Superior, I shall make them accountable as is my duty. Above that every superior knows well of the strict account he will have to give to God, in case his indulgence has given cause to weakening of our Rule and Statutes.[59]

He warned that those who might "be driven by audacity" to "scorn" the statutes or introduce "novelties" that would disturb the peace of the monasteries would be treated with "all severity" according to the statutes and would be "punished" according to the law.[60]

Proceeding on the principle that old law is good law, the Alexian statutes were printed and distributed to revive the discipline of the past. Besides listing the duties of the superior general, the prayer schedule, and other provisions discussed above, the rule directed Brothers to sleep on straw mattresses and to wear wool rather than linen undergarments unless travel or illness demanded the use of linen.[61] Before retiring, a Brother was to lock his door, but because it had five "wide holes" through which the superior could observe each cell, Brothers were never entirely cut off from the supervision. If a Brother was caught preventing his superior's right of inspection by blocking the holes in his door, he lost the right to his own key and the superior could decide to have the door removed. After each of the three required "bleedings" per year, the superior was instructed to treat the brothers leniently, but never to allow dancing.[62]

Stabilitas loci was protected by two specific rules. If a Brother successfully appealed for a transfer to another house he lost his seniority and the rights to vote and to possess a key at his new house.[63] Second, each local community was instructed to choose a superior from among its own brothers and if they did choose one from another house that choice had to be confirmed by the superior general.[64] The chapters on offenses and punishments were nearly identical to the ones contained in the 1686 constitution except that they appear to have been more specific.[65]

Austere penances were common to monastic discipline until very recently. A 1587 constitution of the Hospitallers contained the following penalties for violating the rules, many of which are identical to the Cellite prescriptions for discipline:

". . . eating on the floor, fasting in the ordinary way on bread and water, begging food on one's knees from confreres during the common meal, kissing the feet of the brethren, taking the discipline in public, prostration on the ground while the community passes, public reprimand, privation of active and passive voice for a time or forever, privation of office, taking one or more disciplines, being bound in fetters, being confined in the prison room of the monastery."[66]

The religious character of the Cellite ministries was stressed in the constitution. The Brothers were directed to "care diligently for the spiritual health of the souls of the sick."[67] Specific directives for such pastoral ministry included speaking "about the history of the Old and New Testament, about the suffering of our Lord or about other Spiritual subjects."[68] Though all the Brothers were considered versed in spiritual care, no brother was to "practice medicine or healing"[69] without special permission. This reference to their ministry was one of the few positive points in the statutes. Brother Hendrik set the rather negative tone and, as he himself vowed, it was a document meant to be rigidly enforced by superiors and provincials.

There is no evidence that either the Brabant or the German reform movement was successful. Conditions in the Cologne house continued to deteriorate. Brother Peter von Efferen, who was elected pater in 1702, was gradually exposed as having violated the trust of his confriars; as Brother Bernhard states, "He squandered the income of the monastery and led a scandalous life."[70] Some conscientious Brothers appealed to their house visitator, the prior of Crosiers, to censure their superior and impose a penance. Though the latter inspected the monastery on May 27, 1707, it was not until June 10, 1710 that the provincial chapter took up the reform issue. The papal nuncio at Cologne appointed the prior of Crosiers, Paul Dohmen, to be a general commissioner. At this chapter Tridentine reforms were discussed along with "new agreements for raising the discipline of the order."[71] The authority situation in the Cologne house continued to erode. Again some of the Brothers urged the papal nuncio to intervene; in the mean-

time Pater Effren was removed from office and Vice Pater
Grell was made administrator. Effren's friends appealed to
the nuncio, who reappointed him as pater on September 13,
1717. The Aachen and Trier houses, which since the mid-
fifteenth century acknowledged the Cologne pater as provincial, had been alienated by the Cologne crisis over the years
and viewed Effren's return to authority as abusive.[72]

The conflict between Aachen and Cologne originated in 1701
before Effren's first term of office. The Aachen Brothers
charged that the provincial had appointed one of the Cologne
Brothers as their official visitor, an action which they interpreted as a gross violation of tradition.[73] According to Brother
Ignatius Wiegers, who has researched this conflict, the Cologne
Alexians successfully convinced the papal nuncio to support
them.[74] In the autumn of 1717 the Aachen vice pater, Brother
Peter Strum, journeyed to Cologne to negotiate an agreement.
The conflict remained unresolved, with the result that the
Aachen Brothers authored a notarized statement declaring
"that each House shall go its own way under its respective
ordinary, and they would separate in peace."[75] Because this
statement was drawn up and signed by twelve Aachen Brothers
just three weeks after Effren's reappointment as pater, the
issue may have extended beyond the authority principle to
include a rebellion against their provincial's personal record
of misconduct as well. Though the Cologne Brothers attempted to bring Aachen back into the fold, the break became
final when in 1724 the bishop of Liège, upon the advice of two
theologians who certified the justice of the Aachen position,
recognized the independence of the Aachen house.[76]

To clear the clutter from this episode, one must review the
evolution of Cellite authority structures from the fifteenth-
century origins through the post-Trent reform period. The
Cologne house was first recognized as superior to the Aachen
house before the Cellites were recognized as a religious order.
From the available sources it appears as if the German province preserved this traditional preeminent status of the Cologne house. Provincial chapters throughout the order elected
the provincial for life; delegates to German chapters either

confirmed the elected pater of the Cologne house as their provincial or directly elected one of the Cologne Brothers to the office.

During the post-Trent era when bishops and reform commissions were granted extraordinary powers over all exempt religious orders, the privileged autonomy of the Cellites, particularly in Cologne, diminished. As abuses, factionalism, and conflicts between the Cologne Cellites and the city council increased, intervention by the papal nuncio also increased. The devolution of Cellite autonomy in Cologne reached its nadir when in 1717 the nuncio was empowered to name their pater. After the 1717 rupture the Aachen and Trier communities became de jure diocesan congregations with none of the privileges of an exempt religious order. Ironically 150 years later the situation was reversed; the Aachen house successfully appealed for Papal-Congregation status and the houses which had remained under their provincial assumed the status of Diocesan Congregations, ultimately accountable to their ordinaries. In 1717 Aachen was an unaffiliated house. Today the Brothers of the three provinces that were established by the Aachen Motherhouse refer to the offspring of the Cologne house—the Neuss and Siegburg communities—as unaffiliated Alexians.

Rome approved the 1724 decision by the Liège bishop recognizing the independence of the Aachen Brothers. During the Cologne-Aachen crisis the papal nuncio appointed diocesan Vicar General de Reux as the temporary commissioner (i.e., superior) of the German province.[77] To heal the wounds and encourage reform de Reux transferred Brothers from house to house, thereby violating the spirit of *stabilitas loci*. Aachen and Trier rejected both the transfer and a request to attend the 1722 chapter for the election of a provincial.[78] The new provincial, Pater Goelle, eventually appealed to Rome for protonotary clarification of the status of the order. In 1726 the apostolic protonoter, Prosper Colonna, as a spokesman for the Pope, confirmed the exempt status of the Cellites, citing the 1472 bulls of Sixtus IV as evidence that the Cellites were directly responsible to Rome. Also, on February 5, 1772 Pope

Clement XIV confirmed the bull of Julius II (1506), which was an even stronger endorsement of papal authority over the Cellites. Nevertheless, on the eve of the French Revolution, after many conflicts between the Cologne Brothers and the diocese, the archbishop clearly violated the privileges contained in those papal bulls by placing the German province under his direct rule.[79] Houses in the Brabant province which had been struggling with the bishops apparently followed a similar pattern through the seventeenth and eighteenth centuries and suffered the final defeat when, after the French Revolution, they became Diocesan Congregations.

As an independent house, Aachen was without a rule. The following introduction (written anonymously) to a rule imposed upon them by their bishop in 1763 revealingly narrates the story of the imposition of a new rule.

> The Alexian Brothers had a Province, the Provincialate being in Cologne. Unfortunately the Province was broken up and each House became independent. As a result the Bishop of Aachen appointed a Commissar of the Diocese to write up a new set of Constitutions for the Aachen Brothers.
>
> In this matter the Brothers were not consulted, they were simply asked to accept the new Constitutions and to follow them. The former Constitutions made up by the Brothers were far more satisfactory than these latter.
>
> There were many abuses in the various houses which resulted in the separation. However, had the Bishop's Commissar endeavored to correct the abuses it might not have been necessary to force the new Constitution on us. We, also, were at fault. Had the Provincial's visitations, and the chapters, taken action for correcting abuses things might have been different. Finally, it might be said that all this occurred because of a failure to observe the Rule and Constitutions, resulting in a so-called "Constitution" being forced upon us.[80]

In conrast to the rather lengthy 1686 document, which contained twenty-six chapters, the 1763 constitution was very brief, a mere twelve chapters. With no distinction as to professed status, every Brother had the right to vote for the superior. Only in the case of two deadlocked ballots could the bishop's "Commissar" cast a vote to break the tie.[81] The superior possessed ultimate authority on matters of discipline, but if he wished to make "an important proposal" the constitution directed him to seek "the opinion of the Brothers . . . by vote" before making a final decision. "This, however, must be done in a respectful manner without noise or arguments."[82]

The author of the constitution was very concerned about the danger of overindulgence in alcoholic drinks. Chapter II forbade the Brothers "while traveling to go into public houses of refreshment or recreation, even though priests go to them."[83] Chapter IV warned the Brothers to "drink but little" when they were invited to attend a gathering outside the house and when they had an extraordinary recreation, e.g., a brother's feast day.[84] Chapter VI—"Women in the Monastery—Religious Conduct"—expressly forbade women to attend "investitures, professions, etc." as well as admission to the monastic enclosures—the refectory and the Brothers' "living quarters."[85] The chapter on "Serious Faults" lists three major "crimes"— fourteen-day absence without permission, stealing, committing an "impure act"—for which the punishment was not specifically prescribed, merely a "heavy penance" and the loss of keys, symbols of trust and independence.[86] In contrast to the tone and scope of the 1711 constitution, this appears as a formulistic code for diocesan congregations.

These statutes remained effective until 1835 but they were virtually inoperative during the era of the French Revolution. Other than the introduction quoted above, there are no extant documents revealing the Cologne, Aachen, or Antwerp Brothers' view of the independence of the Aachen community. Because it was primarily a legal break from provincial authority, personal associations were probably maintained. Local autonomy was so etched into their traditions that Aachen's independent status may not have been considered serious by their German and Flemish Brothers. As evidenced from their constitutions throughout the eighteenth century the Cellites of Cologne, Aachen, and Antwerp were conscious of the need for reform. Ironically, Cellite revival actually occurred not by a return to the purity of their legal foundation but by encountering the adversities of the French Revolution, which threatened to extinguish them. Because the modern Alexians emerged out of these bitter encounters with the anticlericalism and secularism of the revolutionary era, that portion of the Alexian story will form the introduction to Volume II.

With hindsight it appears as if the eighteenth-century Cellites were drifting: as they gained prosperity they became more conscious of decline. Because of their ahistorical perspective, reform was interpreted as legal restoration of the past. There is little objective evidence to indicate that "decline" meant the Cellites were dwelling in luxury. In contrast to scandalous monasteries in which concubinage was the rule and in which the desire to reform never surfaced, the Cellite consciousness of abuses and decline seem to indicate that the descent from the spirit and forms of their foundation was not deep. It seems as if the Aachen and Cologne Brothers were aware of their lack of strict monastic life and were floundering for want of charismatic leadership. Their late medieval forms of spirituality and governance needed to be infused with fresh vitality, which was best derived from vibrant ministerial experience. Their late medieval role as tamers of death was no longer a vital one in a culture that was rapidly replacing ritual with rational analysis. Indeed, of the three communities that concern us, only the Aachen Brothers were strongly engaged in the burial ministry. The rise of professional undertakers in Cologne and Antwerp greatly diminished the demand for Cellites at the graveside. Had each community still been involved in their traditional burial and funeral services, this form of religious witness would not have been a source of strength. With the final disappearance of the plague in the early eighteenth century, their ministry to its victims was terminated.

Hence their original charism was not vigorously and visibly expressed on the eve of the French Revolution. Though young men eagerly aspiring to travel the monastic *via caritatis* may not have perceived the sparks of the Cellite charism, the Brothers were engaging in one ministry to the outsider that would eventually mark them as modern Alexians, care for the mentally ill.

11

The Passage Brothers

In spite of the fact that many Brothers may have limited their view of the Cellite ministries to that of income-producing tasks, the original Cellite charism seems to have prevented the Brothers from becoming professional social workers and undertakers. To dwell with contagious disease became more heroic as the knowledge of the need to quarantine victims expanded. The Brothers appear never to have suffered drastic departures from their religious calling to this ministry. The real measure of the spirituality of an order is not how remote it is from the economic marketplace but, rather, how closely it dwells to its unique ministerial calling. To fully appreciate the story of their plague and *Seelbrüder* ministries, it is necessary to turn to the Antwerp community, which has a richly documented account of its service to pest victims.

There were many tragic plague years in the sixteenth and seventeenth centuries, of which the worst were in the 1550s and 1660s.

Since 1345 the Brothers in Antwerp had been living in the house on the Cattlemart that had been given to them by Henry Suderman. One may recall that in the latter part of the fourteenth century the board of aldermen had asserted responsibility over the Brothers and afforded them protection. In the early sixteenth century that area of the city had become very valuable and many property owners near the house of the plague workers were pressuring the aldermen to compel the Brothers to move. In 1548 the Brothers moved to a location further from the town center. As ministers to the outsider pest victims they were compelled to live on the edge of town.

On January 21, 1555 the city fathers passed an ordinance regulating the burial privileges of the Brothers. Of the twelve articles, two specified their responsibilities during the plague. As cited in the introduction, the Brothers had incurred heavy debts during the construction phase of their new house, and because the income from their burials was diminishing (lay people, particularly of the "trades," were burying their own), the Brothers were in a desperate situation.[1] They were so hard pressed that some of the Antwerp Brothers were transferred to other houses in order to lighten the financial burden. The aldermen noted that the Cellites' services were "indispensable" to the city.[2] After an investigation into the Brothers' financial situation, partially caused by the city's forcing them to move from their original location, and after consultation with the lawyers of the affected trades, the aldermen passed the following articles, which are worthy of quoting in full.

1. In the first place, that from now on all bodies within this City shall be carried and buried only by the Cellites and no one else, except, that only the guild's members shall carry each other and those respectively in the guilds and trades and no others, and the Cellites shall not be allowed this but it is to be understood that those of de Meerse [place name]' shall be carried by the little old man, who lives in Saint-Niclaes Chapel, or others who are in de Meerse or have been there, and where the deceased has died of the plague.

2. At the funeral services, no one shall be allowed to serve but the Cellites except the afore ascribed exempt persons and the Cellites will have the following pay: to wit for a religious sinking each Cellite shall be given the amount which the friends of the deceased desire, for the funeral service itself they will have 3 nickels.

3. For each body which is carried together by 4 brothers to the burial, they each shall be paid 2 nickels.

4. For every woman, where both the service and the burial are performed together before noon, the brothers each shall be paid one nickel and no more. If it happens that someone has not belonged to a guild or trade, at the desire of friends be carried to

the grave by some of the guild or by the little old men and desire the service to be performed by them also, and not by the Cellites then they shall be allowed to have the body carried and have the funeral service performed by a person as they would like, then the friends shall owe and pay the Cellites half of the pay which they would have had for the burial and the funeral service but if any women will be carried to the grave by some else then the Cellites their pay above . . . .

5. That from now on no one shall be allowed to put into the coffin or carry any bodies of plague victims of men or their boys [servants] in any other manner than by the Cellites alone and they shall be paid for the aforementioned placement into the coffin eight nickels and the same also for the carrying 8 nickels.

6. If it happens, that some of the aforementioned plague victims are put into the coffin or carried by some other persons and it appeared to the neighbors or others, that the deceased had died from the plague, then in that case the Cellites will have to be paid their full pay in all manners as if they had laid the body in the coffin and carried it to the grave.

7. So when the service is performed for someone who died from the plague and who has been carried by the Cellites, then the Cellites shall also perform the funeral service, notwithstanding that the deceased has belonged to a guild or trade, except where the friends desire the guilds or trades or the little old men to perform the funeral services, in which case the Cellites shall be paid half of their pay, as mentioned above.

8. Anyone who wishes to do so, may carry his child to the grave, if one man can carry it, and if it has not died from the plague, with only one person, without having to pay the Cellites anything.

9. The Cellites will carry the alms children and the poor children of the holy spirit [those dependent upon the charity of the Table of the Holy Spirit], who leave little, so that not enough is left after the debts are paid, to pay for the laying in the coffin and the burial, for God's will.

10. That the women who died from the plague shall be carried to the grave by the Cellites, without anyone else.

11. That the Cellites, when requested, owe the care of the sick at their homes or wherever he is lying sick, for the seemly cost of about 2 nickels between the day and the night, without being allowed to demand more.

12. The Cellites shall have to arrange to always have a rather good number of brothers in order to serve the community easily, in times of pestilence as well as during all other contagious sicknesses whatever they are and however they may come, without fraud or guile.[3]

The Antwerp Cellites were, therefore, closely allied with the city charity system. Their care and burial of pest victims led to some conflicts with certain townspeople, as is evident from the following 1565 city council directive:

> The Cellites may not be wronged at night or while carrying dead bodies, which died from the quick sickness [plague], nor while they are transporting the sick infected by the same sickness. Action will be taken against those who have been insolent in front of the converts of the aforementioned Cellites.[4]

Perhaps because the Brothers were instructed to transport the pest victims to a special quarantined place, thereby separating them from their families and friends, the latter would vent their frustrations by harassing the Brothers. It is also likely that during plague time the brothers became scapegoats for general frustration. Regardless, this situation in Antwerp accents the outsider ministry of the Cellites. This became explicit when in 1627 the city council forbade the Cellites and Black Sisters from attending parish churches during the plague under penalty of losing their privileges.[5]

The most significant brother of the Antwerp community during this time was Jan van der Linden, who was pater for twenty years (1618–1638) and provincial of the Brabant province for twelve years. In 1633 he and his confessor, the Dominican Jacob Passenius, journeyed to the Holy Land. Upon his return in 1635 he published his experience, entitled *Divine Journey*, which, according to Prims, "enjoyed more than 20 editions and served for a long time as a school text."[6] He also authored a book on treating the plague. In the late 1620s Antwerp was struck by a five-year plague, during which the Brothers under the leadership of Pater Jan "acquitted themselves with zeal and diligence, especially when the City was without pestmasters. . . ."[7] In 1628, when the pest had subsided, Pater Jan appealed to the city fathers for financial aid which, he said, had been promised to the Cellites during the epidemic. The pater reminded the city council that five Brothers and four novices died nursing the plague victims, many of whom were poor and were "administered to without demanding a nickel."[8]

Pater Jan told the council that because he was a native of Antwerp who "feels a great affection toward the community," he was reluctant to accept an offer from the mayor of Thienen, who was willing to pay him one thousand guilders a year for the "care of the infected sick."[9] Though there is no record of the council's immediate response, on July 27, 1632 the council appointed Brother Jan pestmaster of Antwerp and the next month it granted the Brothers a two-thousand-guilder subsidy.[11] After Pater Jan returned from the Holy Land he served again as pestmaster with a salary of five hundred guilders a year.[12]

The pestmaster's responsibilities included visiting those suspected of plague infection, transporting them to a special district, and supervising the nursing and funeral duties of the Cellites. He worked closely with the police and was given policelike authority. For example, a city council directive stated that the sick person lying on the Sleutelstreet who, though suspected of being a plague victim and refusing to accept a visit by the pater of the Cellites, must accept the visit or be fined fifty guilders.[13] Pater Jan, who was a Knight of Jerusalem, must have been an extremely energetic leader, one who held the confidence of the entire Brabant province as well as the Antwerp community. Though Pater Jan does illustrate the Brothers' evolution toward a literate analytical view of their life and work, he appears to be more of a precursor of the modern Alexian than a typical seventeenth-century Cellite (for example, the 1711 constitution would refer to many literate Brothers).[14] One may conclude, therefore, that since the Cellites were closely tied to the increasingly complex welfare structure of local government the sophistication of Pater Jan became increasingly more common, particularly among the superiors and provincials of the order.

By the time of Pater Jan's death in 1638 the Antwerp Brothers were caring for some sick in their Cellite house, were asked to take in orphans, and were attending to the sick in the house of correction and the local hospital as well as carrying on their traditional ministries to plague victims dying in their homes and to the dead.

The Lungenbrüder in Cologne were also plague brothers. During six months of the tragic epidemic of 1665–1666, twenty-two brothers and novices died as a result of their contact with patients. The one remaining Brother, Pater Gottfried Undorp, placed the habits of the dead Brothers on the communion rail as an invitation to young men to unite themselves with the sacrifice of the community.[15] Within a few month six novices who had joined the community died of the pest.[16] Apparently Pater Gottfried, who was also the German provincial, transferred Brothers to Cologne as the community continued to thrive as the most significant house in the Rhineland. Their plague ministry was commemorated by a large painting contained in the Rhenish Museum collection. The Cologne Brothers' plague ministry was not so tightly regulated as in Antwerp; it was generally assumed that they would bury all the pest victims. The burial ministry was rigorously directed by the city council, as is indicated by a January 14, 1636 ordinance that stipulated the times of burials and instructions for the proper notification concerning the Brothers' attendance at funerals.[17] Among the various ministerial expressions, none was more dramatic than the Brothers' presence on the executioner's scaffolding. On December 11, 1556 Gerhard von Brouwiehr gave the Brothers the first annual gift of ten *Karolus* gulden on the condition that each time a criminal was sentenced to death one of the Brothers would stay with him in jail from the evening before the execution and accompany him to the scaffold the next day. Throughout that time he was to provide the criminal with Christian comfort and exhort him to resign himself to his doom in faith. Immediately before the executioner lowered the ax, the Brother would hand the criminal a picture of the crucified Jesus to kiss.[18] On one occasion (1682) the city council directed the Brothers to imprison the rebel Nichola Gülick, who lay sick in their house on the Lungengasse. The Brothers were sympathetic to the rebel; and though the council threatened to terminate their privileges the Brothers refused to cooperate on the grounds that their house was not a jail, nor could they guarantee the security of the prisoner. In spite of this display of independence the council did not obstruct their ministry to Gülick.[19]

In their pastoral care for prisoners the Brothers even administered to "witches," though on these occasions not one but two Brothers would attempt to comfort the criminal. In 1629 one witness records that "when the witches were taken to jail, a feast was cooked for the criminals, the two Lungenbrüder, the executioner and the others. When the execution was over, as is the custom, the executioner and other invited guests gathered for a meal in the burgrave's home."[20] The Lungenbrüder attempted to withdraw from the services for witches (perhaps because of the low fees or because they traditionally did not attend to women), but the council rejected their pleas.[21] Hence they were compelled to provide their services until 1655 when the last Cologne witch was executed. Besides their regular and extraordinary ministries, the Cologne Brothers also housed the sick, "bad priests," unruly boys, and a variety of penitents and pensioners.[22] The original charism to administer to sick outsiders evolved into a general ministry to physical, social, and moral "exiles."

Brother Leo von Ratingen was pater of the Aachen community for almost fifty years, during which the city council granted the Cellites the privilege of compiling a Register of Burials.[23] In spite of numerous crises—war, revolution, depression—the Brothers recorded burials uninterruptedly from 1592 to 1922. Their burial fees were regulated by the council with the stipulation that the poor be buried gratis. The degree of prosperity derived from their burial ministry may be estimated by noting that in 1640 there were 355 funerals, which provided the Brothers with 1,394 florins of Aachen value.[24]

Though the Aachen Brothers sheltered the sick in their hospice, they were primarily in-home nurses. On September 20, 1651 Brother John Mungen received 17½ florins for "35 night watches at the home of Secretary Missen."[25] They were even asked to travel outside Aachen, as Brother Ruetger von Linden nursed for four weeks and three days in a Maastricht home during August 1663.[26] As in other towns, the Cellites of

Aachen were absorbed into the city charity system. Though their major task appears to have been to bury the dead, they were also known for their plague ministries. According to a city council decree of the mid-fifteenth century, Aachen established a special pestilence hospital in which four Alexian Brothers were to serve as nurses.[27] For such services to the Aachen community, the city council provided an annual donation of forty talers.[28] As a further symbol of gratitude the city council donated a stained-glass window (1687) for the Brothers' new chapel.[29]

Brother Ruetger von Linden, who was pater during the Thirty Years' War (1618–1648), resembles his counterpart in Antwerp, Jan van der Linden. The identical surnames are coincidental; they both seem to have shared a common identity as great leaders. Brother Ruetger's portrait, which is a treasured illustration of late baroque painting in the collection of the Aachen Alexian house, testifies to the prosperity of the community during his term as pater. Unlike Pater Jan, whose leadership is well documented, we have but fragmentary evidence of Brother Ruetger's impact. One document tells how Brother Ruetger was stabbed three times with a "large butcher knife" by a Henry Borzelt, who was a pensioner in the Alexian hospice.[30] During that same year, 1634, another pensioner, Konert Keull, struck Brother Peter.[31] Brother Ignatius Wiegers concludes that because Borzelt and Keull were mentally ill these incidents mark 1634 as the earliest year for this new ministry that was to become characteristic of Alexian service.[32] By 1634 when Father Binet wrote his book on the founders of religious orders, the Cellites were well known for their ministry to the mentally ill: "They devote themselves to the service of the dead, the *insane* and the pestilence or plague victim."[33]

Actually, the earliest document illustrating the Alexian care for the mentally ill is from Nijmegens. Petre de Hoogh, who had spent 202 days in the stocks, was directed to stay with the "Cellebroeders" in 1569.[34] In 1571 the city council gave the pater of the Cellites twenty guilders and a year later thirty-one guilders for such care.[35] In 1585 a woman "oiver viff sinnen beroefft" (who was bereft of her senses) was locked up in the Cellite house.[36] By 1592 the Brothers in Nijmegens were known for their care of "kranckzinnighe menschen" (mentally ill men). From that year the Brothers' house was called a "Dolhuys" (Madhouse).[37]

To explore the evolution of the Nijmegens Madhouse is beyond the scope of our narrative. Its sixteenth-century foundation clearly marks a fresh development in Cellite ministerial expression. By the nineteenth century when trends in local government and commercial undertaking were preempting the Cellite burial work, the Brothers in Germany and Belgium were primarily—though not exclusively—engaged in caring for the mentally ill. This was the foundation time for the large asylums where patients were treated as "sick" rather than as "mad."

But the Cellite response to the "mad" emanated from their charism to the outcast. The exile status of the "mad" was vividly portrayed in the *Narrenschiff* (Ship of Fools) symbol of the late fifteenth century. Sebastian Brant's *Narrenschiff* (1494) is a commentary on the human condition, but his symbol was derived from real ships of fools "that conveyed their insane cargo from town to town."[38] Some towns exiled the mad by placing them on board a boat. Michel Foucault speculates: "It is possible that these ships of fools, which haunted the imagination of the entire early Renaissance, were pilgrimage boats, highly symbolic cargoes of madmen in search of their reason: some went down the Rhineland rivers toward Belgium and Ghiel; others sailed up the Rhine toward the Jura and Besançon."[39] The shrines, renowned for their cures of madness, were the destination of these voyaging madmen. Many cities provided for their insane by confining them in a special prison. In Germany such places were called Narrtürmer because they were prisons for the mad (*Narr*) located in the towers of the city gates (*Türme*). "The madman's voyage is at once a rigorous division and an absolute Passage. In one sense, it simply develops, across a half-real, half-imaginary geography, the madman's *liminal* position on the horizon of medieval concern—a position symbolized and made real at the same time by the madman's privilege of being *confined* within the city *gates*; his exclusion must enclose him; if he cannot and must not have another *prison* than the *threshold* itself, he is kept at the point of passage. He is put in the interior of the exterior, and inversely."[40]

The symbols, passage and threshold, could apply equally to death and dying. Indeed, just as there was *Totentanz*—dance of death—so there was a *Narrentanz*—dance of madness—portrayed in literature, art, and popular festivals of the sixteenth century. As in the *Ars Moriendi* and the *danse macabre*, the madness theme was primarily didactic. Yet death and madness possessed identical qualities of nothingness. Erasmus's *Praise of Folly* "is constructed on the model of a long dance of madness in which each profession and each estate parades in turn to form the great round of unreason."[41] It is as if death were garbed in fool's clothing and foolish men were by their madness heralding the end of time.

The Cellites, tamers of death, became tamers of madness. Their distinctive response to the outsider, particularly the plague victim, marked them as residents on the threshold, the ditch or graben that surrounded the medieval city. On that threshold and beyond the gates were the vagabonds, the lepers, the plague victims, that floating population in passage. Unlike the Aachen house, which was actually situated on the graben, the Cologne and Antwerp houses were on the inside. Yet, as the Brothers performed their plague and burial ministries they were marked as attendants to those in passage. City councils that evinced a concern for mad persons and families willing to pay for the care of their mad relatives turned to the Cellite "Passage Brothers." The Nijmegen Dolhuys appears to have been the exception; most of the Cellite communities remained tied to burial, home nursing, and plague care until the nineteenth century. The Aachen, Cologne and Antwerp Brothers only gradually shifted from tamers of death to tamers of madness.

Unlike the famous "Madhouses," Bethlehem (Bedlam) Hospital in London and the Paris Hôpital Général, the Nijmegen Dolhuys was relatively small. The Cellite institution and Bedlam both introduced a common fund-raising practice, which reveals the general attitude toward the insane.[42] Each "Madhouse" became a popular entertainment spot; the public was charged a moderate fee for viewing the "funny" madmen in their "cages." The animal symbolism contained in what we would consider as a pathetically bizarre form of entertainment is not mere coincidence. The person was not considered sick, but because he was bereft of rationality he was indeed a mere animal; like the beasts of the jungle the madman was a non-person who could withstand all sorts of discomforts.[43] What would be brutal treatment for a person compelled to live in filthy squalor was for the brutish animal easily tolerated. Though Bedlam continued the zoolike practice until the nineteenth century, the Nijmegen Dolhuys closed its doors to the public in 1650 because the Brothers complained to the city council that the visitors, particularly the children, interfered with efficient care of the insane.[44]

The Brothers of Nijmegen could not escape the confines of their culture but they probably avoided an exaggerated animal image of the "mad" as symbols of the netherworld and instead infused a spiritual—"there but for the grace of God go I"—dimension into the general cultural posture. Life in the Dolhuys was certainly an advancement beyond the Narr-türmer—the jail for the mad in the city gates. The moral responsibility of the Brothers—though grounded in their culture —must have raised the minimum of decency beyond the jail-house cell.

Because Aachen, Cologne, and Antwerp houses were not large confinement institutions until the nineteenth century, the Brothers of these houses were not primarily concerned with the problems of care for the mentally ill. The few such boarders they did have illustrate the almost instinctive Cellite reflex to respond to all kinds of outsiders as well as the laity's instinctive reflex to turn to the Cellites for care of the "exiled." Because the Aachen house was not equipped for the custody of the acutely insane, the instances of violence referred to earlier were probably the exception. Hence, until the nineteenth century when their hospice became an asylum the typical patients were probably the neurotic, the feebleminded, and the epileptic. The small numbers of insane who daily mixed with the other pensioners lived in a more health-producing environment. Unlike the Nijmegen Madhouse, which was under authority of the city council, there is no evidence that the Aachen, Antwerp, or Cologne Brothers accepted the mentally ill as wards of the city. On the contrary, their acceptance of this type of patient was the product of a privately negotiated contract between the Brothers and physicians and the families of the mentally ill. On May 31, 1751 Dr. Schoenmelzer Mannheim committed a councillor of the high court of justice to the Aachen Brothers' convent because he had an attack of "melancholico-depochondricus."[45]

Brother Ignatius reports that it was not unusual for families to rid themselves of unwanted relatives by having them committed to the Brothers. He quotes one such report in which one Le Fevre was "maliciously and secretly confined here with the Alexians"[46] by his son. It must have created a minor scandal; the mayor of Antwerp lodged a complaint against the injustice of this action with the Aachen city council on October 17, 1726.[47] Brother Ignatius concludes that this and other like cases probably led the council in 1747 to decree that the Brothers were forbidden to accept the mentally ill without prior approval by the city council.[48]

There is little evidence specifying the exact dates at which the Antwerp and Cologne Brothers began caring for the mentally ill. Prims merely refers to such care in the eighteenth century as if it had been a traditional practice of the Antwerp Brothers.[49] Brother Bernhard notes that the Cologne Brothers had been taking in pensioners since 1549.[50] We may infer that they gradually accepted mentally ill patients. He reports that on April 11, 1786 the numbers of pensioners totaled fifteen, two of whom were secular priests and the remainder mentally ill and feebleminded.[51] Meanwhile the Aachen, Cologne, and Antwerp Brothers remained tied to their traditional ministries.

Epilogue

As the plague threat diminished, care for the mentally ill eventually became the Brothers' most characteristic ministry. During the eighteenth century the Brothers were floundering between their medieval and modern vocations. They were still rather small communities, busy at many of their original ministries, but their *Seelbrüder* perspective was no longer strongly supported by medieval symbol and ritual. As the cultural vision shifted to a more analytical scientific focus on the profound events of life and death, so the tendency grew to view the Brothers as morticians and pallbearers rather than *Seelbrüder*.

The secular climate, with its cosmopolitanism and rationalism, probably did not filter far down into the Cellite communities. However, the commercial and industrial character of city life was reflected in the enterprising spirit of at least the leadership of the Cellites. The expansion of their properties and their business dealings, regardless of the intended goals, required sophisticated leaders who, with business skill, could manage the affairs of the community. Perhaps these leaders set a secular tone that led to abuses of poverty. Indeed, one is led to ask two paramount questions: Were the Brothers of the eighteenth century practicing a "ministry" or a "work"? Are the names *Seelbrüder* and Passage Brothers appropriate descriptive terms for the eighteenth-century Cellites? If we focus on the abuses, and the implications that the general observance of the rule had declined, then one would infer that the Brothers were workers rather than *Seelbrüder* and Passage Brothers. However, the persistence of their ministries to outsiders brought the Brothers into constant contact with those on the limits of existence. Their original charism may have been obstructed by their eighteenth-century way of life, yet it was present in their traditional posture toward the exiled. The fact that many Brothers may not have been touched by the Cellite charism does not diminish the reality of their authentic motivating spirit. Their services at grave and bedside were medieval expressions of their charism, which persisted in some towns to the twentieth century. Perhaps their routine burial services had diminished the *Seelbrüder* image they had of themselves because of the evolution of the attitudes toward death and the waning of medieval symbol and ritual. The relatively new ministry for the mentally ill and feebleminded was not generally imposed upon them by the city halls, but was, rather, of their own choosing, a fresh manifestation of their original response to the outsider. Though it was not their only ministry in the eighteenth century, it does suggest the vitality of their original charism. Thus the term "Passage Brothers" still seems most appropriate to their eighteenth-century existence.

They administered to the pest victims outside the city walls. To these wretched people the Brothers brought physical and spiritual comfort, a sort of Viaticum to those who were in immediate passage. The Brothers also attended to those mentally ill whom society itself had placed "in passage." They brought them within their own walls where they mingled with them throughout the entire day. The Cellite houses became "islands of fools," where secular society had exiled the insane but where they were cared for by religious who had themselves dwelt on the fringes of society for five centuries.

The eighteenth-century chapter of Cellite history may be characterized by a decline in their medieval ministry and the ascendancy of the modern ministry. During the transition between medieval and modern life they were without strong leadership. Their abuses of poverty and the routine ways in which they viewed their burial services would be violently challenged during the period of the French Revolution. From these encounters with adversity, which threatened them with extinction, the Brothers drew new vigor, a vigor engendered by the spark of their original charism:

God's foundation is my foundation and my foundation is God's foundation. Here I am on my own ground, just as God is on his own ground. Actions spring up from this ground without asking *why?*

NOTES

Introduction

1. David Tracy, *Blessed Rage for Order: The New Pluralism in Theology* (New York: Seabury Press, 1975), p. 105.

2. G. G. Coulton, "The Historical Background of Maritain's Humanism," in *Ideas in Cultural Perspective*, ed. Philip P. Weiner and Nolan Aaron (New Brunswick: Rutgers University Press, 1962), p. 559.

3. Because some readers may not be acquainted with terms regularly used by church historians, the following is a guide:

pauperes Christi—the poor of Christ, in imitation of the communalism of the early church and the poverty of Jesus and his followers.

via media—the middle path where the original Alexians were situated as members of a "lay institute." They separated themselves from the parish but they were not members of a religious order.

via religiosa—the path paved by the three principal vows for the religious life: poverty, chastity and obedience.

vita apostolica—apostolic life derived from the original disciples.

Chapter 1

1. Ernst W. McDonnell, *The Beguines and Beghards in Medieval Culture* (New Brunswick: Rutgers University Press, 1954), p. 432.

2. Henry Charles Lea, *A History of the Inquisition of the Middle Ages* (New York: S. A. Russell, 1955), II, p. 355.

3. McDonnell, *Beguines and Beghards*, p. 436.

4. "Introduction to the Synoptic Gospels," *Jerusalem Bible*, ed. Alexander Jones (Garden City, N.Y.: Doubleday & Company, 1966), p. 14.

5. Ibid.

6. Ibid., p. 205; cf. Acts 4:32–35.

7. Ibid., pp. 207–208.

8. Ibid., p. 210.

9. O. P. Chenu, M.D., *Nature, Man and Society in the Twelfth Century*, selected, ed., and trans. Jerome Taylor and Lester K. Little (Chicago: University of Chicago Press, 1957), p. 214; cf. Herbert Grundmann, *Religiöse Bewegungen im Mittelalter* (Hildesheim: Georg Olms, 1961), pp. 503–513.

10. Chenu, p. 214.

11. Ernst W. McDonnell, "The Vita Apostolica: Diversity or Dissent," *Church History*, XXIV, No. 2 (March 1955): 17.

12. Chenu, p. 221.

13. McDonnell, "The Vita Apostolica," p. 17.

14. Quoted by Chenu, p. 221.

15. Walter J. Ong, S.J., *The Presence of the Word: Some Prolegomena for Cultural and Religious History* (New York: Simon and Schuster, Clarion Books, 1970), p. 128.

16. Ibid.

17. John Dolan and Hubert Jedin, *Handbook of Church History*, trans. Anselm Biggs (New York: Herder and Herder, 1970), IV, pp. 186–187.

18. Richard W. Southern, *Medieval Humanism and Other Studies* (Oxford: Basil Blackwell, 1970), p. 32.

19. Ibid., p. 15.

20. Walter Ullman, *A Short History of the Papacy in the Middle Ages* (London: Methuen & Co., 1972), p. 221.

21. Ibid., p. 226.

22. Ibid.

23. John Moorman, *A History of the Franciscan Order from Its Origins to 1519* (Oxford: Clarendon Press, 1968), p. 46.

24. Southern, *Medieval Humanism*, p. 21.

25. Ibid.

26. Franz Pfeiffer, *Deutsche Mystiker des XIV. Jahrhunderts,* II *Meister* (Leipzig, 1857; 4th ed. Göttingen, 1924); English trans. E. de B. Evans (London, 1924), Sermon 5b.

27. Johann Huizinga, *The Waning of the Middle Ages* (Garden City, N.Y.: Doubleday & Co., Anchor Books, 1954).

28. Ibid., p. 155.

29. Robert E. Lerner, *The Age of Adversity* (Ithaca, N.Y.: Cornell University Press, 1968).

30. Lynn White, Jr., "Death and the Devil," in *The Darker Vision of the Renaissance*, ed. Robert S. Kinsman (Berkeley: University of California Press, 1974), p. 26.

31. Ibid.

32. Ibid.

33. Ibid., pp. 26–46.

34. Denys Hay, *Europe in the Fourteenth and Fifteenth Centuries* (New York: Holt, Rinehart and Winston, 1966), pp. 31–35.

35. Ullman, p. 270.

36. Ibid., pp. 270–278.

37. R. F. Bennett, *The Early Dominicans* (New York: Russell & Russell, 1937), pp. 31–51.

Chapter 2

1. Jeffrey Russell, ed., *Religious Dissent in the Middle Ages* (New York: John Wiley and Sons, Inc.,), pp. 143–147.

2. Herbert Grundmann, *Religiöse Bewegungen im Mittelalter* (Hildesheim: Georg Olms, 1961), pp. 519–524.

3. Bruder Bernhard Giergen, *Das Alexianer Kloster in Köln-Lindenthal in seiner geschichtlichen Entwicklung* (from the manuscript of the then deceased Thomas Paas) (Köln-Lindenthal, 1934), pp. 8–9.

4. Ibid., p. 7.

5. Ibid., p. 9.

6. Archbishop Henry's designation has a variety of spellings. "Virneburg" is from Giergen.

7. Ernst McDonnell, *Beguines and Beghards in Medieval Culture* (New Brunswick, N.J.: Rutgers University Press, 1954), p. 142.

8. Clement Raymond Orth, O.M.C., *The Approbation of Religious Institutes* (Washington, D.C.: Catholic University of America, 1931), pp. 30–31.

9. By the mid-thirteenth century the Franciscans required their novices to have a knowledge of grammar.

10. McDonnell, *Beguines and Beghards*, p. 509.

11. Robert E. Lerner, *The Heresy of the Free Spirit in the Later Middle Ages* (Los Angeles: University of California Press, 1972), p. 45.

12. Ibid., p. 66.

13. Ibid., p. 67.

14. Giergen, p. 12.

15. Ibid.

16. Anna Groh Seesholtz, *Friends of God* (New York: AMS Press, 1934), p. 50.

17. Quoted by Seesholtz, p. 68.

18. Ibid., p. 76.

19. Lerner, *Heresy of the Free Spirit*, p. 20.

20. Norman Cohn, *The Pursuit of the Millennium* (2d ed.; New York: Harper Torchbooks, 1961), p. 149.

21. Gordon Leff, *Heresy in the Later Middle Ages: The Relation of Heterodoxy to Dissent, c. 1250–c. 1450* (Manchester: Manchester University Press; New York: Barnes and Noble, 1967), I, p. 310.

22. Lerner, *Heresy of the Free Spirit*, p. 8.

23. Leff, I, pp. 311–313.

24. Henry Charles Lea, *A History of the Inquisition of the Middle Ages* (New York: S. A. Russell, 1955), II, p. 123.

25. Ibid. Cf. also Lerner, *Heresy of the Free Spirit*, pp. 71–83. He elaborates on the most recent literature on Marguerite, some of which clears her of doctrinal error.

26. Lerner, *Heresy of the Free Spirit*, p. 82.

27. Leff, I, pp. 314–315.

28. Quoted by McDonnell, *Beguines and Beghards*, p. 524.

29. Leff, I, pp. 316–317.

30. Quoted by Lerner, *Heresy of the Free Spirit*, p. 67.

31. Ibid., p. 95.

32. Ibid., p. 94.

33. Ibid., p. 95.

34. Lea, II, p. 373.

35. Leff, I, p. 376.

36. Lerner, *Heresy of the Free Spirit*, pp. 111–112.

37. Leff, I, pp. 371–372.

Notes

38. Lerner, *Heresy of the Free Spirit*, p. 108; Leff, I, p. 372.
39. Quoted by Leff, I, p. 372.
40. Quoted by Leff, I, p. 373.
41. Ibid.
42. Ibid., pp. 373–374.
43. Ibid., p. 376.
44. Ibid.
45. Rufus M. Jones, *Studies in Mystical Religion* (London: Macmillan and Co., 1909), p. 215.
46. Ibid., p. 214.
47. Lerner, *Heresy of the Free Spirit*, p. 110.
48. Ibid., p. 111.
49. Ibid.
50. Ibid.
51. Giergen, pp. 13–14, and Johannes von Asen, "Die Begarden und die Sackbrüder in Köln," *Annalen des historischen Vereins für den Niederrhein insbesondere das alte Erzbistum Köln* (hereafter *AHVN*), CXV (1929): 170–171; Eva Gertrud von Neumann, *Rheinisches Beginen- und Bagardenwesen* (Meisenheim am Glan: Anton Hain K.G., 1960), p. 139.
52. Giergen, p. 14.

Chapter 3

1. Albert Huyskens, "Die Anfänge der Aachener Alexianer im Zusammenhang der Ordens- und Ortsgeschichte," *Zeitschrift des Aachener Geschichtsvereins*, 1928 (English translation, Alexian Brothers Archives, Signal Mountain, Chattanooga, Tennessee), p. 2.
2. Ibid., pp. 2–3.
3. Ibid.
4. Richard Pick, "Das Kapuzinerkloster in Aachen," *Aus Aachener Vergangeheit, Beitrage zur Geschichte der Alten Kaiserstadt* (Aachen, 1895), pp. 74–95.
5. Huyskens, p. 5.
6. Ibid., p. 6.
7. Ibid.
8. "Die letzten mittelalterlichen Laienbrüder," *Alexiana*, 12 (1950): 89.
9. Huyskens, p. 6.
10. Jan van Acker, *Antwerpen van Romeins veer tot werneldhaven* (Antwerpen: Uitgave Mercurius, 1975), p. 10.
11. Ibid., p. 27.
12. Floris Prims, *Geschiedenis van Antwerpen* (Antwerp, 1929), II, p. 202.
13. *Oxford English Dictionary* (Oxford: Clarendon Press, 1961), VI, p. 403.
14. Dietrich von Kurze, "Die festlandischen Lollarden," *Archiv für Kulturgeschichte*, 47 (1965): 76.
15. Ibid.
16. Prims, II, p. 264.
17. Ibid.
18. Chronicle of Bertrijn, p. 19; found on a typed copy of "Notes about the convent of the Cellbrothers at Antwerp—Condensed from old documents, historical works, etc.," Alexian Brothers Archives, Boechout, Belgium.

19. Prims, I, pp. 200–203.
20. Ibid.
21. Ibid.
22. Ibid.
23. Ibid.
24. Ibid.

Chapter 4

1. Quoted by Philip Zeigler, *The Black Death* (London: Collins, 1969), p. 18.
2. William M. Bowsky, ed., *The Black Death: A Turning Point in History?* (New York: Holt, Rinehart and Winston, 1971), p. 1.
3. Zeigler, p. 85.
4. Ibid.
5. John J. A'Becket, "Alexians," *The Catholic Encyclopedia* (New York: Robert Appleton, 1907), I, pp. 306–307.
6. "On the Frontpiece," *Saint Alexius-Almanac, Aachen*, 7 (1934) : 7.
7. Johanne Nohle, *The Black Death, a Chronicle of the Plague*, trans. C. H. Clarke (New York: Harper & Brothers, 1924), p. 121.
8. Ignatius Wiegers, C.F.A., *Die Aachener Alexianerbrüder ihre Geschichte und ihr Ordengeist* (Aachen, 1956), p. 42. (Private English translation in Alexian Brothers Archives, Signal Mountain, Chattanooga, Tennessee.)
9. A. Sanford, "The Alexian Brothers," *New Catholic Encyclopedia* (Washington, D.C.: Catholic University of America Press, 1967), I, pp. 306–307.
10. McDonnell, *Beguines and Beghards*, p. 267.
11. Walter John Marx, *The Development of Charity in Medieval Louvain* (Ph.D. dissertation, Columbia University, 1936), p. 9.
12. McDonnell, *Beguines and Beghards*, p. 267. Also cf. "On the Alexian Brothers of Ghent," *Alexiana*, 12 (1950) : III.
13. Ibid. Also cf. Marx, p. 69.
14. Zeigler, p. 106.
15. Ibid., p. 88.
16. Ibid., pp. 92–95.
17. Quoted by Nohle, p. 239.
18. Zeigler, p. 93.
19. Ibid.
20. Henry Charles Lea, *A History of the Inquisition of the Middle Ages* (New York: S. A. Russell, 1955), II, p. 385.
21. Floris Prims, *Geschiedenis van Antwerpen* (Antwerp, 1929), II, p. 264.
22. Robert E. Lerner, *The Heresy of the Free Spirit* in the Later Middle Ages (Los Angeles: University of California Press, 1972), p. 131.
23. McDonnell, *Beguines and Beghards*, p. 563. Cf. also Lerner, *Heresy of the Free Spirit*, pp. 133–134, and Lea, II, pp. 388–391.
24. Lerner, *Heresy of the Free Spirit*, p. 133.
25. Lea, II, pp. 391–392.
26. Albert Huyskens, "Die Anfänge der Aachener Alexianer im Zusammenhang der Ordens- und Ortsgeschicte," *Zeitschrift des Aachener Geschichtsvereins*, 1928 (private trans.), p. 11.
27. McDonnell, *Beguines and Beghards*, p. 566.

28. Ibid., p. 568.

29. Huyskens, p. 13. This may be the same complaint as noted by McDonnell.

30. Ibid., pp. 13–14.

31. Ibid., p. 14.

32. Ibid., pp. 14–15.

33. McDonnell, *Beguines and Beghards*, p. 568.

34. Quoted by McDonnell, *Beguines and Beghards*, p. 569.

35. Lerner, *Heresy of the Free Spirit*, p. 97.

36. Ibid.

37. Ibid., p. 99.

38. Quoted in a 1434 bull by Pope Eugene IV directed to "The Venerable Brothers, Archbishops of Cologne, Treves and Mayence as well as their Suffragans throughout Germany, Brabant and Flanders. . . ." English translation, Alexian Brothers Archives, Signal Mountain, Chattanooga, Tennessee.

39. Ibid.

40. Ibid.

41. Ibid.

42. Huyskens, pp. 11–12.

43. Lerner, *The Heresy of the Free Spirit*, p. 141.

44. Huyskens, p. 12.

45. Lerner, *The Heresy of the Free Spirit*, p. 141.

46. Huyskens, p. 16.

47. Ibid., pp. 16–17.

48. Prims, II, p. 264.

49. Walter Ullman, *A Short History of the Papacy in the Middle Ages* (London: Methuen & Co., 1972), p. 298.

50. Lerner, *The Heresy of the Free Spirit*, p. 148.

51. English translation of this papal bull is in the Alexian Brothers Archives, Signal Mountain, Chattanooga, Tennessee.

52. Ibid.

53. Ibid.

54. Huyskens, pp. 22–23.

55. Prims, II, p. 264.

56. Ibid.

57. Ibid.

58. Ibid.

59. Ibid.

60. Lerner, *The Heresy of the Free Spirit*, p. 198.

61. Quoted by Albert Hyma, *The Brethren of the Common Life* (Grand Rapids, Mich.: Eerdmans, 1950), p. 33.

62. Ibid., p. 54.

63. Quoted by R. R. Post, *The Modern Devotion* (Leiden: E. J. Brill, 1968), pp. 273–274.

64. Lerner, *Heresy of the Free Spirit*, p. 149.

65. Huyskens, p. 34.

66. Ibid., pp. 24–25.

67. Ibid., pp. 26–32.

68. Ibid.

69. Ibid., pp. 27–28.

70. Ibid., pp. 31–32.

71. Grabon's story is found in Lea, II, pp. 409–410; Gordon Leff, *Heresy in the Later Middle Ages: The Relation of Heterodoxy to Dissent, c. 1250– c. 1450* (Manchester: Manchester University Press; New York: Barnes and Noble, 1967), I, pp. 349–350; Lerner, *Heresy of the Free Spirit*, p. 162; Post, pp. 290–291.

72. Quoted by Huyskens, p. 32. Also cf. Bernhard Giergen, *Das Alexianer Kloster in Köln-Lindenthal* (Köln-Lindenthal, 1934), p. 22.

73. Huyskens, pp. 32–33.

74. Ibid., p. 33.

75. Ibid.

76. Ibid.

77. Ibid., p. 34.

78. Bull of Pope Eugene IV, English translation in the Alexian Brothers Archives, Signal Mountain, Chattanooga, Tennessee.

79. Ibid.

80. Ibid.

81. Ibid.

82. Ibid.

83. Ibid.

Chapter 5

1. Albert Huyskens, "Die Anfänge der Aachener Alexianer im Zusammenhang der Ordens- und Ortsgeschichte," *Zeitschrift des Aachener Geschichtsvereins*, 1928 (private trans.), p. 35.

2. Ibid., p. 43.

3. Ibid.

4. Ibid., pp. 43–44.

5. Ibid., p. 44.

6. Ibid.

7. Martin Birken, who is working on a history of the Cellites, origins to the Reformation, said that the Amsterdam Cellites professed as early as 1454.

8. Huyskens, p. 46.

9. Cf. chap. VI, below.

10. Huyskens, p. 46.

11. Ibid., p. 45.

12. Ibid.

13. Ibid., p. 48.

14. Cf. chap. VI, below.

15. Joseph Greving, "Protokoll über die Revision der Konvente der Beginen und Begarden zu Köln im Jahre 1452," *AHVN*, LXXIII (1901): 25–77.

16. Ibid., p. 43.

17. Huyskens, p. 46.

18. Ibid., pp. 48–49.

19. Ibid., p. 49.

20. Ibid., p. 51.

21. Richard Vaughan, *Charles the Bold* (New York: Harper & Row, 1974), pp. 25–30.

22. Huyskens, p. 51.
23. Ibid.
24. Ibid.
25. Ibid.
26. Ibid.
27. Bernhard Giergen, *Das Alexianer Kloster in Köln-Lindenthal* (Köln-Lindenthal, 1934), p. 36.
28. Huyskens, p. 54.
29. Clement Raymond Orth, *The Approbation of Religious Institutes* (Washington, D.C.: Catholic University of America Press, 1931), pp. 30–31.
30. Papal bull of Pope Julius II, English translation in the Alexian Brothers Archives, Signal Mountain, Chattanooga, Tennessee.
31. Ibid.
32. Ibid.
33. Ibid.
34. Outram Evennett, *The Spirit of the Counter-Reformation* (Notre Dame, Ind.: University of Notre Dame Press, 1970), p. 103.
35. John Dolan et al., *Handbook of Church History*, trans. Anselm Biggs (New York: Herder and Herder, 1970), IV, p. 560.
36. Ibid.
37. Evennett, p. 68.
38. Ibid., p. 68.
39. Ignatius Wiegers, C.F.A., *Die Aachener Alexianerbruder* (private trans., Aachen, 1956), p. 8.
40. Huyskens, p. 54.
41. Ibid.
42. Ibid.
43. Floris Prims, *Geschiedenis van Antwerpen* (Antwerp, 1929), VII, p. 265.
44. Ibid.
45. Giergen, pp. 37–38.
46. Ibid., p. 38.
47. Ibid., pp. 45–46.
48. Ibid., p. 47.

Chapter 6

1. Johann Huizinga, *The Waning of the Middle Ages* (Garden City, N.Y.: Doubleday and Co., Anchor Books, 1954), pp. 225–242.
2. Robert S. Kinsman (ed.), *The Darker Vision of the Renaissance* (Berkeley: University of California Press, 1974).
3. For a comprehensive analysis of ritual, cf. Louis Bouyer, *Rite and Man, the Sense of the Sacral and Christian Liturgy* (London: Burns and Oates, 1963), p. 57.
4. Ferdinand Tönnies, *Community and Society* (*Gemeinschaft und Gesellschaft*), trans. and ed. Charles P. Loomis (East Lansing: Michigan State University Press, 1957), p. 33.
5. Ibid., p. 43.
6. Ibid., p. 49.

7. Albert Huyskens, "Die Anfänge der Aachener Alexianer im Zusammenhang der Ordens und Ortsgeschichte," *Zeitschrift des Aachener Geschichtsvereins*, 1928 (private trans.), pp. 39–40.

8. Ibid.

9. Ibid., p. 40.

10. Ibid., pp. 40–41.

11. Ibid., pp. 41–42.

12. Ibid., p. 43.

13. Tönnies, pp. 33–34.

14. Aberdingk Thijm, ed., "Statuta et Modus Vivendi Fratrum et Sororum de Cella Vulgariter Nuncupatorum in Villis Gandavensi, Brugensi et Aldenardensi Tornacensis Dyocoesis Residentium," in *Gestichten van Liefadicheid in Belgie*, p. 376.

15. Ibid.

16. Ibid.

17. Ibid.

18. Ibid.

19. Ibid., p. 377.

20. Ibid., p. 378.

21. Ibid., pp. 378–379.

22. Ibid., p. 378.

23. Ibid.

24. Ibid.

25. Ibid., p. 377.

26. Ibid.

27. Ibid., p. 378.

28. Ibid., p. 379.

29. Ibid.

30. Ibid. "Bevestiging en statuten der cellebroeders te diest—1462," p. 380.

31. Ibid.

32. Ibid.

33. Ibid.

34. Ibid.

35. Ibid., p. 381.

36. Ibid.

37. Ibid.

38. Ibid., p. 380.

39. Ibid.

40. Quoted by Huyskens, p. 45.

41. Ibid., pp. 49–50.

42. Ibid., p. 47.

43. Ibid.

44. Ibid.

45. Ibid., p. 48.

46. Ibid.

47. Floris Prims, *Geschiedenis van Antwerpen* (Antwerp, 1929), VII, p. 265. VII, p. 265.

48. Bernhard Giergen, *Das Alexianer Kloster in Köln-Lindenthal* (Köln-Lindenthal, 1934), p. 42.

Notes

49. *Regel van den Heiligen Vader Augustinus, Tot Gebruk van de orde der Cellebruders, Te samed met Hune Statutes* (Sint-Truiden, 1862), p. 45.

50. Giergen, p. 42.

51. *Regel, etc.*, p. 65.

52. E. K. Francis, "Toward a Typology of Religious Orders" in *Religion, Culture and Society*, ed. Louis Schneider (New York: John Wiley, 1964), p. 519.

53. Ibid.

54. Jean Leclercq, O.S.B., "Profession according to the Rule of St. Benedict," in *Rule and Life, an Interdisciplinary Symposium*, ed. Basil M. Pennington (Spencer, Mass.: Cistercian Publications, 1971), p. 143.

55. Ibid.

56. Rev. J. C. Dickinson, *The Origins of the Austin Canons and Their Introduction into England* (London: Church Historical Society, 1950), p. 257.

57. *Regel, etc.*, pp. 20–42.

Chapter 7

1. Malcom David Lambert, *Franciscan Poverty: The Doctrine of Absolute Poverty of Christ and the Apostles in the Franciscan Order 1210–1323* (London: S.P.C.K., 1961), p. 150.

2. Ibid.

3. Ibid., p. 178.

4. Ibid., pp. 179–181.

5. McDonnell, *Beguines and Beghards*, p. 150.

6. Dom François Vandenbroucke, "Laity and Clergy in the Thirteenth Century," in *The Spirituality of the Middle Ages*, ed. J. Leclercq, F. Vanderbroucke and L. Bouyer (New York: Desclee Company, 1968), p. 360.

7. Quoted by ibid., p. 362.

8. David Tracy, *Blessed Rage for Order* (New York: Seabury Press, 1975), p. 93.

9. Cf. Walter J. Ong, S.J., "World as View and World as Event," in *Environ/Mental: Essays on the Planet as Home*, ed. Paul Shepherd and Daniel McKinley (Boston: Houghton Mifflin, 1971).

10. Cf. chap. IV, above.

11. Richard Kieckhefer, "The Radical Tendencies in the Flagellant Movement of the Mid-Fourteenth Century," *The Journal of Medieval and Renaissance Studies*, IV, No. 2 (1974): 17.

12. Vandenbroucke, p. 401.

13. Dolan et al., *Handbook of Church History*, trans. Anselm Biggs (New York: Herder and Herder, 1970), IV, p. 438.

14. Quoted by G. G. Coulton, *Five Centuries of Religion* (Cambridge: Cambridge University Press, 1950), IV, p. 154.

15. Ibid., p. 155.

16. Dolan et al., *Handbook of Church History*, IV, p. 589.

17. Ibid., pp. 585–594.

18. Quoted by Huyskens, "Die Anfänge der Aachener Alexianer im Zusammenhang der Ordens- und Ortsgeschichte," *Zeitschrift des Aachener Geschichtsvereins*, 1928 (private trans.), pp. 58–61.

19. R. R. Post, *The Modern Devotion* (Leiden: E. J. Brill, 1968), p. 517.

20. E. F. Jacob, "The Fifteenth Century, Some Recent Interpretations," a reprint from *The Bulletin of the John Ryland Library* (Manchester, England, July 1930), Vol. 14, No. 2, p. 13.

21. Ibid.

22. Episcopal Letter from Louis de Bourbon to the Cellites of Aachen, March 18, 1469. English translation, Alexian Brothers Archives, Signal Mountain, Chattanooga, Tennessee.

23. Dolan et al., *Handbook of Church History*, IV, p. 14.

24. Gabriel Russotto, *Hospitaller Spirituality* (Sydney, Australia: Cresta Printing Co., 1961), p. 92.

25. Quoted in Dolan et al., *Handbook of Church History*, IV, p. 442.

26. R. W. Southern, *Western Society and the Church in the Middle Ages* (Grand Rapids, Mich.: Wm. B. Eerdmans Publishing Company, 1970), p. 318.

27. Louis Zambarelli, C.R.S., "The Story of St. Alexius," in the *St. Alexius Calendar* (Signal Mountain, Chattanooga, Tennessee, Congregation of the Alexian Brothers), p. 19.

28. Ibid., pp. 19–20.

29. Henry Dedeck, V.L., *The Life of St. Alexis* (New York: Publications of the Institute of French Studies, 1931), p. 4.

30. Ibid., p. 2.

31. Zambarelli, p. 36.

32. C. E. Stabbins, "Les origines de la Légende de Saint Alexis," in *Revue Belge de Philologie et d'Histoire*, 50 (1973): 507.

33. Quoted in "Report on the Authenticity of Saint Alexius," submitted to the second session of the 21st General Chapter (1969) of the Alexian Brothers, p. 1. Alexian Brothers Archives, Signal Mountain, Chattanooga, Tennessee.

Chapter 8

1. Robert McAfee Brown, *The Spirit of Protestantism* (New York: Oxford University Press, 1961), p. 192.

2. Ibid.

3. Ibid.

4. Ibid., p. 103.

5. Ibid.

6. Ibid.

7. Dolan et al., *The Handbook of Church History*, trans. Anselm Biggs (New York: Herder and Herder, 1970), IV, p. 183.

8. Ibid.

9. Joseph and Francis Giess, *Life in a Medieval City* (London: Arthur Baker, 1965), pp. 116–117.

10. Eva von Neumann, *Rheinisches Beginen- und Begardenwesen* (Meisenheim am Glan: Anton Hain K. G., 1960), p. 138.

11. Albert Huyskens, "Die Anfänge der Aachener Alexianer im Zusammenhang der Ordens- und Ortsgeschichte," *Zeitschrift des Aachener Geschichtsvereins*, 1928 (private trans.), p. 6.

12. Joseph Biergans, "Die Wohlfahrtspflege der Stadt Aachen in den letzten Jahrhunderten des Mittelalters," *Zeitschrift des Aachener Geschichtsvereins*, 31 (1909): 86.

13. Asen, "Die Begarden und die Sackbrüder in Köln," *AHVN*, CXV (1929): 170–171.

14. Neumann, p. 139.

15. George Deux, *The Black Death* (London: Hamish Hamilton, 1969), p. 32.

16. Ibid.

17. Ibid., p. 32.

18. Ibid., p. 189.

19. Ibid.

20. Quoted by G. G. Coulton, *Ten Medieval Studies* (Gloucester, Mass.: Peter Smith, 1967; first published 1930), pp. 228–229.

21. Walther Rehm, *Der Todesgedanke in der Deutschen Dichtung von Mittelalters bis Romantik* (Tübingen: Max Niemeyer, 1967), pp. 58–74.

22. Phillipe Ariès, *Western Attitudes toward Death* (Baltimore, Md.: Johns Hopkins Press, 1974), p. 13.

23. Ibid., p. 18.

24. Ibid., p. 22.

25. Rehm, pp. 75–93.

26. Ariès, pp. 29–31.

27. Meister Eckhart, *Treatises and Sermons of Meister Eckhart*, selected and translated from the Latin and German by James M. Clark and John V. Skinner (New York: Harper & Brothers, 1958), p. 84.

28. Ibid., p. 85.

29. Ibid., p. 86.

30. Bernard Poschmann, *Penance and Christian Anointing* (New York: Herder and Herder, 1964), p. 245.

31. Ibid.

32. Ibid., pp. 243–244.

33. Ibid., p. 244, n. 30.

34. Heinrich Boos, *Geschichte der rheinischen Stadtkultur* (Berlin: J. A. Stargard, 1897), III, p. 208. Also cf. Dolan et al., *Handbook of Church History*, trans. Anselm Biggs (New York: Herder and Herder, 1970), IV, p. 484.

35. "Die letzten mittelalterlichen Laienbrüder," *Alexiana*, 12 (1950): 89.

36. Huyskens, p. 21.

37. Ibid., p. 32.

38. Ibid.

39. Ibid., p. 33.

40. Ibid.

41. John Carroll Futrell, "Discerning the Founder's Charism," *The Way*, Supplement No. 14 (Autumn 1971), p. 62.

42. Ibid., p. 63.

43. K. Muret, *Rites of Funerals Ancient and Modern in use throughout the known world*, trans. P. Lorraine (London, 1683), pp. 258–259.

44. Ibid., p. 77.

45. Quoted by Betrand Puckle, *Funeral Customs, Their Origins and Development* (London, 1926), p. 63.

46. Ibid.

47. Louis Bouyer, *Rite and Man* (London: Burns and Oates, 1963), p. 158.

48. Cf. Joseph and Francis Giess, *Life in a Medieval City*, p. 75, and Puckle,

Funeral Customs, p. 149, and J. A. Jungmann, *Public Worship*, trans. Clifford Howell (London: 1957), p. 82.

49. Neumann, p. 138.

50. Huizinga, *The Waning of the Middle Ages* (Garden City, N.Y.: Doubleday and Co., Anchor Books, 1954), p. 52.

51. Ibid., p. 53.

52. Dolan et al., *Handbook of Church History*, IV, pp. 388–389.

53. Quoted by Sister Mary Catherine O'Connor, *The Art of Dying Well* (New York: Columbia University Press, 1942), p. 6 n. 35.

54. Ibid., p. 3.

55. Ibid., p. 23.

56. Nancy Lee Beaty, *The Craft of Dying: The Tradition of the "Ars Moriendi" in England* (New Haven: Yale University Press, 1970), p. 5.

57. Leonard Kurtz, *The Dance of Death and the Macabre Spirit in European Literature* (New York: Columbia University Press, 1934), p. 210.

58. *Todtentanz der Stadt Basel* (Basel: Otto Stuckert, 1858), p. 67.

59. Beaty, p. 12.

60. O'Connor, p. 5.

61. Huizinga, pp. 138–151.

62. Ibid.

63. Quoted by Huizinga, p. 151.

64. Quoted in Dolan et al., *Handbook of Church History*, IV, p. 439.

65. Dom Vincent Skelly, ed., *Meditations and Sermons on the Incarnation, Life and Passion of the Lord, to wit, from the advent of the Lord in the Work of Thomas a Kempes* (London, 1907), IV, p. 201.

66. Quoted in "An Enthusiastic Eulogy to the Old Cellites or Alexians," *St. Alexius Almanac* (Aachen: Alexian Brothers, 1934), VII, p. 9.

Chapter 9

1. Peter Geyl, *The Revolt of the Netherlands 1555–1609*, 2d ed. (New York: Barnes and Noble, 1962), pp. 94–95.

2. Floris Prims, *Geschiedenis van Antwerpen* (Antwerp, 1929), VIII, p. 319.

3. Ibid.

4. Ibid.

5. Ibid.

6. Ibid.

7. Ibid.

8. Ibid.

9. Ibid.

10. Ibid.

11. Bernard Moeller, "Piety in Germany around 1500," in *The Reformation in Medieval Perspective*, ed. Steven E. Ozment (Chicago: Quadrangle Books, 1971), p. 53.

12. Ibid., p. 54.

13. Ibid.

14. Ibid., p. 57.

15. Gerald Strauss, ed., *Discontent in Germany on the Eve of the Reformation* (Bloomington: Indiana University Press, 1971), pp. 140–145.

Notes

16. Louis Bouyer et al., *Orthodox Spirituality and Protestant and Anglican Spirituality* (New York: Desclee, 1969), pp. 63–70.
17. Outram Evennett, *The Spirit of the Counter-Reformation* (Notre Dame, Ind.: University of Notre Dame Press, 1970), p. 40.
18. *Constitution of the Alexian Brothers, 1686*, Alexian Brothers Archives, Signal Mountain, Chattanooga, Tennessee.
19. Ibid.
20. Ibid.
21. Ibid.
22. Cf. Evennett, pp. 43–66.
23. Thomas Frederick Simmons, ed., *The Lay Folks Mass Book* (London: N. Turner & Co., 1879), p. 346.
24. Josef Andreas Jungmann, S.J., *Brieverstudien* (Trier, 1958), pp. 75ff.
25. Ignatius Wiegers, C.F.A., *Die Aachener Alexianerbrüder ihre Geschichte und ihr Ordensgeist* (Aachen, 1956), p. 13.
26. Dom Gabriel Brasso, O.S.B., *Liturgy and Spirituality* (Collegeville, Minn.: The Liturgical Press, 1976), p. 43.
27. Ibid.
28. Evennett, p. 36.
29. Ibid.
30. Gabriel Russotto, *Hospitaller Spirituality* (Sydney, Australia: Cresta Printing Co., 1961), pp. 24–37.
31. Ibid., p. 92.
32. Joseph Andreas Jungmann, S.J., *The Good News Yesterday and Today* (New York: W. H. Sadlier, 1962), p. 61.

Chapter 10

1. *Regel van den Heiligen Vader Augustinus, Tot Gebruk van de orde der Cellebruders, Te samed met Hune Statutes* (Sint-Truiden, 1862), p. vii.
2. The following account is derived from Brother Damien Steyaert's extensive research of the authority issue.
3. *Regal, etc.*, p. vii.
4. W. J. Marx, *The Development of Charity in Medieval Lourain* (Ph.D. dissertation), p. 76.
5. Bernhard Giergen, *Das Alexianer Kloster in Köln-Lindenthal* (Köln-Lindenthal, 1934), p. 38.
6. Ibid., p. 39.
7. Ibid., pp. 49–51.
8. Ignatius Wiegers, C.F.A., *Die Aachener Alexianer brüder ihre Geschichte und ihr Ordensgeist* (Aachen, 1956), p. 12.
9. Ibid.
10. Ibid., p. 16.
11. Giergen, pp. 73–74.
12. Ibid., p. 74.
13. Ibid.
14. Ibid., p. 78.
15. Ibid., p. 79.
16. Ibid., pp. 79–80.

17. Ibid., p. 80.
18. Ibid., p. 82.
19. Ibid., p. 87.
20. Ibid.
21. Ibid., pp. 83–84.
22. Ibid., p. 87.
23. Wiegers, pp. 13–14.
24. Ibid., p. 14.
25. Ibid.
26. Ibid., p. 16.
27. Figures from ibid.
28. Ibid.
29. Van Schevensteen, A.F.C., *Documents Pour A L'Etude Des Maladies Pestelentielles Dans Le Marqisot D'Anvers Jusqu'e La Chute De L'Ancien Regime*, ed. Lamertin (Brussels: Commission Royale d'Histoire, 1931), I, p. 48.
30. Ibid.
31. *ACTE* Van Syne Keyserlijcke ende Conincklijcke majesteyt Carel den sesden vergunt in synen Souvereynen Raede van Brabant, raeckende de twee guldens competerende de Cellebroeders van ieder Lyck by hun, ofte eenige andere niet wesende van het ambacht van den Meersche gedraegen worndende (Eugenius Henricus Fricx, drucker van Syne Majestey (Tote Brussel, 1713), pp. 3–4. (Taken from a photocopy of this *ACTE*, in the Alexian Brothers Archives in Boechout, Belgium).
32. Ibid., pp. 5–6.
33. Hubert Jedin, *Crises and Closure of the Council of Trent* (London: Sheed and Ward, 1967), p. 134.
34. Giergen, p. 88.
35. Ibid.
36. Ibid., p. 89.
37. Ibid.
38. Ibid.
39. *Constitution of the Alexian Brothers, 1686*, Alexian Brothers Archives, Signal Mountain, Chattanooga, Tennessee, p. 3.
40. Ibid., p. 8.
41. Ibid.
42. Ibid.
43. Ibid.
44. Ibid.
45. Ibid.
46. Ibid., p. 9.
47. This entire story is derived from Brother Damien Steyeart's research notes compiled at the Mechlin Archdiocesan Archive.
48. This bull appears as an appendix to *Regel, etc.*, pp. 76–79.
49. Ibid., p. 77.
50. *Regel, etc.*, p. 43.
51. Ibid., p. 9.
52. Ibid.
53. Ibid., pp. 9–10.
54. Ibid., p. 135.

55. Ibid.
56. Ibid., p. 15.
57. Ibid., p. 16.
58. Ibid.
59. Ibid., pp. 16–17.
60. Ibid., p. 18.
61. Ibid., p. 56.
62. Ibid., p. 69.
63. Ibid., p. 68.
64. Ibid., p. 62.
65. Ibid., pp. 66–74.
66. Gabriel Russotto, *Hospitaller Spirituality* (Sydney, Australia: Cresta Printing Co., 1961), pp. 94–95.
67. *Regel etc.*, p. 62.
68. Ibid.
69. Ibid.
70. Giergen, p. 92.
71. Ibid.
72. Ibid.
73. Wiegers, pp. 20–22.
74. Ibid.
75. Ibid.
76. Ibid.
77. Giergen, p. 93.
78. Ibid.
79. Ibid., p. 94.
80. The constitution of 1763, Alexian Brothers Archives, Signal Mountain, Chattanooga, Tennessee.
81. Ibid.
82. Ibid.
83. Ibid.
84. Ibid.
85. Ibid.
86. Ibid.

Chapter 11

1. Van Schevensteen, A.F.C., *Documents Pour A L'Etude Des Maladies Pestelentielles Dans Le Marqisot D'Anvers Jusqu'e La Chute De L'Ancien Regime*, ed. Lamertin (Brussels: Commission Royale d'Histoire, 1931), I, p. 48.
2. Ibid.
3. Ibid.
4. Ibid., p. 79.
5. Ibid., p. 409.
6. Floris Prims, *Geschiedenis van Antwerpen* (Antwerp, 1929), VIII, p. 319.
7. Van Schevensteen, II, p. 12.
8. Ibid.
9. Ibid.
10. Ibid., p. 26.

11. Ibid., p. 28.

12. Ibid., p. 43.

13. Ibid., p. 106.

14. *Regel van den Heiligen Vader Augustinus, Tot Gebruk van de orde der Cellebruders, Te samed met Hune Statutes* (Sint-Truiden, 1862), p. 17.

15. Bernhard Giergen, *Das Alexianer Kloster in Köln-Lindenthal* (Köln-Lindenthal, 1934), p. 60.

16. Ibid.

17. Ibid., p. 67.

18. Ibid., p. 68.

19. Ibid., p. 69.

20. Ibid.

21. Ibid., p. 71.

22. Ibid.

23. Ignatius Wiegers, C.F.A., *Die Aachener Alexianerbrüder ihre Geschichte und ihr Ordensgeist* (Aachen, 1956), p. 12.

24. Ibid.

25. Ibid., p. 15.

26. Ibid.

27. Joseph Biergans, "Die Wohlfahrtspflege der Stadt Aachen in den letzten Jahrhunderten des Mittelalters, *Zeitschrift des Aachener Geschichtsvereins*, 31 (1909) : 86.

28. Ibid., p. 397.

29. Wiegers, p. 14.

30. Ibid., p. 14.

31. Ibid.

32. Ibid.

33. Quoted in *St. Alexius Almanac* (1934), VII, p. 7.

34. H. D. J. van Schevichaven, *Oud-Nijmegens, Kerken, Klooster, Gasthuizen, Stichtingen en opengare Gebouwen* (Nijmegens: Firma H Ten Hoet, 1909), p. 60.

35. Ibid.

36. Ibid.

37. Ibid., p. 61.

38. Michel Foucault, *Madness and Civilization, a History of Insanity in the Age of Reason* (New York: Pantheon Books, 1965), p. 8.

39. Ibid., p. 9.

40. Ibid., p. 11.

41. Ibid., p. 13.

42. van Schevichaven, p. 65.

43. Foucault, p. 68.

44. van Schevichaven, pp. 65–66.

45. Wiegers, p. 22.

46. Ibid.

47. Ibid.

48. Ibid.

49. Prims, IX, p. 160.

50. Giergen, p. 54.

51. Ibid., p. 63.

INDEX